poetry: an introduction through writing

POETRY: an introduction through writing

Lewis Turco

RESTON PUBLISHING COMPANY, INC., Reston, Virginia
A Prentice-Hall Company

©1973 by
RESTON PUBLISHING COMPANY, Inc.
A Prentice-Hall Company
Box 547
Reston, Virginia 22090

10 9 8 7 6 5 4 3 2 1

ISBN: 0-87909-637-3

Library of Congress Catalog Card Number: 72-91118
Printed in the United States of America.

dedication:

HONKYTONK REVISITED
For Fay, Russ, D.A., Matt, Elizabeth, Don, John,
Dennis, Ron, Steve, P.J., Kevin, Sam, and
all my other students and young poet friends,
past, present, and future.

Once: young, drunk,
roaring with floorshows,
bursting with beer,
white as a lamb in my swabbie clothes,
free of the sea, free
of anchors, capstans, captains,
coils of ratline, wallows, waves —
once: wild, wayward,
I would a knuckle around a pencil,
pummeled a napkin, pounded
the table and snaked a sheepshank
of graphite about glorious grammar:

I made a poem.

Dedication

"Honkytonk" I called it in that
honkytonk: the sax honked,
we hooted at fat shills,
skinny frills, naked girls —
fools in the lewd who outhoused
the farmer's lass; we foamed,
fumed, fondled infamy —
ah! we were grand that night!
Our eyeballs were nude,
ah! we were grand!

So was my poem.

Then it was back to the ship,
bank to bunk out, flake out,
sack out: we were not truly free.
But in my jumper there was a pocket,
in it a napkin, a greatness —

on it a poem.

At dawn it was a scratch and a
scrawl, a tall story, a tale
untrue and wanton . . . ,

it was no poem.

In a flash and a tear it was gone,
torn, tossed to frothing waters,
fallen on seas, washed unto fishes:
now I recall it: young, drunken,
rampant and oaten,
badly unbalanced, lacking meter, marvelously
disorganized, dissembling and dirty, ah!

That was a poem!

acknowledgements

Vito Hannibal Acconci, "Re," reprinted from YOUNG AMERICAN POETS edited by Paul Carroll, Follett Publishing Company, Chicago, Ill., by permission of the publisher.

Richard Londraville, "Rod Mckuen Formula," reprinted by permission of the author. Copyright 1972 by Richard Loudraville.

H. Idris Bell and David Bell, several short passages from the introductory essays in DAFYDD AP GWILYM by permission of Honourable Society of Cymmrodorion, London, England.

Lewis Turco, "Mon Coeur" (Fall 1970), reprinted from NORTHWEST REVIEW, Volume XI, #1, Eugene, Oregon, by permission.

Lewis Turco, "The Glass Nest," reprinted from AMERICAN CHRISTMAS, 2nd edition, edited by Schott and Myers (copyright 1967) by Hallmark Cards, Inc., by permission of the publisher.

Artwork for Joyce Kilmer's "Trees" by Socrates Sampson.

Lewis Turco, "Defining the Poet," reprinted from CONCERNING POETRY, copyright 1971 by Lewis Turco, by permission of the author.

Marianne Moore, "To Military Progress," and "Poetry," reprinted from COLLECTED POEMS (copyright 1935 by Marianne Moore and renewed 1963 by Marianne Moore and T.S. Eliot) with permission of Macmillan Company, New York, N.Y.

Geoffrey Chaucer, "The Complaint of Chaucer to His Purse," reprinted from the WORKS OF GEOFFREY CHAUCER, edited by F.N. Robinson, Houghton Mifflin Company, Boston, by permission of the publisher.

E.E. Cummings, "1(a," reprinted from 95 POEMS (Copyright 1958), by E.E. Cummings, by permission of Harcourt Brace Jovanovich, Inc., New York, N.Y.

Lewis Turco, "The Moment Before," reprinted from IN THE POET'S HAND, with permission of Frostburg State College Library, Frostburg, Maryland.

Thomas H. Johnson, "Acrostic Love Poem to Elizabeth Fitch," reprinted from THE TOPICAL VERSES OF EDWARD TAYLOR," an article in PUBLICATIONS OF THE COLONIAL SOCIETY OF MASSACHUSETTS, no. 34, 1943, pp 513-54, with permission of the editor.

Richard Kostelanetz, "Nymphomania," reprinted from VISUAL LANGUAGE (Assembling Press, Box 1967, Brooklyn, New York) by permission of the author.

Alfred Kreymborg, "Nun Snow: A Pantomine of Beads," reprinted from SELECTED POEMS OF ALFRED KREYMBORG, (Copyright 1945 by Alfred Kreymborg) published by E.P. Dutton & Co., Inc. and used with their permission.

Lewis Turco, "The Student," "The Pilot," (Copyright 1966 and 1969 by the SATURDAY REVIEW), reprinted with permission of the SATURDAY REVIEW, New York, NY 10017.

Langston Hughes, "Go Slow," reprinted from THE PANTHER AND THE LASH, copyright 1967 by Arna Bontemps and George Houston Bass, by permission of Alfred A. Knopf, Inc.

Dylan Thomas, "Triolet," "Vision and Prayer," "Of Any Flower," and "Fern Hill," reprinted from THE POEMS OF DYLAN THOMAS, edited by Daniel Jones, copyright 1946, and copyright 1971 by New Directions Publishing Corporation, by permission of the New Directions Publishing Corporation.

Walter H. Kerr, "The View From Khufu's Tongue," reprinted from POETRY (December 1971) by permission of the Editor of POETRY.

Maxine W. Kumin, "400-Meter Free Style," reprinted from HALFWAY by Maxine W. Kumin, Holt, Rinehart, & Winston, 1961, copyright by Maxine W. Kumin, by permission of the author.

Richard Frost, "Climbing the Tower at Pisa". . ., reprinted from GETTING DRUNK WITH THE BIRDS, by Richard Frost (Copyright 1971), Ohio University Press, with permission of the author.

Carl Sandburg, "Cool Tombs," reprinted from CORNHUSKERS by Carl Sandburg, copyright 1918 by Holt, Rinehart and Winston, Inc., and 1946 by Carl Sandburg), by permission of Holt, Rinehart and Winston, Inc.

Allen Ginsberg, "A Supermarket in California," reprinted from HOWL AND OTHER POEMS (copyright 1956, 1959) by permission of City Lights Books, San Francisco, Calif.

William Carlos Williams, "On Gay Wallpaper," and "The Red Wheelbarrow," reprinted from COLLECTED EARLIER POEMS (copyright 1938 by William Carlos Williams) by permission of New Directions Publishing Corporation.

Lewis Turco, "The Door," "The Guestroom," "The Kitchen," "The Livingroom," (Copyright 1970 by Lewis Turco), reprinted from THE INHABITANT with permission of Despa Press.

Robert Creeley, "The Hero," reprinted from FOR LOVE, (Copyright 1962 Robert Creeley) by permission of Charles Scribner's Sons, New York, N.Y.

Lewis Turco, "Pines," (copyright 1971), reprinted from INNERSPRING QUARTERLY, by permission of the author.

Russell Salamon, "She," reprinted from PARENTHETICAL POPPIES, by Russell Salamon (Copyright 1964) Renegade Press, with permission.

Lewis Turco, "The Morbid Man Singing," (Copyright 1969 by POEM), reprinted from POEM (No. 7, Nov. 1969), Huntsville, Alabama, by permission.

Donald Justice, "To Waken A Small Person," reprinted from NIGHT LIFE, by Donald Justice (Copyright 1966) by permission of Wesleyan University Press. First Appeared in *The New Yorker*.

Lewis Turco, "Parenthetics for Langston Hughes" (Langston Hughes issue), reprinted with permission of FREE LANCE, Cleveland, Ohio.

Burton Raffel, "The Husband's Message," reprinted from POEMS OF THE OLD ENGLISH translated by Burton Raffel (Copyright 1960, 1964), University of Nebraska Press, by permission.

Lewis Turco, "Image Tinges with No Color," (Copyright 1966 by Lewis Turco), reprinted with permission of the author.

Vachel Lindsay, "General William Booth Enters Into Heaven" (Jan 1913), "A Negro Sermon: Simon Legree" (June 1916), "John Brown" (June 1916), reprinted from POETRY with permission of the Editor of POETRY.

Vachel Lindsay, "General William Booth Enters Into Heaven," reprinted with permission of the MacMillan Company, New York, New York.

Wallace Stevens, "The Bird With The Coppery Keen Claws," and "Thirteen Ways of Looking At A Blackbird," (copyright 1923 and renewed 1951 by Wallace Stevens), reprinted from COLLECTED POEMS OF WALLACE STEVENS by permission of Alfred A. Knopf, Inc.

Irving Feldman, "Scratch," (Copyright 1961 by Irving Feldman), reprinted from WORKS AND DAYS, Little, Brown and Co. with permission of the author.

John Fandel, "Monday's Vision," reprinted from TESTAMENT & OTHER POEMS by John Fandel, Sheed and Ward (Copyright by Sheed and Ward 1959), by permission of the author.

Robert Frost, "Mending Wall," reprinted from THE POETRY OF ROBERT FROST, edited by Edward Connery Lathem (copyright 1930, 1939, and 1969 by Holt, Rinehart and Winston, Inc., and 1958 by Robert Frost, copyright 1967 by Lesley Frost Ballantine) by permission of Holt, Rinehart and Winston, Inc.

Lewis Turco, "On Being Disappointed at a Basketball Game," (Copyright 1959 by Lewis Turco) reprinted by permission of FINE ARTS MAGAZINE, University of Connecticut.

Howard Nemerov, "The Goose Fish," reprinted from NEW AND SELECTED POEMS by Howard Nemerov, copyright 1960 by University of Chicago, by permission of the author.

Raymond P. Staszewski and Lewis Turco, "Graduation," (Copyright 1972 by Lewis Turco), reprinted with permission of the authors.

Thomas Hardy, "The Temporary the All," reprinted with permission of the MacMillan Company, New York, New York.

Benjamin K. Bennett, "Alcaics," reprinted from POETRY (Oct. 1969) by permission of the Editor, (Copyright 1969) by POETRY.

Ogden Nash, "Kindly Unhitch That Star, Buddy," reprinted from VERSES FROM 1929 ON, by Ogden Nash (Copyright 1935) by permission of Little, Brown and Company, Boston, Mass.

Theodore Roethke, "Words for the Wind," reprinted from COLLECTED POEMS OF THEODORE ROETHKE (copyright 1955) by permission of Doubleday & Company, Inc., New York, N.Y.

Claire McAllister, "A Pantoum for Morning," (copyright 1964 by Claire McAllister) reprinted from ARMS OF LIGHT by Claire McAllister by permission of Alfred A. Knopf, Inc.

Russell Atkins, "Night and a Distant Church," reprinted from OBJECTS 2 by Russell Atkins, Renegade Press, Copyright 1963 by Russell Atkins, by permission of the author.

Lewis Turco, "A Dedication," "An Old Acquaintance," "An Ordinary Evening in Cleveland," "Burning the News," "Millpond," "Raceway," "Scarecrow," "The Old Professor and the Sphinx," (Copyright 1968 by Lewis Turco), reprinted with permission of the UNIVERSITY OF MISSOURI PRESS.

Ezra Pound, "In A Station of the Metro," reprinted from POETRY (April 1913) with permission of the Editor of POETRY.

Lewis Turco, "The Weed Garden," (Autumn 1971), reprinted from POETRY NORTHWEST, Vol. 12, No. 3, Seattle, Washington, by permission.

Vern Rutsala, "Evenings at Home," reprinted from *Northwest Review* with permission of the author. Copyright 1970 by *Northwest Review*.

Morton Marcus, "Hand," reprinted from ORIGINS, Kayak Press (copyright 1969 by Morton Marcus) by permission of the author.

Lewis Turco, "Seasons of the Blood," reprinted with permission of the Slow Loris Press. Copyright 1972 by Lewis Turco, by permission.

Lewis Turco, "The Dead Sailor," (Copyright 1968 by THE NATION), reprinted from THE NATION, New York, N.Y., with permission.

William Carlos Williams, "Marriage," reprinted from POETRY (November 1916), with permission of the Editor of POETRY.

William Heyen, "The Return." Published in POETRY (Copyright 1972 by William Heyen), reprinted with permission of the author.

A.R. Ammons, "Shore Fog," reprinted from BRIEFINGS: POEMS SMALL AND EASY, copyright 1971, by permission of W.W. Norton & Company, Inc., New York, N.Y.

J.V. Cunningham, "Epigram 11" and "Epigram 49," reprinted from THE COLLECTED POEMS AND EPIGRAMS OF J.V. CUNNINGHAM, copyright 1971, by permission of The Swallow Press, Chicago.

Margaret Macy, "Nahant," reprinted from INNERSPRING, I:2, 1971, by permission of the author. Copyright 1971 by INNERSPRING.

Dave Etter, "Country Graveyard," reprinted from THE LAST TRAIN TO PROPHETSTOWN by Dave Etter, copyright 1968 by University of Nebraska Press, by permission of the author.

Lewis Turco, "Pocoangelini 4," "Pocoangelini 7," "Pocoangelini 18," "Jasper Olson," (Copyright 1971 by Lewis Turco), reprinted with permission of Despa Press.

Kenneth Fearing, "Dirge," reprinted from NEW AND SELECTED POEMS by permission of Indiana University Press, Bloomington, Indiana.

Lewis Turco, "An Immigrant Ballad," "A Pastorale of Sorts," "Chant of Seasons," "Dead End," "Party Game," "Sabrina," "Street Meeting," "The Old Professor," "Totentanz," "Visitor," (Copyright 1960 by Golden Quill Press), reprinted with permission of THE GOLDEN QUILL PRESS, Francestown, New Hampshire.

Carl Sandburg, "Chicago," reprinted from POETRY (March 1914), with permission of the Editor of POETRY.

Lewis Turco, "Words for White Weather," (copyright 1970, 1971 by Lewis Turco), reprinted with permission of the author.

Weldon Kees, "After the Trial," reprinted from THE COLLECTED POEMS OF WELDON KEES by permission of the University of Nebraska Press.

Lewis Turco, "Balsamum Apoplecticum," and "A Talisman" (Copyright 1971 by MODERN POETRY STUDIES), reprinted with permission of MODERN POETRY STUDIES, Buffalo, New York.

Rudyard Kipling, "Soldier, Soldier," reprinted with permission of Thomas Y. Crowell Company, Inc.

Lewis Turco, "Odds Bodkin's Strange Thrusts and Ravels," (Copyright 1966 by Lewis Turco), reprinted with permission of THE OBERLIN QUARTERLY, Oberlin, Ohio.

John Crowe Ransom, "Bells for John Whiteside's Daughter," (copyright 1924 and renewed 1952 by John Crowe Ransom) reprinted from POEMS AND ESSAYS by John Crowe Ransom by permission of Alfred A. Knopf, Inc.

Williams Butler Yeats, "Crazy Jane and the Bishop," reprinted from COLLECTED POEMS (copyright 1933 by Macmillan Company) by permission of The Macmillan Company, New York, N.Y.

Alberta T. Turner, "From My Mother's Mother," reprinted from NEED, Ashland Poetry Press, copyright 1971 by Alberta T. Turner, by permission of the author.

W.D. Snodgrass, "April Inventory," (copyright 1957 by W.D. Snodgrass) reprinted from HEART'S NEEDLE by W.D. Snodgrass by permission of Alfred A. Knopf, Inc.

Henry Martin's cartoon copyright by New York Times Company and reprinted by permission.

Wallace Stevens, "Sunday Morning," reprinted here by permission of Alfred A. Knopf, Inc., Copyright 1923 and renewed 1951 by Wallace Stevens. From COLLECTED POEMS OF WALLACE STEVENS, Alfred A. Knopf, Inc., New York.

Richard Emil Braun, "Goose," reprinted from CHILDREN PASSING by Richard Emil Braun, University of Texas, copyright 1962 by Richard Emil Braun, by permission of the author.

Daryl Hine, "Bluebeard's Wife," reprinted from THE WOODEN HORSE, by Daryl Hine (Copyright 1965), by permission of Atheneum Publishers, New York, N.Y. First appeared in *Glamour* magazine.

Charles Causeley, "Ou Phrontis," published in UNION STREET (Copyright 1957 (London) 1958 (USA by Charles Causeley), reprinted with permission of the author.

Edwin Arlington Robinson, "Cliff Klingenhagen," reprinted from CHILDREN OF THE NIGHT, Charles Scribner's Sons, New York by permission of the publisher.

Acknowledgements continued on Page 405.

CONTENTS

INTRODUCTION

This book is *not* intended as a text in "creative writing." It is meant to introduce college students to the genre of poetry *from the writer's point-of-view*, by presenting them with the same problems that aspiring poets encounter as they develop into true poets. The book proceeds from some general observations to simple, and then through more complex exercises set forth in clear language, with many examples from all of English and American poetry.

This has never been done before—at least, not to my knowledge—on the college level, if on any level. In high school students are turned off poetry by teachers who have been trained to believe there are only two ways to write poetry, namely, in accentual-syllabic, usually rhymed, verse, or in "free verse," which none seem to be able to define. Although poets have been writing poems in a thousand different ways for centuries, students in high school are turned off poetry. . . . As a result, teachers often try to jam everything into metrics, and when it can't be done, both teachers and students know something is wrong, but they don't know what. So the teachers pretend everything is all right, and call the exceptions *free verse* or *sprung rhythm* or something equally undescriptive. At this point, students turn off and go to college.

In college they meet professors who also do not know the different prosodies of poetry (while I was writing this text, I explained *dipodics* to several of my colleagues, one of whom is a Ralph Hodgson scholar. Hodgson wrote in dipodics, and the scholar had never heard of it). These professors are scholars or critics, for the most part, and for their purposes *how* a poem is built doesn't matter. They are interested in more esoteric things.

It's as though a group of freshmen were taken out into the desert on a guided tour. They come to a beautiful palace called "Poetry," which is built high in the air on four marble pillars. When they arrive, the guide calls out, and someone lets down a golden ladder. The students climb up to the palace and are met by a professor who immediately ushers them into a vast baroque hall called "The New Criticism Throneroom." When they have finished there, the students visit the Freudian Wing for a time, with its loveseats and ornate couches. Then they enter the Jungian Parlor to look at the myths, depicted in great murals on the walls, and when they are tired they rest in the Transcendental Suite, full of starlight and Cosmic Muzak played through loudspeakers.

When they leave, it is night. The students climb down the golden ladder and are led blindly away—no one has shone a torch upon the marble pillars that support this marvel in the air. If someone had struck a light at the right time, the pupils would have seen signs on the four pillars: "The Typographical Pilaster," "The Sonic Pilaster," "The Sensory Pilaster," and "The Ideational Pilaster." If one had examined these pillars, he would have discovered how the magnificent Palace of Poetry was supported in the heavens by simple stone—the work of the craftsman.

I have just spun an *allegory*; a metaphorical construct that, in this case, talks about a genre of literature in terms of a fictive palace. It is one of the methods of poetry. This book will examine the *methods* of poetry. We will throw some light on the pillars, and leave it to others to conduct the major tours upstairs. Those tours, the points-of-view of scholars and critics are valid, *but so is the point-of-view of the writer*, whose work it is that the scholars and critics study. J. V. Cunningham has written an epigram (page 328) about this. It is writers who *built* the palace in the first place.

Many students will groan when they look at the exercises they will be asked to do. "But poetry is a gift of the Gods," they may say. "It is soul-stuff. Why do you want to tamper with my soul?"

My answer is, "Yes, poetry *is* soul-stuff. But it is the soul of humanity expressed in *language*, and the more one knows about language, the *material* of poetry, the better he can express what is in the heart.

Nothing but bad poetry is destroyed by examination. Even then, it is not the examination that destroys it; rather, it is the poetry that destroys itself. Bad poetry (a contradiction in terms, poetry is not bad, since poetry is consummate expression through language. Say, rather, failed attempts at writing poetry) contains a self-destruct mechanism: its badness is masked only by the ignorance of the perceiver. Do away with ignorance, and the knowledge of its badness shows up the failure.

For instance, many students—and his publishers—believe that Rod McKuen is the Great American Poet. No amount of contrary opinion can sway the students who so believe.
a Yeats scholar who teaches at the State University of New York College at Potsdam, brought in some typical McKuen poems to study . . . but let Londraville tell his own story:

"Last year I taught a course numbered Literature 102, which in our college is an introduction to literary genre. I have taught the course before, with generally satisfactory, if unspectacular, results. The students learn about the novel, short story, drama, and poetry. It is a course for beginners, unpretentious and modest. I am not looking for budding poets, or even budding critics. I would like to have my students leave the course with an elementary appreciation of literary form, and trust that their own taste and three more years of literature courses will develop a choice of reading which force feeding seldom can effect.

"Poetry, since it is the most demanding of the genres, is usually the least popular part of the course. I don't let this upset me, since I have learned that the most vehement detractors of poetry are often those same students who, later in their college careers, come to love it best. As freshmen, they are often the only students with a strong point of view; and since good poetry is often difficult and obscure, they are put off. None of us is that fond of frustration, and a poem can be every bit as puzzling as non-Euclidian geometry.

"I was surprised, therefore, that my latest class of 102 students "loved" poetry; they were genuinely eager to get to that part of the course. I do believe that students are, on the average, improving year by year, and so I first thought that some massive breakthrough had been engineered by ingenious high school teachers. There was also a marked increase in the number of unsolicited poems that students wanted me to comment on.

"These student attempts have always been a problem. If they are horrendous, I tend to beg off criticism; if they show some promise, I try to make suggestions for rewriting. The number of rewritten poems I have seen over the years has not been encouraging. Most students cannot or will not make the distinction between an emotion that they feel and the emotion contained in a poem. They know that they have *felt* sincerely while they were writing the poem; they see no reason why the emotion isn't apparent to me. They read their effort again, and the original emotion is recalled to them; the generalities which they have written become translated in their minds to the specific feeling which generated the attempt to write a poem.

"All of this is, of course, no news to anyone who has taught college freshmen. But it does, I believe, account in a large part for the appeal of Rod McKuen.

"When we began to study poetry, there was an initial interest from the class—excitement is too grand a term—but they did show a general enthusiasm, which unfortunately began to wane after the first two lessons. They wanted to hear nothing about form, which was not surprising, but they talked a great deal about the emotion generated by poems. There seemed to be a consensus that form and density could do little else than hinder poetry.

"Finally one of the more outspoken students asked if we could read some 'relevant' poetry, something from 'this century.' I was a bit taken aback, since we had just finished Allen Ginsberg's *Howl*, but I asked her if she had anyone particular in mind. She did, and her choice of McKuen elicited approving murmurs among her classmates. I had heard of him before, even had his poems thrust upon me by an undergraduate who felt there was something in me worth saving, but I must admit that I had not read much of the book. What I had read, however, struck me as especially mawkish. I asked the class what they liked about McKuen's poetry. 'He's real.' 'He tells it like it is.' 'He knows what it's like between a man and a woman.' Even the men in the class declared that if they had to read poetry, they would prefer McKuen to anyone I had offered to date.

"Certainly such enthusiasm shouldn't be squelched, so I promised to read *Listen to the Warm* and *Lonesome Cities.* I read them, and my opinion didn't change. The ideas were sentimental, and the execution was sloppy; but I did understand the appeal that he would have made to the undergraduate. The subject material was hip and topical; a few years ago it would have been too overtly sexual for its audience, but that has changed. Even the most stolid of the women's magazines would not now think of going to press without at least one article concerning orgasm.

"But sentimentality is not limited to mother, babies, and small animals: it is a deliberate attempt to make a point by excluding all of the facts except those which reenforce your view, and it may be used by a Secretary of State as well as by Elizabeth Barrett Browning.

"Sentimentality had lured my students, who were avowedly the least sentimental of humans. They had been tricked because the traditional subject matter of the sentimentalist had been replaced with 'relevant,' 'new' material. Not that I blame them. In a world as uncompromisingly complex as ours, simple solutions have tremendous appeal. I enjoy the sentimental myself, but I am not, I hope, deceived by it. It is much easier to give oneself to the easy generalization of a McKuen than to the paradoxes of a Donne or a Yeats; it requires a singular tough-mindedness which we are not always ready to assume. We are lazy animals, all of us, and understanding poetry is almost always a job we would rather work at tomorrow.

"Imagine the joy, then, of a young student with some pretensions to the intellectual who first reads McKuen. All of the ingredients seem to be there—the stuff certainly looks like poetry—and he enjoys it. If he cannot quite isolate the emotions that are elicited, at least they are pleasant emotions.

"As I have said before, I have no quarrel with his enjoying it; I enjoy some quite pathetic art myself. But how could I show the students in my class that their enjoyment of some work did not necessarily make it art? Certainly any argument would be rejected with, 'That's only your opinion.' I was over thirty, and 'too intellectual' to appreciate real emotion.

"I looked the books over more carefully, remembering that the poet Lewis Turco had told me that formula was always easier than form. I discovered that McKuen's poems conformed to a formula which could be

applied with embarrassing exactness to almost all of his work. The formula
is as follows:

"1. *Nostalgic tone.* The present for the persona is a time to be endured.
The really good times of his life are gone, never to return.

"2. *A lonely setting, emphasizing the separateness of the persona.* He is
either physically removed from others, strolling down a deserted strand
at low tide, for example; or he may be 'alone in a crowd,' surrounded
by people who are insensitive to him.

"3. *A male persona with female fantasies.* This statement may smack
of 'male chauvinism,' but the male is usually the one to break off a
love relationship. In McKuen's poems the situation is reversed. The
man pines for a woman who has left him, and he is powerless in his
love for her.

"4. *One contrived, 'pretty,' image,* usually having to do directly with
the sensuous appreciation of a woman or the warmth of remembered
and 'cuteness' than by appropriations. His use of syllepsis in 'A Cat
Named Sloopy' ('my arms full of canned liver and Love') is a fair
example.

"5. *Brevity.* The poem should not exceed twenty lines. Half that
length is better.

"6. *'Free verse'.* Rhyme may be used of course, but lack of craft
may be more easily concealed where there are fewer rules to follow.

"I knew that no mere analysis of this formula would convince my
students against their will, for their feelings about McKuen's poetry were not
based upon logic. I devised an alternate plan.

"I had noticed how similar McKuen's work was to undergraduate
attempts to write poetry. He was slicker of course, but the elemental
ingredients remained the same. With his formula in mind I wrote the
following three poems in seven minutes and twenty-three seconds:

FOR CASSANDRA

How long has it been
Cassandra, my Cass,
Since we dissolved our love's language
In fiery ecstasy?

As I was tasting the sweet
Marmalade sunshine of your body,
You were already planning
Your escape.

I am without you
And the sun filtering through
Tall buildings into my dusty room
Mocks me with its promise of warmth.

THE BRIDGE

I stand looking
On waters infinitely
Below me. The palings are
Parting the turbulent
River, as you severed
The unity that was our love.

I do not blame you.
I remember only
The sunlight in the
Hair of our love
Making fantastic patterned flowers
That once seemed indestructable.

AT THE SUPERMARKET

The decision for peanut butter
Jarred long rows of memories
And sent them scattering across the aisles.

I saw the back of your head
Through the maze of push-carts
And was stabbed, again,
By that succulent, cloudy mane
That always used to mingle
With our kisses.

Has it been only a year?

"I ran off copies of the poems and handed them out to my class.
The response was immediate. Not only did they recognize the author as
McKuen, but some of them even remembered having read the poems before.
I let them talk approvingly for a while, then I told them. They didn't
believe me, of course, so I wrote another on 'shoestrings,' a topic of their
choice, in under two minutes. (Speed comes with practice.)

"They were angry, certainly, but they were ready to listen. I explained
the formula to them, and they began to see that their favorite was as
predictable as a *Lassie* re-run. Some felt cheated, but I reminded them that

they had hoodwinked themselves. I also told them that they shouldn't now feel obliged to dislike McKuen's work, but to separate their judgment concerning a poem from any isolated emotional effect it might have upon them. Someone who has recently lost a parent, for example, will react a great deal differently to a poem dealing with death than will someone who has not had that experience. But the same kind of emotion might also be elicited by a photograph, or a piece of clothing belonging to the dead person. We must finally judge the poem on the consistency and honesty of its internal emotion, not on whether or not it tells us what we want to hear."

With this very simple formula in hand nearly anyone can write the "poems" of Rod McKuen. Both Landraville and I have had some of our students try it.

But how many people could write the poems of Yeats, or Shakespeare, or Alexander Pope? And *why* can't they?

The answer is again simple: Because there is a vast difference between the *formula* and the *formal*. Formulas pander to those who prefer not to have to use their minds very much. The formal appeals only to those who care enough about language to want to use or respond to it totally, in the best kind of way, in order to express or understand what is deepest inside the human mind and spirit. Formulas demand nothing except that one respond to them in superficial, automatic ways, like Pavlov's dogs salivating at the sound of a bell, as they had been programmed to do.

Poetry, on the other hand, is always formal. Whether the writer or reader knows it consciously or not, it has *form* in order to reach deeply, to touch finely, to say what is most meaningful to generations, not merely what is popular to a single generation. Rod McKuen is this present generation's Edgar Guest. I have asked my students on occasion if they knew who Edgar Guest was, and they have usually said they do not. But ask their grandparents, and they will know, though they have never heard of Rod McKuen.

The word *form* is another student turnoff. Say "form" to pupils; they think "sonnet." "The sonnet is dead," is a frequent claim, by elders as well as the young.

But "the sonnet" is not dead. It cannot die. It is merely a specific form. What people usually mean is that, in their opinion, nobody can write a sonnet anymore because the form has been done to death.

It isn't the form that's dead, though—it is the burden of tradition that lies upon the sonnet. When one thinks "sonnet," one doesn't think merely of the form, one thinks of all the sonnets he has had to read. And when one goes to write a sonnet, he *still* thinks of all those sonnets he has read. As a result, he often winds up writing a sonnet like Shakespeare, or Milton, or somebody. And he thinks, "I want to write like *me,* not like somebody else." And he grunts in disgust as he crumples the paper and tosses it into a wastebasket.

But if one can unburden himself of tradition, the form remains waiting to be used in a new way. It is neutral, merely a technique. Take the triolet, for instance—that form which Edgar Lee Masters puts down in his poem "Petit the Poet". Every little old lady from Dubuque to Oshkosh has written a triolet. Its burden of tradition is that the triolet is a pretty little thing, fit only for writing about fluffy cloudlets on a spring day, and daffodils on a lawn. Even the poet Dylan Thomas, when he was a child, wrote a triolet, and fell under the weight of the burden of tradition:

TRIOLET

The bees are glad the livelong day,
For lilacs in their beauty blow
And make my garden glad and gay.
The bees are glad the livelong day,
They to my blossoms wing their way,
And honey steal from flowers aglow.
The bees are glad the livelong day,
For lilacs in their beauty blow.

DYLAN THOMAS

A truly awful piece of work, unless one looks at it simply as an exercise in metrics. But even then, one need not have written a triolet about flowers and bees. This is a triolet, too:

JASPER OLSON

I take my women any way they come—
I'm Jasper Olson, brother, hard and fast
I play this game. Though some folks think I'm dumb,
I take my women any way they come,
and come they do. There's no time to be numb
in this life—grab it now and ram the past.
I take my women any way they come.
I'm Jasper Olson, brother, hard and fast.

from BORDELLO

I suppose one of the reasons I wrote "Jasper Olson" was just to see if, for once, someone couldn't dump the burden of tradition that encumbers the triolet. I found that the form *wasn't* dead. Only imagination is smothered by tradition, and all the poet needs to do in order to use an old form is to push the pillow off his face so he can breathe again.

"But form itself is restricting," one might answer. "Why can't I just do what I want, the way I want to do it?" My reply is, "You can—go ahead. But *know* what you're doing, because anything you do can be analyzed and judged—after all, you're using *my* language too."

"And I won't' use forms, either."

"Then what will you use?"

"Free verse. I want to be free."

"How free? As free as this?"—

```
                RE

(here)   (        )  (        )
(    )  (there)    (                  )
(    )  (              ) (here and there—I say here)
(                     ) (I do not say now) (                    )
( I do not say it now ) (        ) (                            )
                 )    (then and there—I say there) (           )
                            ) (        )  (say there)          )
(    )  (I do not say·then) (
(I do not say, then, this )  (            ) (      )
(              ) (then I say) (          )
(      )  (         ) (here and there)
            )  (first here)1 (              )
(I said here second) (        )  (                )
(                 )  (I do not talk first)   (             )
(              )  (              ) (there and then)
(         )  (here goes) (            )
(I do not say what goes) (        )  (          )
(                 )  (I do not go on saying)  (            )
(             )  (              ) (there is)
(      )  (that is not to say) (          )
(I do not say that) (         )  (       )
(              )  (here below) (            )
(        )  (              ) (I do not talk down)
(              )  (under my words) (              )
(under discussion)   (         )  (      )
(             )  (all there)   (                )
(    )  (       ) (I do not say all)
(             )  (all I say)  (           )
```

VITO HANNIBAL ACCONCI

"Yes, I'd like to be that free," students have answered when I showed them this poem.

"Look at the poem—just look at it: Hold it at arm's length. What do you see?"

"A lot of sets of parentheses."

"Right. How many?"

"Three in each line."

"Do all sets contain words?"

"No. Only one set in each line."

"Is there any pattern to which set is filled from line to line?"

The students study the poem. Then, invariably, at least one student raises his hand and says something like, "The first is filled in the first line; the second in the second; the third in the third; the second in the fourth, the first in the fifth . . . ."

"So the pattern of filling is 1–2–3–2–1–2–3–2–1, etc.?"

"Yes."

"Is it a form?"

Very unwillingly the answer: "Yes."

And I usually add, to rub it in a bit, "It is more formal and 'restrictive' than any sonnet I have ever read. But does the poem work? Does the form help the poet say what he wants to say (or doesn't want to say, in this case)?"

"Yes."

"Then the poem works. Its form is utilized to advantage. That's all anybody can ask of a form. *And all I mean by form is structure*—I don't mean something as narrow as you want to think I mean. *All* poems have structure—even failed poems. As likely as not, in a failed poem it is the structure that has fallen apart."

So this book will study all of the formalisms and structures of poetry. We will touch the marble pillars, examine the mortices and the colors of the stone, the material of language.

And, lest anyone think that I myself was brainwashed by some professor who was hung up on technique, let me say that this way of doing things comes naturally to me. In high school I wrote an answer to Walt Whitman's "Mannahatta"—years later I discovered I had written it in a prosody that was nearly perfect Anglo-Saxon prosody. Again, in high school I wrote a poem that I much later found to be strict quantitative accentual-syllabic verse. During four years in the Navy after high school, I taught myself many of the things I knew I needed to know if I were ever to hope to be that thing called a "poet." By the time I set foot in a college classroom, I was publishing in the literary magazines.

The reason I did these things was largely because when I first began to send poems out, I received a reply from an editor who told me just how badly I handled the language. She told me, "Perhaps in ten years you'll be a poet," if I worked hard, wrote much, experimented, and read a great deal.

She got me so angry I dove furiously into books and into myself. Within a year—when I was 19—the same editor accepted my first two poems for publication.

If this introduction has gotten you angry, too, all to the good.
I intended for it to upset you, at least. I hope it gets the poets angry, too,
because in this book I am going to be like the magician who shows the
audience how his tricks work—spilling the beans and dispelling the aura of—
mystery that surrounds the art of legerdemain. For too long, poets
have been like the members of the ancient cult of Magi—investing the simplest
rituals and concepts with mists and taboos.

Anyone can learn to write poetry. Individually, the techniques are
simple, though it takes concentration to learn them—concentration and
practice. No one can teach someone to write *great* poetry, however.
Only God or the Muses give talent—all the teacher can give is knowledge.
One thing I can guarantee: *Anyone* who reads this book and does the
exercises will know a great deal more about poetry than when he started—
and that's all this book is about, after all.

Poetry: An Introduction Through Writing has been tested in practice.
It is, in essence, the course that has been taught now for two years at
the State University of New York College at Oswego under the title
"The Nature of Poetry." More than 200 students have taken this course at
Oswego during the first two years. Furthermore, this book is based upon
the State University of New York's correspondence course study-guide titled
Creative Writing in Poetry, and many other students are currently enrolled
in the course through the various campuses of the University.

When S.U.N.Y. asked me to write the study-guide *Creative Writing
in Poetry*, examples of poems to illustrate the techniques were needed.
Since there was no money to pay permission fees to reprint poems by
contemporary authors, I was forced to use a number of my own poems as
examples.

In *Poetry: An Introduction Through Writing* I intended to use only
poems by other poets, but the publisher of this text asked me to retain
my poems from the study-guide, upon which this present work is based,
for the following reasons:

First, because students might be less hostile to discipline if they knew
that the author of the book had himself done the things he is asking the
students to do;

Second, because the book is by a practicing writer, and not by
someone who comes to poetry through scholarship or criticism;

Third, because many of those of my poems used here were written
at ages equivalent to the ages of college students (18-26 years);

Fourth, because there were in some cases simply no other examples
available—as, for instance, in the cases of Welsh *cynghanedd* and many of the
Japanese forms.

To these reasons, I would like to add one of my own: The impossibly
large reprint fees required by publishers of major poets who are now, for

the most part, passed away. In a sense, this has been a good thing, because it has served to remind me that I was not editing a comprehensive anthology of British and American poetry, but an introductory poetry text.

As a result, I have used a fair number of poems by major poets of the 20th century (as well as of other centuries, of course), but many more poems by young poets whom I consider to be fine writers.

I have tended to select the best poems I could find to illustrate the structures examined in the book. Wherever possible, I have used not only my own work, but the work of craftsmen—work I personally admire, at the same time that I maintained a catholicity of overall selection. I hope that I've come somewhere near my goal: To make a readable book out of a text that asks a good deal of the students who use it.

Lewis Turco
Oswego, N.Y.

FOREWORD

TO THE INSTRUCTOR

This will seem, at first glance, like a ridiculously tough book to hand freshmen and sophomores—but that is only because no one has ever attempted to teach a course in poetry in the same way that freshman composition has been taught for years.

There are no harder, and no easier, techniques covered in a good book on grammar.

What was wrong with the old approach to freshman composition was not that techniques "turned off" students, but that it violated a basic law of education: *There is no learning without motivation to learn.* We tried to teach 100% of our freshmen how to write discursive prose, and many of them were not interested in discursive prose. In fact, most of the *teachers* weren't interested, either, and the students knew it.

One cannot teach 100% of any group how to do a particular thing (nor can one interest 100% of an English department in teaching a particular course).

This book is intended to be used in a course which is not required for 100% of freshmen or sophomores, but which is an elective. There must be prior interest in poetry, on the parts both of students and instructor, before learning can take place.

If you are teaching a course which is required of students—*don't use this book*. Use one of the many "pop-zap," "feely-groovy" texts available. They will "turn on" your students; i.e., your students will learn little and be delighted with a course that requires little of them.

But if you feel, as I do, that students want to be challenged, then perhaps this is the text for you.

The publisher and i have been told many times that the approach used in this text is too rigorous. To this charge I can only reply, This is the course that has been in use at S.U.N.Y. College at Oswego since 1970, and it seems to work well. Many students who merely had an "interest" in poetry have discovered not only that they learned something about that in which they were interested, but also that they can write it. A few—freshmen and sophomores—have even begun to publish their work, not only on campus, but in national literary outlets as well—little magazines and student anthologies.

For years I was afraid to teach poetry this way. I did what we have all done—let the students decide what poetry is, and taught *down* to them. Circumstances helped me decide I was doing the wrong thing—that my teaching was not *actually* teaching, but largely public performance. I began to teach this course, and within a year other instructors, including a graduate teaching assistant, were teaching the course as well. We all discovered that our classes filled up each semester, and that most of our students enjoyed the work they were asked to do.

Not 100% of them enjoyed it, of course, but our proportions were no higher or lower than the proportions in other demanding courses. There are no panaceas, notwithstanding the fact that publishers keep trying, and the textbooks keep including more and more graphics and poor selections, less and less substance.

But these remarks will convince no one. Only a trial can do that, and an open mind to attend the open question.

1

DEFINING
THE POET

TREES

by Joyce Kilmer

I think that I shall never see
A poem lovely as a tree.

A tree whose hungry mouth is prest
Against the earth's sweet flowing breast;

A tree that looks at God all day,
And lifts her leafy arms to pray;

A tree that may in Summer wear
A nest of robins in her hair;

Upon whose bosom snow has lain;
Who intimately lives with rain.

Poems are made by fools like me.

But only God can make a tree.

Is that a poem? Perhaps most people would say yes, but most *poets*
would say no, it's not—it's a series of versified aphorisms, clichés dressed
up in rhymes and meters. Then what *is* poetry? It's a difficult question—
so difficult, in fact, that a truism has been invented by poets and others
who, for one reason or another, wish to avoid the necessity of giving an
answer: "Poetry is that literary art which is indefinable and mysterious."

If this answer does not satisfy us, we must turn to the lexicographer
who, unfortunately, is equally unsatisfactory: "Poetry," says the *Oxford
Universal Dictionary*, is "the art or work of a poet." The dictionary
defines the word in terms of its practitioner. And when we look up the
word *poet*, we discover that he is "one who composes poetry; a writer
of verse."

We have gone in a circle, and we stand almost where we started.
Almost, but not quite, for we have now "a writer of verse" besides our
circular definition. But if we pursue the dictionary further, we discover
a secondary definition of *poet*: "A writer in verse (or sometimes in
elevated prose) distinguished by imaginative power, insight, and faculty
of expression." This is important for us to remember: *much poetry is not
written in verse at all, but in prose*—"The Song of Songs," for instance,
and the prose poems of the French symbolists. Therefore, it will not do
simply to define the poet as "a writer in verse."

What do we have now? We have this: That a poet is one who writes
verse (which anyone might do) and sometimes prose, though an "elevated"
prose. That word *elevated* is going to be important eventually, when we
disentangle these snarled threads of definition. But right now it is vague
and frustrating, as is this entire attempt to pin down a reasonable
definition of *poetry*.

We ought, perhaps, to begin clean. Maybe we can take a clue,
though, from the definition of a poet as *one who writes poetry*. And it
may help if we shift our attention to other kinds of writers for a moment:
What is a novelist, for instance? A novelist is one who writes novels.
What is a novel? A novel is a long fictional narrative. All right, then,
what is a novelist? He is a writer of long fictional narratives. No trouble
at all there.

What is the novelist's (and the story writer's, for that matter) primary
job? To tell a fictive story—*to tell a story*. The fictionist, then, focuses on
narration, and his main use of language is as a vehicle for storytelling.
To tell his story he needs four basic elements: *character*, *plot*,
atmosphere, and *theme*, and he needs, besides, a number of narrative
language techniques.

What does the dramatist do? He writes drama. What is drama?
Drama, says the dictionary, is "a composition in prose *or* verse [my

emphasis], adapted to be acted on the stage, in which *a story is related* by means of *dialogue and action* [my emphasis again]. . . ." What is the difference between the dramatist and the fictionist?

The answer is, *there is none* except that the dramatist is more severely limited in the range of language techniques at his disposal. There is not even a difference in *mode*—that is, prose or verse— because some novels have been written in verse, for instance; the novels of the 20th century writer Christopher La Farge. In fact, the first novels were called *epics,* and they were written in verse. The dramatist must, like the fictionist, use the basic ingredients of the story: character, plot, atmosphere, and theme; however, he can ordinarily use only the narrative language technique of dialogue. Unlike the fictionist, the dramatist may supplement this narrative technique with theatrical techniques, such as representation (scenes, costumes, and physical actions). The dramatist's focus, in his play, is still upon the narrative—he, too, is a storyteller.

What about the essayist? What does he write? The question is rhetorical by now. All right, then, what is an essay? In its modern sense, an essay (according to the *Oxford Universal Dictionary*) is "A book or writing which treats of some particular subject; now always one containing a methodical discussion or exposition of the principles of a subject." Why does one write an essay?—*to prove a point regarding a subject.*

The essayist's focus, then, is upon the subject he is examining, and his techniques are generally those of rhetoric rather than of narration. The basic elements of the essay are 1) the *subject* being examined; 2) the *thesis,* or statement of the point to be made concerning the subject; 3) the *argument,* or the logical proofs and data required to back the thesis statement; and, 4) the *conclusion* reached, which is usually identical with the thesis.

A summary of literary focuses may be in order at this point: The fictionist focuses on the narrative; the dramatist does likewise; the essayist focuses on the examination of a subject. We are left with the poet. What is his focus? What's left?

There is nothing left but the language itself.

The poet focuses his attention upon the literary resources of the language. He may use *all* of the techniques of the fictionist, the dramatist, the essayist; he has at his disposal exactly the same things that other writers have, but the difference between the poet and other writers is in focus: The poet regards language as a material, much as a graphic artist regards his pigments, clay, or ink. *To the poet, language is a substance to be molded and shaped.* All else is secondary, because the poet realizes that *how* something is said often has more to do with *what* is said than anything else: Something said well is something well-said; *but something said superbly is a poem.*

It is time to return to that vague word "elevated" that we found in our original attempt to define "poet." How does Oxford define *elevated?* —"Raised up; at a high level. Also . . . exalted in character; lofty, sublime . . . elated . . . slightly intoxicated."

That last definition, Oxford says, is intended to be used in a jocular sense, but it is perhaps most to the point, for a good definition of a poet might be, "A writer who is intoxicated with language."

Some people will think that too jocular a definition, though many poets would be quite happy to leave it at that. On the other hand, very few poets would be satisfied with the definition, "A writer of verse." Why? Because verse is merely *one* language technique, not *all* of them, and the poet refuses to be limited in any way. He refuses to be satisfied with knowing only one or a few things about language, he insists upon knowing everything he can about the medium in which he works. He may learn these things by himself, and never consciously learn a single definition of any of the techniques he is using, *but merely because he doesn't know what he is doing doesn't mean he isn't doing it.* And learning the definitions won't hurt him. In fact, making conscious a knowledge of the techniques at his disposal may open up new reaches and vistas of possibility to him, for the poet takes as his province the entire realm of language. He should not cut himself off from any aspect of language unless he has tried it and found that it doesn't suit his purposes.

To write only in verse is limiting and, to reiterate an earlier point, anybody can write in verse—advertising men writing jingles, song writers, the lady next door who does sonnets for the garden club. The word *poet*, Robert Frost has said, is a "praise-word." The poet elevates the language. He does everything any other writer does, but he concentrates upon using these things more completely—he wrings everything he can out of every word: denotation, connotation, sound, association, stress, imagery, and so on and on. He handles and forms the language as a potter handles and shapes clay; he molds language into an art object. That is to say, poetry is not to be defined in terms of a particular mode, such as prose or verse, but rather in terms of intensity of concentration *on* mode, on language of whatever species.

Any writer, in either mode, whose main focus is upon the resources of the language itself, is a poet. He may write rhymed quatrains, or he may write prose-poems. He may narrate a story; he may, in fact, be called a novelist by some people—one thinks of James Joyce, who wrote a modern "novel" in prose, but followed the epic form, and even titled it after a character in an epic: *Ulysses.* James Joyce is much more the poet in his novels than in his *Pomes Penyeach,* which are very rigid, old-fashioned lyrics written in metered forms. Not that there is anything wrong with meters and forms—merely that Joyce doesn't use them with anything like the genius he displays in his prose.

The poet may write plays in verse, as Shakespeare did, winning the honorific title "The Bard of Avon"—we don't call him "The Playwright of Avon." Or the poet may write in "elevated" prose, like the playwright Synge. But as long as the narrative is secondary to language, to *how* he does what he does—and, one might add, provided that his work is qualitatively successful—he is a poet, not something else.

On the other hand, someone may write a narrative in verse—one thinks of a person like Robert Service who wrote humorous verse narratives such as "The Cremation of Sam McGee." Service's interest is in the narrative and in the humor, not particularly in the language—he is a fictionist, a story-writer in verse, not a poet, for his concern is not the molding and elevation of language (and, thereby, the molding and elevation of observation, of thought, of a thousand things that can be done only in language).

One can, of course, always get into a debate about whether or not a particular piece is a poem, about whether a particular writer is a poet or a novelist. Opinion will always play a large part in the evaluation of literature. The object here isn't to pigeonhole people or genres—merely to clear up some general vagueness and ambiguity in the definition of the genre of poetry.

My remarks to this point may help to explain why poetry, for many people, is so "difficult" to experience. In our reading, we are used to focusing upon narrative or explanations of how to make or do things, or upon arguments; not upon the language itself, not upon language as substance. We, as readers, are adept at following techniques such as plot and exposition, but not so adept at responding to language as it simultaneously operates on a variety of levels. Every true poem is a complex (but not necessarily *complicated*) organism comprised of several interdependent patterns.

2

OF PROSODICS:

an overview

This chapter will make a quick survey of many of the elements of language art which will be treated at greater length elsewhere. If, in this quick view, it seems that the art of poetry is very complicated, don't be discouraged. Each of the elements is basically quite simple, and you will be led through them one at a time, in as clear a manner as possible. The complexity of poetry does not derive from single elements, but from manipulating these elements simultaneously in the total art object that we call a "poem." But if each element is mastered individually, the unconscious mind will absorb it and eventually enable one to write better than he might have thought possible. The elements become "second nature," and the resultant poems are "natural." The poet, when he has developed his techniques, just sits down and writes—he doesn't have to say to himself, "Now I'm going to build a metaphor." He just does it, because he has learned *how* to make metaphors. But while he is learning his art, he must expend as much sweat as the beginning painter, or architect, or musician. It's a long way from piano finger exercises to the concert hall, but the early training is essential, and the final performance *seems* effortless. It is in this *seeming* that art lies, and poetry is as much an art as any other.

Very often, even when he is unaware of it—when he is out shopping, or sitting in contemplation—the poet's mind is at work sorting things out, organizing. Then, suddenly, the urge to write will strike, and he will sit down and write a real poem. Some call this "inspiration," but what it really is is the signal that the poet is ready to create, and his mind tells him so. But if he has no techniques with which to work, he will write on a lower level than he would have if he had mastered his craft. Writing cannot take place in a vacuum, though it must take place in the solitary act.

In order to create, in order to mold the language, the poet must have some kind of system, or *prosody*—a theory of poetic composition or *organizing principle* —within the bounds of which he can build his structure. Form, then, whether it be "internal" and "organic," or "external" and "formal," is of major importance.

Unfortunately, when one says "form," many people think only of some structure that is traditional, such as the sonnet. But *every element of language is a form of some kind.* The letters of the alphabet are forms, conventions we have agreed upon in order to communicate. So are words, phrases, and sentences. The poet is interested in all of these things, since his medium is language. He may also be interested in sonnets, which are metrical forms, but at the very least, he is interested in words and in how to put them together, and in language structures.

This is not to say that poetry depends upon a particular organizing principle, a particular prosody, such as rhymed metrical verse. Meter is only one kind of prosody, and a prosody can be based upon any aspect of language, be it rhythm, or grammar, or figures of speech, or syllables, or words, or letters, or what-have-you. All that is necessary is that the system be unified and coherent, and that the products of the system be successful in terms of the system, and in terms of the reader's perception of and response to the system.

That any coherent prosody is acceptable is not readily understood by many readers of English verse, for they are so used to metrical structures that all other prosodies seem alien. However, there are at least *four* different prosodies traditional to the English language; all are ancient, and all are still in use in the twentieth century.

The first, and perhaps the original prosody, is ACCENTUAL VERSE, which is as old as Old English. The major form of English accentual verse is Anglo-Saxon prosody. This prosody is that in which *Beowulf* is written, not to mention such later poems as *Piers Plowman* and *Sir Gawain and the Green Knight.* Anglo-Saxon prosody has been written in our own era, and other accentual forms—some of them, like "sprung rhythm," derived from Anglo-Saxon prosody—have been used by poets as disparate as Gerard Manley Hopkins and Wallace Stevens. What is the basis for accentual verse?—*The counting of stressed* (accented) *syllables in a line of verse,* paying no attention to the unstressed syllables.

Thus, in the broad sense of the word, accentual verse is a *meter* too—a
measure, a counting.

Here is a poem written in accentual verse. Although it is not
Anglo-Saxon prosody, it comes very close. Each line has two stressed
syllables. In fact, each *pair* of lines might be considered one *stich* (which
means *line*), and each single line would then be considered a *hemistich*
(or *half-line*). Each pair of lines—each stich—has in its center a rhythmic
pause or *caesura*. In this poem, the pause is often set off by punctuation,
but sometimes only by a phrasal pause (a place where one naturally
pauses to take a breath, or where one briefly hesitates in order to
separate phrases that might otherwise run together in a confusing
manner), or by a typographical layout which makes the eye briefly pause
before it goes on to the next hemistich:

MON COEUR

He will live,
                    hew love. His limb
is the dove's perch,
                    time's lurching,
a green waking.
                    No mind's nor world's
fool—rather,
                    the meadow's madman
who is spared by wind,
                    whose spirit
has no ending. He
                    sings everything,
no one thing.
                    None know his
sense, yet all
                    may understand him.
Of this bright earth,
                    of bone's and blood's
humor, still
                    he is sky's as well.
That stone, sterile,
                    in the brown hand of the
poet shall turn
                    to loam. That stone
is the world's fruit
                    to be held, hurled in
an arc, eaten,
                    beaten, driven as an
ass is driven
                    over the good ground.

Who is he,
　　　　this holy man who
thinks with his flesh?
　　　　　　He is none but
himself, he is no one
　　　　　　and he is all,
a bridegroom, a bride,
　　　　　　bird and snake,
priest, prophet,
　　　　the namer and the sayer.

SYLLABIC VERSE is also "metrical" in the final analysis. It is based
upon *the counting of all syllables* in a line of verse, whether they are
stressed or unstressed. Japanese verse is syllabic, but more to the point,
so was Celtic verse—the poetry of the ancient Gaels of Scotland, Ireland,
Wales, and Cornwall, among other regions of the British Isles. There is
even a native American form of syllabics—the *cinquain.*

The cinquain is an example of *quantitative syllabic verse,* which
simply means that each line is of a different syllabic length, but the
lengths are *pre-set*: One must always observe the traditional syllabic
lengths of each line.

Originally, the poem was done in iambic meters (we will study
iambics later): In the first line there was one iamb, in the second there
were two, in the third there were three, in the fourth there were four, and
in the final line there were again two. But over the years this iambic base
was abandoned, and only the syllable-count remained: There were two
syllables in line one, four in line two, six in line three, eight in line four,
and two syllables in the last line. There are no rhymes in the cinquain.

One may invent one's own quantitative syllabic structures. If the
poem is of more than one stanza, each line of succeeding stanzas has the
same syllable-count as the corresponding line in the first stanza. Here is
an example of an unrhymed poem written in quantitative syllabics:

AN OLD ACQUAINTANCE

As we stand talking, his eye
　drops out. I am amazed.
　His socket looks funny.
　It's a nice day, I say.
His scalp is scattered on the

carpet. What's the matter with
　your nose, I ask—but it
　is too late. He laughs. His
　teeth hit something on their
way down. I must be getting

on, I suggest. But I am
  too slow to catch his ear.
  Can't you say something, I
  inquire: he opens his
mouth to show me. That's too bad,

I say, but he shakes his head
  too hard. I try looking
  into his mind, but he
  is thinking of nothing.
A spider is spinning her

web in a white cave. It is
  awkward. Well, it's getting
  late, I say. The spider
  has caught something. I smile
at him; he stands there grinning.

One may also write poems written in *normative syllabics*: The poet
chooses to write all the lines of his poem in a single length, with only
minor variations—one or two syllables, perhaps—in the lengths of
particular lines. Here is a poem written in *decasyllabics,* or lines that are
each ten syllables in length:

THE GLASS NEST

The angel hair of winter—come down to
Spring from the Feast of the Nativity—
lies among crocus under the lilac:
a moss of spun glass among spears of green
and cream. Pendulous upon a limb, seed
and suet dangle in the wind straining
through the straining bush: a roof of birds.
Nuthatch and black-capped chickadee, grackle
and cowbird—white with grey, black upon brown—
move among the branches and the sunlight
(like a bright ladder for wings) which coaxes
life out of the bark in furious buds.

The snow has melted, all but the false snow,
filaments spun from silica, mica
ice made for a metal tree topped by a
star of tinsel whose light was wired to our
wall. Carpets and curtains between us and
the wind, winter's emblem glistened above
gifts no Magi could have dreamt in their sands
or tamarinds: glistened for a space.
                                        Now
the birds come tearing the angel hair, their

eyes bright with birth. Our useless artifice
shall make a glass nest in a real tree. Its
dangle will be rare among sunlight and
showers, leaves, limbs, explosions of true wings.

Syllabics are perhaps as old as accentuals, and are traditional to our
language through Gaelic and French influences; for, if we consider the
Celtic to be peripheral to English, French is not, and the traditional
French prosody is syllabics. In fact, it was the French language which,
after the Norman invasion of England in 1066, dominated and helped to
transform Old English—basically a Germanic language—until our
language re-emerged later as Middle English, the immediate predecessor
of our modern tongue. For two or three centuries the poetry of England
was largely Norman French; it was syllabic (see the plate "The Literary
Languages of Britain" for illustrations of the languages and prosodies
used in British lands throughout history). It had to be syllabic because,
whereas Old English was an inflectional language—that is, a language
which at root was based on sequential stressed and unstressed syllables—
the French language (or so the French maintain) is not. When a rare
syllable in French is stressed, it must be so indicated by an *accent grave*
or *aigu*.

Thus, the French are prohibited from basing a prosody upon
sequential stressed and unstressed syllables. They therefore count, they
measure, all syllables. The English-language poet, on the other hand, has
no such limitation—he may count *either* stresses *or* syllables . . . or *both,*
as we shall see shortly. The modern American poet Marianne Moore
chooses to count syllables rather than stresses. The Welsh poet Dylan
Thomas, who wrote in English, also chose syllabics as his meter. Both
these poets chose to rhyme their syllabic poems. Here is a poem by
Marianne Moore in rhymed quantitative syllabics; it contains only one
variation in the syllabic lengths of the lines—line two of stanza one is six
syllables long. All other second lines are of five syllables. *By no means is
this a defect of the poem.* Only a poor poet is slave to form. Form is
merely the backbone of the poem; it releases meanings, it does not
imprison them if it is used well. If it is necessary for the poet to break
his *form* for the sake of the *poem,* he will do so without hesitation. The
poem is the important thing, after all, not *rigid* structure:

TO MILITARY PROGRESS

You use your mind
like a millstone to grind
    chaff.
You polish it

and with your warped wit
   laugh

At your torso,
prostrate where the crow
   falls
on such faint hearts
as its god imparts,
   calls

and claps its wings
till the tumult brings
   more
black minute-men
to revive again,
   war

at little cost.
They cry for the lost
   head
and seek their prize
till the evening sky's
   red.

MARIANNE MOORE

The English language has borrowed and absorbed so much from other languages that there are limitless possibilities for invention within it. For instance, it is possible to postulate a prosody which might be called MORAICS—a system based upon *only the counting of unstressed syllables in a line of verse,* paying no attention at all to the stressed syllables, though whether anyone has actually done this is a question. It would be a difficult prosody to analyze. Moraics would look a great deal like "free verse," about which we will have more to say shortly.

In English there is a fourth possibility for a *metrical,* or counting, prosody: One may choose to *count the number of syllables in the line,* and then *count the number of stressed syllables as well.*

When Middle English had reasserted the dominance of our tongue over French in the high middle ages, writers such as Chaucer and his contemporary John Gower felt that a new metric was necessary. They knew that English had both stressed and unstressed syllables, and, too, they had been influenced by the French syllabic prosody to a great degree. Thus, they needed a verse vehicle which could accommodate both elements, both the old and the new. They were very successful, for their invention, ACCENTUAL-SYLLABIC VERSE, has become the accepted norm for verse in English.

Accentual-syllabic prosody counts both the number of syllables in the line and the number of accents. Moreover, the accented syllables will alternate *more or less* regularly with the unaccented syllables. We call this type of verse "metrical," but in fact it is no more metrical than syllabics, accentuals, or moraics. All four prosodies count.

Here is "The Complaint of Chaucer to His Purse" in Middle English. Poetry is often held to be untranslatable, and the reason for this is that poetry, being language art, cannot be taken out of the context of the language and time at which it is written because too much will be lost: The sound of the words and sentences; the overtones of words as they may have existed in another period—many things. It is easier to translate fiction, drama, or nonfiction, because any narrative may be told in any tongue, any argument made in another language. But poetry, in a very real sense, *is* the language. Something will always be lost in the translation of any genre, but poetry is always almost totally lost in translation. Nevertheless, Middle English is close enough to Modern English so that a translation of this poem may give readers who are unfamiliar with the earlier tongue some idea of its original effect. A modern version follows the original:

COMPLAINT TO HIS PURSE

To yow, my purse, and to noon other wight
  Complayne I, for ye be my lady dere!
I am so sory, now that ye been lyght;
  For certes, but ye make me hevy chere,
  Me were as leef be layd upon my bere;
For which unto your mercy thus I crye:
Beth hevy ageyn, or elles mot I dye!

Now voucheth sauf this day, or yt be nyght,
  That I of yow the blisful soun may here,
Or see your colour lyk the sonne bryght,
  That of yelownesse hadde never pere.
  Ye be my lyf, ye be myn hertes stere,
Quene of comfort and of good companye:
Beth hevy ageyn, or elles moote I dye!

Now purse, that ben to me my lyves lyght
  And saveour, as doun in this world here,
Out of this toune helpe me thurgh your myght,
  Syn that ye wole nat ben my tresorere;
  For I am shave as nye as any frere.
But yet I pray unto your curtesye:
Beth hevy ageyn, or elles moote I dye!

GEOFFREY CHAUCER

THE COMPLAINT OF CHAUCER TO HIS PURSE

To you, my purse—to no one else in sight—
  I make complaint, for you're my lady dear!
I am so sorry now that you are light
    For, certainly, you make such heavy cheer
    I'd just as soon be laid upon my bier.
I throw myself upon your mercy, cry,
Be heavy, a gain, or else I must die!

Grant me this day—lest it be turned to night—
  Your blissful jingle ringing on the ear,
Or let me see your sunshine color bright:
    Its yellowness has never owned a peer.
    You are my life, heart's helmsman at the steer,
Queen of comfort and of good company.
Be heavy again, or else I may die!

Now, purse, that are to me my lifetime's light
  And savior (that is, down in this world here),
Help me get out of town with all your might,
    Since you refuse to be my treasurer
    (For I am shaved as close as any friar).
Yet, again, I pray unto your courtesy,
Be heavy again, or else may I die!

Chaucer wrote his poem in a traditional stanza form—*rime royal.* All lines are iambic pentameter (five iambic feet in each line). The stanza is a septet (seven lines long) rhyming *ababbcc.* In most poems written in rime royal the rhymes change after the first stanza, but Chaucer *chose* to continue the poem with the original rhymes, and in addition he made the last line a *refrain* (a line that is repeated at set intervals throughout the poem, usually at the end of each stanza). In this case, the refrain is an *incremental refrain,* because he changed a word in some way each time the refrain reappeared, so that the meaning of the line changed slightly each time as it gained momentum toward the climax of the poem.

Here is a contemporary poem written in another traditional stanza form—*quatrains* (four-line stanzas). The meter is iambic tetrameter (four iambic feet in each line). The poem, written in a college writing arts workshop, *does not rhyme*—it uses *consonance* (similarity of sound) rather than rhyme (identity of sound). The poem *consonates abab, cdcd,* and so forth:

DEAD END

DEAD END shouted black-on-yellow.
Yet I, unbelieving, drove
On until I reached a fallow
Field beside a gutted grove.

There the road derived its dying
From a fang that tore the lip
Of the earth. The grove, unseeing
How its fate had changed in shape

Owing to a bulldog boulder,
Stood and meditated death:
Passively denied The Builder
And the light that loves the moth.

Where the civilized macadam
Halted at the brooding rock,
There I stood and cursed my Sodom,
Knowing that I, too, must look

And, in seeing, rub the pillared
Salt that was my soul in wounds
That had turned the field thrice pallid,
Made the grove devoid of sounds.

Finally I turned my back and
Went the way that I had come;
Left the sign still shouting DEAD END—
Grove and field and boulder, dumb.

At this point, a note concerning QUANTITATIVE ACCENTUAL-SYLLABIC VERSE may be called for. The prosody of the ancient Greeks depended upon a system in which each syllable was assigned its particular "length," much as notes in the musical scale may be eighth notes, or quarter notes, or half notes, or whole notes. Many English writers, particularly in the Renaissance, experimented with quantitative accentual-syllabics, assigning English syllables specific lengths. None of these experiments was really successful, perhaps because English intonations are not codified—no system of syllable "lengths" is widely accepted.

As a result, quantitative accentual-syllabics can really be understood only in terms of a sub-order of NORMATIVE ACCENTUAL-SYLLABIC VERSE: We can *pre-assign* certain verse feet in a line of verse—i.e., as in a line of *Sapphics;* trochee (-◡), trochee, dactyl (-◡◡), trochee, trochee—rather than simply setting an accentual-syllabic norm, say iambic pentameter, and then following the meter with variations.

Sapphics is a Greek form. It is unrhymed. The *Sapphic line* is eleven syllables long, and it contains five *verse feet*, as described above. The *Sapphic stanza* is made up of three such lines followed by a shorter line, an *adonic,* which is a single dactyl (-◡◡) followed by one trochee. This is the Sapphic stanza (◡ stands for an unaccented syllable; - stands for an accented syllable):

-◡ -◡ -◡◡ -◡ -◡

-◡ -◡ -◡◡ -◡ -◡

-◡ -◡ -◡◡ -◡ -◡

-◡◡ -◡

And here is an example of a poem written in Sapphic stanzas:

VISITOR

Visitor, you've come and have gone while I was
gone, while winds were moving through open windows,
billowing the drapes in my vacant chambers,
    sounding the silence;

come and gone, whoever you were, and left no
note but quiet sliding among the shadows.
Here before my house, by the stolid doorway,
    I remain watching—

listening where you must have lingered, waiting.
I stand listening for the bell's thin echo,
knowing for a certainty you were here and
    left without echo.

All will turn out differently now. Behind this
door there stands an alien future. Words that
needed speaking have not been spoken, and the
    time that has not been

spent correctly now must be handled strangely,
sold less truly: used in another manner.
Sounds have not been breasted. The stillness thickens
    over your footfalls.

Visitor, between us are tunnels sealed and
hollow; there are depths where once there were crossings.
There are windows, too, gone opaque with wonder,
    darkling with questions.

The first and last lines of the first stanza of this poem have been *scanned*. *Scansion* enables one to see where the stressed and unstressed syllables fall in a line of verse. The perpendicular line (|) plays no part in the actual scansion; it is merely a *divider,* showing the separations between the verse feet.

The rhythms of each line are *falling rhythms*: in each verse foot the accent falls on the *first* syllable. If a line ends in a falling rhythm, it is called a *feminine ending.* Conversely, if the rhythms of a line are *rising rhythms,* in each verse foot the accent falls on the *last* syllable, and lines ending in rising rhythms are *masculine endings.*

In a Sapphic poem there may be any number of stanzas, which are a form of the quatrain. Certain substitutions for some of the verse feet are allowable in these pre-set meters: One may substitute a spondee (– –) for a trochee in lines one and two, feet numbers two and five, and one may do the same in line three, foot number five.

We will have more to say about quantitative accentual-syllabics later on.

3

OF NON-METRICAL PROSODIES:

an overview

Earlier, we noted that there were "at least four" prosodic systems (excluding moraics) that are traditional to the English language. What is there left? We have gotten used to calling it "free verse," but the term is erroneous in that "free verse" is a catch-all term that we use to "describe" (in fact, to *avoid* describing) a large number of prosodies that have nothing to do with counting syllables of any kind. Second, it is wrong because it is a French term translated and misapplied to the English language.

The term "free verse" is derived from the French term *vers libre* which Ezra Pound, Amy Lowell, and others began to popularize during the 'tens and 'twenties of this century, in the pages of Harriet Monroe's *Poetry* magazine and elsewhere. But as it is applied to English prosodies, the term is misleading, if not actually inapplicable.

As one may easily see by examining French verse forms, the French prosodic system is syllabic, not accentual. The reason for this, as has already been mentioned, is that the French consider their language to be *without* stresses; thus, they are precluded from using any accentual or accentual-syllabic system.

It should be clear, then, that if the French refrain from writing lines that contain specific numbers of syllables, their verse is "free." However, this is *not* the case with verse written in English.

The English language is obviously a stressed language—we can hear the cadences of our words. It has been said, in fact, that English is basically an iambic language. And we say, further, that any English-language poet, whether he be a "free verse" poet or otherwise, must have an "ear" . . . that is, an ear for cadences, for rhythms.

Therefore, English poetry can never be "free" in the sense that French poetry may be *libre*. No matter what the English-speaking poet may do, his verse will be basically accentual (though he may use other systems besides accentuals). In fact, one might go so far as to point out that *most free verse poems in English are basically iambic, or mixtures of iambic and anapestic measures.*

To go even farther, since the poet's work is to mold and "elevate" the language within some organizing principle (some prosody), it is evident that any poet, even the French poet, is never really "free" of structure, so the term is wrong in French as well, except in a very narrow sense. Actually, rather than talk about "free verse," we ought to isolate the elements upon which a non-metrical (non-counting) poet bases his prosodic organizing principle, and then give his system a name that is descriptive of his method.

NON-METRICAL PROSODIES

Some non-metrical prosodies are based upon grammar rather than on counting, and, generally, these systems should properly be called GRAMMATICS. Only in a very loose sense can they be called "verse" at all—they are really forms of *prose,* if we mean by *verse* a measured line. Many "free verse" forms, then, are prose forms—but, as we have argued, they may still be poems: One may write poems in either the prose mode or the verse mode.

One such theory was practiced by the ancient Hebraic poets who derived their system from the even more ancient Chaldeans. Grammatic prosodies, then, are really the oldest (and simplest) systems traditional in the western world, if not in the whole world. The work of the Hebraic poets may be found in English in the *Bible;* specifically, in the King James version, published in 1611, though other English versions appeared earlier, and versions in Latin, Greek, French, and other languages have influenced us since Anglo-Saxon times.

In English translation, at least, a large portion of the verses of the *Bible* are written, not in ordinary prose (though that is how it appears to the layman), but in a grammatic prosody; to be precise, in a system of parallel sentence structures. There are four major types of parallel grammatical structures that may be isolated in the *Bible*: SYNONYMOUS PARALLELISM, SYNTHETIC PARALLELISM, CLIMACTIC PARALLELISM, and ANTITHETICAL PARALLELISM.

Synonymous parallelism breaks each verse in two. The first half will say something; the second half will repeat, in different words, the same thing as the first; i.e., "The sun is setting; | heaven's fire flickers in the west."

Synthetic parallelism also divides the verse, but the second half gives a consequence of the first: "In the sky, darkness; | the birds settle out of the air."

Antithetical parallelism, too, breaks the verse in half, but the second half rebuts or contradicts the first half: "Silence among all things; | quietude is a tumult."

Climactic parallelism is easiest of all: Each succeeding verse builds upon the preceding verses until a climax is reached (in longer poems, a series of climaxes):

The sun is setting; heaven's fire flickers in the west.
In the sky, darkness; the birds settle out of the air.
Silence among all things; quietude is a tumult.
Night walks out of the mountains to lie upon the land.

The last line, of course, is the climactic parallel.

In Hebrew prosody there might be other strictures imposed upon the system. For instance, a *perfect parallel (isocolon)* is one that not only divides the verse, but in each half there might be required the same number of words, even the same number of syllables: "A time to live, | a time to die" is a famous example, and English-language poets have used WORD-COUNT PROSODY either as a system by itself, or in conjunction with grammatic parallels. In any particular poem any one parallel may be used throughout; any combination of the four may also be used.

Here is a prose poem that uses several parallel structures. For now, we need isolate only one: Notice that in almost every paragraph (these are not stanzas) there are only two sentences or independent clauses. There are variations in paragraph four, which is made up of a single sentence, and in paragraph nine, which has two sentences, but three independent clauses:

THE LIVINGROOM

The chairs of his livingroom lounge thinking in groups. Couches remember what it was like here yesterday and the day before.

Lamps dimly recall old shadows in the various corners. The carpet ruminates, sometimes darkly, but again less so, running out perhaps from under a table.

Two candles counterpoint an African violet, broadleafed in a large pot; their sentinel lances prefigure a grey print in a grey frame behind them on the wall.

The gentleman's chair—gainly in complement beside the grace of a lady's rocker, yet separated from her moods by the sewing cabinet—stands in the far corner, a boy's skull growing out of the cutplush of the fabric of the seat.

The boy's ivory jaw falls and closes. The child is singing.

He listens, the Inhabitant of this room, as his furniture is listening, but the boy is not singing to him, obviously, for he can hear nothing. Yet the chairs are enthralled—even the candles seem to lean in the direction of the skull making silence vocal.

The skull is yellow, and there is yellow thread in a needle which lies on the wood of the sewing cabinet, but the dominant tone of the furniture is brown, as brown as the study into which the Inhabitant has sunken. Why can't he hear what the boy is singing, bone against the upholstery and the ornate arms, the frame of bent dark wood like the oval of an egg?

He watches the skull grow upward on its stem of spine; he waits till it is tall as a lily, and the chairs wait, the couches roar quietly.

If the boy begins to stare at him, what will he do? His hair is thinning, it is true, and he has a slight stomach—yet he is a lover of song; it is not his fault.

Perhaps it would be well to applaud in the thin lamplight, among the uneasy things, the unsettling mood of the livingroom. Perhaps he ought, really, to pretend he has heard, for the skull is now as tall as he himself sitting in the gentleman's chair beside the grace of his lady the rocker, her spine curved now against the stair-corner, not straight as it had been when her bride's body would not bend to the will of a stripling.

Perhaps it would be as well not to listen to the song the couches recall; to forget to applaud might be wiser than to listen to the skull's yellow music which, strangely, now that he has decided, comes moving quietly across his teeth like a shadow to stir the leaves of the violet.

                    from *The Inhabitant*

Who has written in English in grammatic parallels—besides the translators of the *Bible,* that is? In the 18th century Christopher Smart

did. In this following poem the parallel structures are very obvious—
just run your eye down the left-hand margin:

OF JEOFFRY, HIS CAT

For I will consider my Cat Jeoffry.
For he is the servant of the Living God, duly and daily serving him.
For at the first glance of the glory of God in the East he worships in his way.
For is this done by wreathing his body seven times round with elegant quickness.
For then he leaps up to catch the musk, which is the blessing of God upon
        his prayer.
For he rolls upon prank to work it in.
For having done duty and received blessing he begins to consider himself.
For this he performs in ten degrees.
For first he looks upon his fore-paws to see if they are clean.
For secondly he kicks up behind to clear away there.
For thirdly he works it upon stretch with the fore paws extended.
For fourthly he sharpens his paws by wood.
For fifthly he washes himself.
For sixthly he rolls upon wash.
For Seventhly he fleas himself, that he may not be interrupted upon the beat.
For Eighthly he rubs himself against a post.
For Ninthly he looks up for his instructions.
For Tenthly he goes in quest of food.
For having consider'd God and himself he will consider his neighbour.
For if he meets another cat he will kiss her in kindness.
For when he takes his prey he plays with it to give it chance.
For one mouse in seven escapes by his dallying.
For when his day's work is done his business more properly begins.
For [he] keeps the Lord's watch in the night against the adversary.
For he counteracts the powers of darkness by his electrical skin & glaring eyes.
For he counteracts the Devil, who is death, by brisking about the life.
For in his morning orisons he loves the sun and the sun loves him.
For he is of the tribe of Tiger.
For the Cherub Cat is a term of the Angel Tiger.
For he has the subtlety and hissing of a serpent, which in goodness he suppresses.
For he will not do destruction, if he is well-fed, neither will he spit without
        provocation.
For he purrs in thankfulness, when God tells him he's a good Cat.
For he is an instrument for the children to learn benevolence upon.
For every house is incompleat without him & a blessing is lacking in the spirit.
For the Lord commanded Moses concerning the cats at the departure of the
        Children of Israel from Egypt.
For every family had one cat at least in the bag.
For the English Cats are the best in Europe.
For he is the cleanest in the use of his fore-paws of any quadruped.

For the dexterity of his defence is an instance of the love of God to him
      exceedingly.
For he is the quickest to his mark of any creature.
For he is tenacious of his point.
For he is a mixture of gravity and waggery.
For he knows that God is his Saviour.
For there is nothing sweeter than his peace when at rest.
For there is nothing brisker than his life when in motion.
For he is of the Lord's poor and so indeed is he called by benevolence
      perpetually—Poor Jeoffry! poor Jeoffry! the rat has bit thy throat.
For I bless the name of the Lord Jesus that Jeoffry is better.
For the divine spirit comes about his body to sustain it in compleat cat.
For his tongue is exceeding pure so that it has in purity what it wants in musick.
For he is docile and can learn certain things.
For he can set up with gravity which is patience upon approbation.
For he can fetch and carry, which is patience in employment.
For he can jump over a stick which is patience upon proof positive.
For he can spraggle upon waggle at the word of command.
For he can jump from an eminence into his master's bosom.
For he can catch the cork and toss it again.
For he is hated by the hypocrite and miser.
For the former is afraid of detection.
For the latter refuses the charge.
For he camels his back to bear the first notion of business.
For he is good to think on, if a man would express himself neatly.
For he made a great figure in Egypt for his signal services.
For he killed the Icneumon-rat very pernicious by land.
For his ears are so acute that they sting again.
For from this proceeds the passing quickness of his attention.
For by stroaking of him I have found out electricity.
For I perceived God's light about him both wax and fire.
For the Electrical fire is the spiritual substance, which God sends from heaven to
      sustain the bodies both of man and beast.
For God has blessed him in the variety of his movements.
For, tho he cannot fly, he is an excellent clamberer.
For his motions upon the face of the earth are more than any other quadruped.
For he can tread to all the measures upon the musick.
For he can swim for life.
For he can creep.

CHRISTOPHER SMART
from *Rejoice in the Lamb*

    During the middle of the 19th century another English poet, Martin
Farquhar Tupper, wrote a best-selling book, mostly of bad prose poems,
called *Proverbial Philosophy.*

The 19th century American poet Walt Whitman also wrote in grammatic parallels. His poems were not nearly as popular as Tupper's, though his simple style was supposed to be appealing to the masses. The parallels in this poem are almost as obvious as those in Christopher Smart's poem:

I HEAR AMERICA SINGING

I hear America singing, the varied carols I hear,
Those of mechanics, each one singing his as it must be blithe and strong,
The carpenter singing his as he measures his plank or beam,
The mason singing his as he makes ready for work, or leaves off work,
The boatman singing what belongs to him in his boat, the deckhand singing on
  the steamboat deck,
The shoemaker singing as he sits on his bench, the hatter singing as he stands,
The wood-cutter's song, the plowboy's on his way in the morning, or at noon
  intermission or at sundown,
The delicious singing of the mother, or of the young wife at work, or of the girl
  sewing or washing,
Each singing what belongs to him or her and to none else,
The day what belongs to the day—at night the party of young fellows, robust,
  friendly,
Singing with open mouths their strong melodious songs.

WALT WHITMAN

One of the interesting things about the structure of this poem is that it is one long sentence. Note how large a part repetition plays in this kind of poem, and how the sentence is merely a listing of things, a *catalog* of kinds of singing and kinds of people singing. George Puttenham, in his Renaissance book *The Arte of English Poesie* called this listing of things "the heaping figure"—the poet heaps nouns, verbs, and other parts of speech one upon the other; the Greeks called it *sinathrismus*. Whitman usually tried, in his poems, to build to a climax in the last parallel. In this case, the climax is undercut somewhat by the superfluous phrase, "with open mouths"—it would be difficult for anyone to sing "strong melodious songs" with closed mouths.

Many other poets in the 20th century—Allen Ginsberg among them —have written in grammatic prosodies, including this oldest of the old, parallelism. It is amazing to think of the furor created by these prose forms during the early days of this century. The only way that the uproar can be explained is by realizing that somehow the idea had grown up over the years that a poet was one who wrote in verse; thus, anyone who wrote in prose must be something else, but not a poet. This misconception is still widespread, but even the Renaissance writer John

Lyly, author of the novel *Euphues,* which gave rise to the stylistic school
of Euphuism, should be considered more poet than novelist, for his
avowed purpose was to elevate the language through grammatics and
rhetoric rather than to narrate a story.

Any number of other grammatic systems, besides parallelism, are
possible. The "metaphysical" poets, including John Donne, based their
organizing principle largely upon the extended metaphor, or *conceit.*
In this poem Donne's metaphor is that the sun is a fool; then the sun
and the room are equated with a number of other things, and the
metaphor, as it is extended, becomes more and more complicated:

THE SUN RISING

> Busy old fool, unruly Sun,
> Why dost thou thus,
Through windows, and through curtains, call on us?
Must to thy motions lovers' seasons run?
> Saucy pedantic wretch, go chide
> Late school-boys and sour prentices,
> Go tell court-huntsmen that the king will ride,
> Call country ants to harvest offices;
Love, all alike, no season knows nor clime,
Nor hours, days, months, which are the rags of time.

> Thy beams so reverend and strong
> Why shouldst thou think?
I could eclipse and cloud them with a wink,
But that I would not lose her sight so long.
> If her eyes have not blinded thine,
> Look, and tomorrow late tell me,
> Whether both th' Indias of spice and mine
> Be where thou left'st them, or lie here with me.
Ask for those kings whom thou saw'st yesterday,
And thou shalt hear, "All here in one bed lay."

> She's all states, and all princes I;
> Nothing else is.
Princes do but play us; compared to this,
All honor's mimic, all wealth alchemy.
> Thou, Sun, art half as happy as we,
> In that the world's contracted thus;
> Thine age asks ease, and since thy duties be
> To warm the world, that's done in warming us.
Shine here to us, and thou art everywhere;
This bed thy centre is, these walls thy sphere.

JOHN DONNE

Although this is a metrical poem, the accentual-syllabics are rough, and the central binding force is metaphor (about which we will have more to say later on).

A grammatic prosody recently invented by the poet Russell Salamon is called PARENTHETICS. As simple as parallels, and effective in a very strange way, a parenthetic structure is built by taking a word, phrase, or clause, such as "Call them what you will"; then by taking another element such as a clause, "They are the black songs," breaking it in half, and enclosing the first element with the halves of the second:

They are the
    Call them what you will
Black songs

This process may be carried on indefinitely, making the poem as long as the poet desires:

PARENTHETICS FOR LANGSTON HUGHES

If you would sing America
  Blues move darkly
    They are the
      Call them what you will
    Black songs
  Along the edge of hymn:
You must sing them all.

If we analyze the poem, we see that it is built of these elements: 1) Call them what you will; 2) They are the black songs; 3) Blues move darkly along the edge of hymn; and 4) If you would sing America you must sing them all.

The modern poet E. E. Cummings used grammatics in related ways. Often he used grammatical *dispersion*: He would first write a poem in a traditional form, such as a sonnet. Then he would disguise the original form by "dispersing" the lines according to some pattern different from its original structure—perhaps breaking it up into lines that were really phrases or a few words, or by breaking the sonnet lines in half and making each half-line a single line (as Langston Hughes said he used to do in order to be paid for a twenty-eight line poem rather than a fourteen-line sonnet), or by cutting lines at caesuras, or by running together two or more lines.

Here is a Cummings poem that operates something like parenthetics, except that here the poet breaks a word in two ("loneliness") and inserts a sentence into the break (*a leaf falls*). In addition, Cummings uses the typographical level of the poem to split the poem into a dispersed picture-poem: The poem falls as the leaf falls:

l(a

l(a
le
af
fa

ll

s)
one
l

iness

E. E. CUMMINGS

    The typographical level is very important in this impressionist poem: It makes its impression very largely through the way the poem *looks* on the page. It plays visually with such things as the letter *I*, which looks like a numeral *1*; it breaks the word "loneliness" in such a way as to emphasize the word *one* buried in the larger word. Techniques like this are what might be called *sight-puns*; plays on words that only the eye can catch—it would be almost impossible to read this poem aloud and have the audience catch this play. It must be seen to be understood.

4

OF POETIC
LEVELS

How many other prosodies are possible?—any number of them.
A poem is composed of patterns on four levels. A poet may use all of
them equally, but he may choose to emphasize any one of them, or any
combination, just as the fictionist may, at one point, wish to write
an action story, minimizing character, atmosphere, theme; and, at other
points, write a character sketch, or a thematic story, or a mood piece,
minimizing plot.

But the poet, since he is specifically concerned with elements of
language, may go further than the fictionist; he may invent or use a
prosody based almost entirely on a particular poetic level. The four
levels of poetry, in ascending order of importance, are these:

the typographical level. That is, the level of print. The first thing
one should do when he begins to analyze a poem is to hold it away from
him at arm's length and just look at it. Does its layout have any
regularity about it? If so, you can be sure you will find regularity in its
prosody. Run an eye down either margin: Are there parallel structures
in the first words, or even *head-rhymes?* Are there *end-rhymes* or
consonances? Does the reader receive an impression simply from the
appearance of the arrangement of lines on the page? Is there a difference
between, say, the looks of a poem by Emily Dickinson—

I DIED FOR BEAUTY

I died for beauty, but was scarce
Adjusted in the tomb,
When one who died for truth was lain
In an adjoining room.

He questioned softly why I failed?
"For beauty," I replied.
"And I for truth,—the two are one;
We brethren are," he said.

And so, as kinsmen met a night,
We talked between the rooms,
Until the moss had reached our lips,
And covered up our names.

EMILY DICKINSON

—and of a poem by Whitman?—

A NOISELESS PATIENT SPIDER

A noiseless patient spider,
I marked where on a little promontory it stood isolated,
Marked how to explore the vacant vast surrounding,
It launched forth filament, filament, filament, out of itself.
Ever unreeling them, ever tirelessly speeding them.

And you O my soul where you stand,
Surrounded, detached, in measureless oceans of space,
Ceaselessly musing, venturing, throwing, seeking the spheres to connect them,
Till the bridge you will need be formed, till the ductile anchor hold,
Till the gossamer thread you fling catch somewhere, O my soul.

WALT WHITMAN

Is there a prosody based on the typographical level? Yes, it is called *spatial prosody*, and there are two major sub-genres. The first—called variously *calligrammes, hieroglyphic verse*, and *shaped stanza*—has as its intention the visual imitation, through the shape of its stanzas, of a particular form—a visual form such as a circle, or square, or something more complicated. Often the shape is related to the subject discussed in the poem.

Spatial poems are relatively popular in our own age. An extreme form of spatials is the second sub-genre of spatials called *concrete verse*.

Concrete verse takes the poem much farther toward graphic art than does hieroglyphic verse. It is really more picture than poem.

Here is an example of a calligramme. Parenthetically, one might note that this is also an example of the poetic *genre* called *occasional poetry*—poetry written for an occasion. This occasion was the death of President Kennedy by assassination, and the form of the poem is meant to imitate the telescopic sight on the rifle used by Lee Harvey Oswald:

THE MOMENT BEFORE

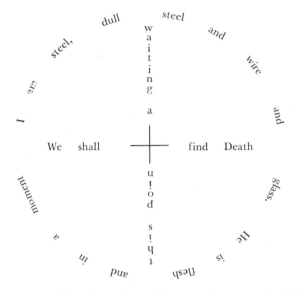

The poem used in Chap. 3 to illustrate the prosody called parenthetics, "Parenthetics for Langston Hughes," was also an example of the genre of occasional poetry—it was an *ode* written to memorialize the life of the Black poet Langston Hughes. There are various literary genres—we have mentioned some of them: fiction, drama, poetry, essay. Others are biography, autobiography, belles lettres.

But within each literary genre, there are sub-genres—and we have mentioned some of the sub-genres of fiction: the action story (plot), mood-piece (atmosphere), thematic story, and character sketch. In poetry there are also sub-genres: lyric poetry, dramatic poetry, satiric poetry, pastoral poetry, occasional poetry, and didactic poetry. We will go more deeply into genres in subsequent chapters.

To get back to the subject at hand, calligrammes can become very complicated, as for instance this poem by the early American poet Edward Taylor, which edges closer and closer toward the pictorial:

ACROSTIC LOVE POEM TO
ELIZABETH FITCH

ACROSTIC LOVE POEM TO ELIZABETH FITCH
This Dove &
Olive Branch to
you
is both a Post &
Emblem too[1]
These for M[y Dove]
Tender & Onely [Love]
Mrs. Elizabeth [Fitch][2]
at her father's house in
N[orwich]

```
[A]spiring Love, that Scorns to hatch a Wish
[B]eneath itselfe, the fullest, chiefest Blisse
[C]ontain'd within          Heav  E  ns Chrystail Pale, & Shine,
[D ot] h wish its Object      a  L ŵ A  yes; So doth mine.
[E lec] t no more              P  res  S  ented in desire:
[F or H] eavens Roofe,      a  Y  e, lets not  A  wish soar higher.
[G ot t] hough too        di  M,    N    ò N  e can get to sign
[H ear] e you, (my      FR  E  I  ND) yⁱˢ stren  G T  h'ned Wish of mine.
[I n d] rossy        Sil  VR        should,      I SH  ould by this,
K eep dull my      P  O S  T,    and staine my    S E  rious Wish.
L est wᶜʰ      pol  L  V  ted bee,          or th' f  E A  rfull Dove
M y Post out    F  O  yl'd                  I ru  N a R  ing of Love,
N ew        P  O  L lisht, wʳᵉ my    cent'red heart  D  o  T  h reek
O ut      hi G  hes  T  Streams of Love,    which here  D  oe  M  eet
P rese      N  ted t  H  us yʳ Heart,      LOVES RI  N  G    yo  V  'll finde
Q uest    I  onlesse,    A  lwayes [the] best    B  E  fitt    S    yᵉ minde.
R ese    R  ve mine      T  hat. Yet let        O  ur    secre  T  breast
S  E  t Love      t  H  e Tune which tu  N  es this Ring yᵉ    B  est.
  H  e Ring of Love my    Ple  A  — sant—  H  eart must      b  E  E
T  RVELY    CONFIND    WI  T      HIN      THE        TRINITIE
```

V { pon your Hearte (I pray you) put Loves Ring
  { nerringly; Loves Swelt (ring) Hearte herein

W { earing a True-Loves-Knot at centre's set.
  { here with I send to you an Alphabet

X { enodick whence all syllables compleat.
  { tracted are to spell what Love can speake.

Y ea, see, then what I send. Yet I design

Z ion my Ring shall Licen(c)e with her Trine

[*Triangle:* The ring of my pleasant heart must bee
trvely confind within the Trinitie]   [*Circle:* Lovs Ring I send
                                                That hath no end]

[1] These words are written inside a crude drawing of a dove holding an olive branch with which Taylor decorated this page of his manuscript.

[2] Taylor's first wife, whom he married on November 5, 1674, was Elizabeth Fitch.
EDWARD TAYLOR

Here is an example of concrete verse, which is almost totally pictorial. Concrete verse is *ideographic* in nature. An *ideograph* is, according to Oxford, "A character or figure symbolizing the idea of a thing, without expressing the name of it, as the Chinese characters, etc. Thus in English the ideograph + may be pronounced 'plus', 'added to', or 'more'. . . . "

NYMPHOMANIA

RICHARD KOSTELANETZ

the sonic level. It is on the sonic level that the *sound of language* is most important: Rhyme, rhythm, alliteration, consonance, assonance, caesura, and many other techniques may be used to make a pattern. Metrical prosodies, (especially accentuals and accentual-syllabics), are often based on the sonic level. Lyrics are written with an emphasis on this level; nonsense verse uses it almost exclusively—think of Lewis Carroll's "Jabberwocky." Here are some lyrics and nonsense poems:

SABRINA

Sabrina was a gentle girl,
    Sabrina was a willow twig.
And all the greengrass days we spent
Have gone to sleep in twilight's tent,
And there is little I can say
Except that she has gone away.

Sabrina danced, her skirts awhirl,
    A windblown summer lilac sprig
Adrift upon a wanton song
When dusks were short and life was long.
But now there's little more to say
Except, Sabrina's gone away.

Sabrina's feet were slight and swift;
    Sabrina's limbs were slim and brown.
Her hair was soft as sun, her eyes
Were lambent moonstones of surprise,
But there is not much more to say
Except that she has gone away.

And she is milkweed flown adrift.
    She is the skybound fledgling's down.
The sprig is plucked, the willow weeps
Outside the house where summer sleeps
And there is nothing more to say
Except, Sabrina's gone away.

"Sabrina" was written in a college class. Its intention is not to say something deep, nor really to characterize the girl who remains an idealization rather than a person. The intention is to use the music of the language to create a mood, leave an impression.

In this poem by the early English Renaissance poet John Skelton, a good deal of the satire lies in the sounds of the poem, particularly in the refrains:

MANNERLY MARGERY MILK AND ALE

Ay, beshrew you! by my fay,
These wanton clerks be nice alway!
Avaunt, avaunt, my popinjay!
What, will ye do nothing but play?
Tilly vally, straw, let be I say!
Gup, Christian Clout, gup, Jack of the Vale!
With Mannerly Margery Milk and Ale.

By God, ye be a pretty pode,
And I love you an whole cart-load.
Straw, James Foder, ye play the fode,
I am no hackney for your rod:
Go watch a bull, your back is broad!
Gup, Christian Clout, gup, Jack of the Vale!
With Mannerly Margery Milk and Ale.

Ywis ye deal uncourteously;
What, would ye frumple me? now fy!
What, and ye shall be my pigesnye?
By Christ, ye shall not, no hardely:
I will not be japéd bodily!
Gup, Christian Clout, gup, Jack of the Vale!
With Mannerly Margery Milk and Ale.

Walk forth your way, ye cost me nought;
Now have I found that I have sought:
The best cheap flesh that ever I bought.
Yet, for His love that all hath wrought,
Wed me, or else I die for thought.
Gup, Christian Clout, your breath is stale!
Go, Mannerly Margery Milk and Ale!
Gup, Christian Clout, gup, Jack of the Vale!
With Mannerly Margery Milk and Ale.

                                        JOHN SKELTON

JABBERWOCKY

'Twas brillig, and the slithy toves
    Did gyre and gimble in the wabe:
All mimsy were the borogoves,
    And the mome raths outgrabe.

"Beware the Jabberwock, my son!
    The jaws that bite, the claws that catch!
Beware the Jubjub bird, and shun
    The frumious Bandersnatch!"

He took his vorpal sword in hand;
    Long time the manxome foe he sought—
So rested he by the Tumtum tree,
    And stood awhile in thought.

And, as in uffish thought he stood,
    The Jabberwock, with eyes of flame,
Came whiffling through the tulgey wood,
    And burbled as it came!

One, two! One, two! And through and through
    The vorpal blade went snicker-snack!
He left it dead, and with its head
    He went galumphing back.

"And hast thou slain the Jabberwock?
    Come to my arms, my beamish boy!
O frabjous day! Callooh, Callay!"
    He chortled in his joy.

'Twas brillig, and the slithy toves
    Did gyre and gimble in the wabe;
All mimsy were the borogoves,
    And the mome raths outgrabe.

Lewis Carroll

Many of the words in this poem are *neologisms*—words made up by the writer, new coinings. Lewis Carroll called these particular neologistic constructions "portmanteau words"—words made up of parts of other words. For instance, "slithy" is made out of *lithe* and *slimy*. He intended the overtones, or *associations* that we have with both words, to continue to be present in the new word.

the sensory level. On the third, the sensory, level, the five external senses, taste, touch, sight, smell, and hearing, are important, as is the internal "sense" of emotion. Patterns of imagery (figurative language, *tropes*), evocations of sensation, mood, atmosphere, and feeling come to the fore on this level. "Imagism," a movement of the 20th century, based its prosody on the sensory. The following is a poem in which sensory impressions and images are of primary importance—they are its organizing principle. The poem's purpose is not to be logical, but to evoke the coldest of moods:

IMAGE TINGED WITH NO COLOR

I smell you coming
with the January wind
buried in your bones, old man,
like a blear of snow in the pines.

Is she your sister,
or your mother, whom I see
dressed in an ice blue shawl,
sweeping the leaves before you?

Often I have thought of you
when the sun strikes aside
the dark leaves like so many webs
spun across the day to tangle my eyes,

and always your image
is tinged with no color, no
touch, only a scent
as of asters lying under a fallen clock.

In your pockets, I can tell,
there are small things wound in pelts—
mice, perhaps, or squirrels
nesting against the chill flesh of your thighs.

I smell you coming, by night,
a skein of white planets
unraveling behind you,
and as you pass I shall greet you coldly.

Winter, in the poem, is seen figuratively as the *personification* of an old man, and the traditional associations of winter-as-death are meant to be evoked. This time death passes the speaker by, but, as the poem implies, it won't always be so.

Here is another impressionist poem, by the modern American poet Alfred Kreymborg. One shouldn't try to make any *logical* sense out of it; the "sense" it makes is that of feeling and mood—one ought simply to try to respond to it on a sensory level. "Nun Snow" doesn't *mean* anything, except what it *is*.

NUN SNOW:
A PANTOMIME OF BEADS

EARTH VOICE:

Can she be
thoughtless of life,
a lover of imminent death,
Nun Snow
touching her strings of white beads?
Is it her unseen hands
that urge the beads to tremble?
Does Nun Snow,
aware of the death she must die alone,
away from the nuns
of the green beads,
of the ochre and brown,

purple and black—
does she improvise
along those muted strings
in the worldly hope
that the answering, friendly tune,
the faithful, folk-like miracle,
will shine in a moment or two?

MOON VOICE:

Or peradventure,
are the beads merely wayward
on an evening so soft,
when One Wind
is so gentle a mesmerist
he draws them and her with his hand?

EARTH VOICE:

Was it Full Moon,
who contrives tales of this order
and himself loves the heroine,
Nun Snow—

WIND VOICE:

Do you see his beads courting hers?—
lascivious monk!—

EARTH VOICE:

Was it Full Moon,
slyly innocent of guile,
propounder of sorrowless phantoms,
who breathed that suspicion?
Is it One Wind,
the wily, scholarly pedant—
is it he who retorts—

WIND VOICE:

Like olden allegros
in olden sonatas,
all tales have two themes,
she is beautiful,
he is beautiful,
with the traditional movement,
their beads court each other,
revealing a cadence as fatally true
as the sum which follows a one-plus-one—
so why inquire further?
Nay, inquire further,
deduce it your fashion!

Nun Snow,
as you say,
touches her strings of white beads,
Full Moon
his lute of yellow strings;
and Our Night
is square, nay,
Our Night
is round, nay,
Our Night
is a blue balcony—
and therewith close your inquisition!

EARTH VOICE:

Who urged the beads to tremble?
They're still now!
Fallen, or cast over me!
Nun, Moon and Wind are gone!
Are they betraying her?—

MOON VOICE:

Ask Our Night—

EARTH VOICE:

Did the miracle appear?—

MOON VOICE:

Ask Our Night,
merely a child on a balcony,
letting down her hair and
black beads in glissando—
ask her what she means,
dropping the curtain so soon!

                    ALFRED KREYMBORG

the ideational level. The fourth level is the level of thought and idea. The poem's theme, moral, meaning, philosophy, argument, and observation will be found here—if, in fact, the poem has any of these things. This is the level of rationality and logic, and *didactic* (teaching) poetry is written largely on this level. The danger is that thought may tend to dominate language if this level is overemphasized, and a writer of didactic poetry may in fact turn out to be not a poet so much as an essayist in verse, as some people argue Alexander Pope was in such pieces as his *Essay on Criticism,* which was written in heroic couplets. Here is a poem—written, by the way, in prose parallels—which emphasizes the ideational level:

THE STUDENT

This student is lost in his books.
I have seen many students lost many ways.
They have been lost in the halls
looking for some door to enter,
afraid to find it because of Minotaur.
They have been lost in words
that fog up their lenses so badly they can't see.
They have been lost in the backstretch.
They have been lost in the woods with some girl
who told her daddy.
They have been lost in my office waiting
for me to come, but I never do.
I have seen many students lost many ways—
even lost in thought, though very few.
This student is lost in his books.
If he looks up, he will find that he is here:
the present is upon him; all books
lead to now at last, and that is
the key to the maze of words.

fusion. The sum of the lower levels of a poem ought to exceed its parts. How do all the elements of appearance, sound, sensation, and idea come together and interact? How do they fuse (if they do) into an organic whole, and is the whole successful in terms of its prosody and the poet's intent as perceived by the reader?

Here is a poem by a 19th-century Englishman. Actually, it's not a poem—it's a failure as a poem. It was meant seriously, but the final effect is ridiculous. It winds up as the caricature of a poem. But even a poem that never fuses on any level may have its uses and its pleasures—if it is bad enough:

A TRAGEDY

Death!
Plop.
The barges down in the river flop.
Flop, plop,
Above, beneath.
From the slimy branches the grey drips drop,
As they scraggle black on the thin grey sky,
Where the black cloud rack-hackles drizzle and fly
To the oozy waters that lounge and flop
On the black scrag-piles, where the loose cords plop,

As the raw wind whines in the thin tree-top.
Plop, plop.
And scudding by
The boatmen call out hoy! and hey!
And all is running in water and sky,
And my head shrieks—"Stop,"
And my heart shrieks—"Die."

My thought is running out of my head;
My love is running out of my heart;
My soul runs after, and leaves me as dead,
For my life runs after to catch them—and fled
They are all every one!—and I stand, and start,
At the water that oozes up, plop and plop,
On the barges that flop
And dizzy me dead.
I might reel and drop.
Plop
Dead.

And the shrill wind whines in the thin tree-top.
Flop, plop.

A curse on him.
Ugh! yet I knew—I knew—
If a woman is false can a friend be true?
It was only a lie from beginning to end—
My Devil—my "Friend"
I had trusted the whole of my living to!
Ugh! and I knew!
Ugh!
So what do I care,
And my head is as empty as air—
I can do,
I can dare
(Plop, plop,
The barges flop
Drip, drop.)
I can dare, I can dare!
And let myself all run away with my head,
And stop.
Drop
Dead.
Flip, flop.
Plop.

THEO. MARZIALS.

Perhaps we should recapitulate here. What is a poet? He is a writer whose primary concern is the resources inherent in language. But that's too cumbersome. Say, rather, that *a poet is an artificer of language.* And let us make the distinction that, by contrast, *the fictionist is an artificer of written narrative; the dramatist is an artificer of theatrical narrative; the essayist is an artificer of rhetorical exposition.*

Let us remember, too, that an artifice of language may or may not be a poem, not because it is written in a particular mode, such as verse, but because its author focused, or did not focus, primarily on the literary resources of the language *as a substance,* the substance of art.

suggested writing assignment

Everyone has written a poem or two at some point. Submit a sample of poetry you have already written. It should not be very long, but long enough to give the reader some idea of your normal style at this point in the course.

5

two prosodies:
SPATIALS AND GRAMMATICS

In Chap. 4 it was mentioned that the typographical level is of some importance. In spatial prosodies it is of primary importance. Look back at the poem "The Moment Before," given as an example on page 43, Chap. 4. It is made up of two sentences: "I am steel, dull steel and wire and glass. He is flesh, and in a moment we shall find Death waiting at this point." The sentences are arranged in the form of a circle and crosshairs—the *t*'s of "a*t*" and "poin*t*" are one + at the center of the circle. The statement the poem makes is primarily a graphic one, not a literary one.

It is *shape,* then, that is the making of a spatial poem. Puttenham illustrated some of the shapes possible in his *Arte of English Poesie*:

LOZENGE   SPINDLE   TRICQUET   QUADRANGLE

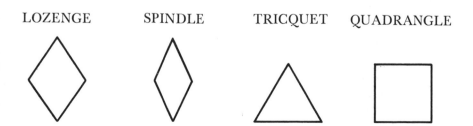

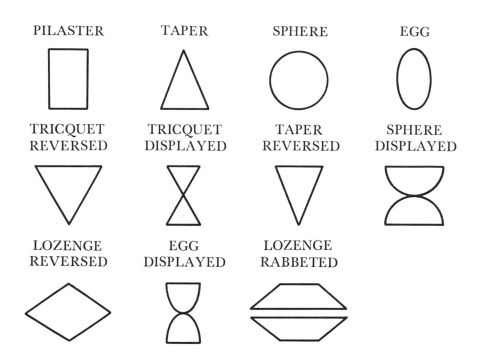

PILASTER   TAPER   SPHERE   EGG

TRICQUET REVERSED   TRICQUET DISPLAYED   TAPER REVERSED   SPHERE DISPLAYED

LOZENGE REVERSED   EGG DISPLAYED   LOZENGE RABBETED

But even in a more or less "normal" poem, the typographical level may play a large part. Here is a poem by Langston Hughes:

GO SLOW

Go slow, they say—
While the bite
Of the dog is fast.
Go slow, I hear—
While they tell me
You can't eat here!
You can't live here!
You can't work here!
Don't demonstrate! Wait!—
While they lock the gate.

Am I supposed to be God,
Or an angel with wings
And a halo on my head
While jobless I starve dead?
Am I supposed to forgive

And meekly live
Going slow, slow, slow,
Slow, slow, slow,
Slow, slow,
Slow
Slow,
Slow?
????
???
??
?

LANGSTON HUGHES

Everything is "normal" . . . until we get toward the end of the poem. There, the repetition of the word "slow" comes slowing down until it turns into a question in the fifth-to-last line—a *rhetorical question*: The answer is obvious. At this point the spatial element, at the climactic moment of the poem, becomes paramount: The tail of question marks descends visibly, carrying on the slowing-down process, but at the same time it ascends climactically to the final question mark, which emphasizes the great question being asked.

At the end of the poem meaning resides primarily in how the poem looks: The medium *is* the message, to quote McLuhan. This is always true of poetry: Style—the *way* in which something is said—has most to do with *what* is said:

SCHOOL DRAWING

There is a road: no
one is walking there. Brown
paper, black paper triangles
wrangle with the air
to make a windmill

striping a crayon
sun. A black arrow points
away from the blades that turn in
fire. It is burning,
and there is no wind

The Dylan Thomas poem "Vision and Prayer" is written in two *movements,* and in two *shapes*—the lozenge, and the tricquet displayed:

VISION AND PRAYER

i

Who
Are you
Who is born
In the next room
So loud to my own
That I can hear the womb
Opening and the dark run
Over the ghost and the dropped son
Behind the wall thin as a wren's bone?
In the birth bloody room unknown
To the burn and turn of time
And the heart print of man
Bows no baptism
But dark alone
Blessing on
The wild
Child.

I
Must lie
Still as stone
By the wren bone
Wall hearing the moan
Of the mother hidden
And the shadowed head of pain
Casting to-morrow like a thorn
And the midwives of miracle sing
Until the turbulent new born
Burns me his name and his flame
And the winged wall is torn
By his torrid crown
And the dark thrown
From his loin
To bright
Light.

When
Then   wren
Bone writhes down
And   the   first   dawn
Furied   by   his   stream
Swarms on the kingdom come
Of the dazzler of heaven
And the splashed mothering maiden
Who bore him with a bonfire in
His mouth and rocked him like a storm
I shall run lost in sudden
Terror   and   shining   from
The once hooded room
Crying   in   vain
In   the   cauldron
Of   his
Kiss

In
The spin
Of   the   sun
In the spuming
Cyclone of his wing
For I was lost who am
Crying at the man drenched throne
In the first fury of his stream
And the lightnings of adoration
Back to black silence melt and mourn
For I was lost who have come
To dumbfounding haven
And the finding one
And the high noon
Of his wound
Blinds my
Cry.

There
Crouched bare
In the shrine
Of his blazing
Breast I shall waken
To the judge blown bedlam
Of the uncaged sea bottom
The cloud climb of the exhaling tomb
And the bidden dust upsailing
With his flame in every grain.
O spiral of ascension
From the vultured urn
Of the morning
Of man when
The land
And

The
Born sea
Praised the sun
The finding one
And upright Adam
Sang upon origin!
O the wings of the children!
The woundward flight of the ancient
Young from the canyons of oblivion!
The sky stride of the always slain
In battle! the happening
Of saints to their vision!
The world winding home!
And the whole pain
Flows open
And I
Die.

ii

In the name of the lost who glory in
The swinish plains of carrion
Under the burial song
Of the birds of burden
Heavy with the drowned
And the green dust
And bearing
The ghost
From
The ground
Like pollen
On the black plume
And the beak of slime
I pray though I belong
Not wholly to that lamenting
Brethren for joy has moved within
The inmost marrow of my heart bone

That he who learns now the sun and moon
Of his mother's milk may return
Before the lips blaze and bloom
To the birth bloody room
Behind the wall's wren
Bone and be dumb
And the womb
That bore
For
All men
The adored
Infant light or
The dazzling prison
Yawn to his upcoming.
In the name of the wanton
Lost on the unchristened mountain
In the centre of dark I pray him

That he let the dead lie though they moan
For his briared hands to hoist them
To the shrine of his world's wound
And the blood drop's garden
Endure   the   stone
Blind host to sleep
In   the   dark
And deep
Rock
A w a k e
No heart bone
But let it break
On the mountain crown
Unbidden by the sun
And the beating dust be blown
Down to the river rooting plain
Under the night forever falling.

Forever   falling   night   is   a   known
Star   and   country   to   the   legion
Of sleepers whose tongue I toll
To   mourn   his   deluging
Light through sea and soil
And we have come
To   know   all
P l a c e s
Ways
M a z e s
P a s s a g e s
Quarters and graves
Of the endless fall.
Now   common   lazarus
Of the charting sleepers prays
Never to awake and arise
For the country of death is the heart's size

And the star of the lost the shape of the eyes.
In the name of the fatherless
In the name of the unborn
And the undesirers
Of midwiving morning's
Hands or instruments
O in the name
Of no one
Now or
No
One to
Be I Pray
May the crimson
Sun spin a grave grey
And the colour of clay
Stream upon his martyrdom
In the interpreted evening
And the known dark of the earth amen.

I turn the corner of prayer and burn
In a blessing of the sudden
Sun. In the name of the damned
I would turn back and run
To the hidden land
But the loud sun
Christens down
The sky.
I
Am found.
O let him
Scald me and drown
Me in his world's wound.
His lightning answers my
Cry. My voice burns in his hand.
Now I am lost in the blinding
One. The sun roars at the prayer's end.

DYLAN THOMAS

The first movement, "Vision," is diamond-shaped, like the stanzas. It is a priceless jewel; it is a prism through which a great light is sent, to be broken down thereby into its elemental parts. Vision sparkles like the fire in a diamond of first water. Thomas never says this in so many words—he *shows* it on the page. Great poetry is a showing, not a telling; it is a work of art, not a speech.

Likewise, "Prayer" is in the shape of an hour-glass, the opposite of the diamond—it is a giving, from the person praying, back to the source of vision. And the prayers filter through the hours of a lifetime like sand through an hourglass. Again, Thomas doesn't say so—he doesn't have to. He simply sets the hourglass beside the diamond, and their mere contrast says most of it. The words of the poem are only *glosses* (commentaries) on the stanza shapes.

Here is a student who has come away from a college basketball game disillusioned—the poem is written in the shape of a simple rectangle or pilaster, meant to imitate the form of a basketball court:

ON BEING DISAPPOINTED AT A BASKETBALL GAME

> The sad arc of a cockeyed shot
> and lights reflecting from one
> unbalanced lad loose upon this
> court are unnerving things for
> any man to watch.
>   There exist
> five unraveled ends out there,
> twining around the brown locus
> of our bouncing eyes, lurching
> at ragged ends, stitching coo-
> coo quilts with warped crochet
> needles.
>   A machine is gremlin
> ridden, the bobbin wobbles and
> the stands are pincushions be-
> neath both buttocks.
>   Not even
> crossed fingers help.
>   What if
> the world were to wind in such
> fashion?
>   And what if it does?
>
> What if that ball were a brown
> world whirling along propelled
> by a rheumatic Arm, aimed with
> rheumy Eyes, zagging in voids?

In this poem, notice that the movement is from something commonplace, a basketball game, outward to a larger philosophical question. This is something else we need to remember: Large issues may be raised out of ordinary experiences. Note, too, that sound has not been forgotten. The sonic element of this poem is not so overt as in the Thomas poem, but it is not unimportant. There are examples of various kinds of sonic devices, as well as imagistic or sensory techniques. When you have come to the chapters covering these elements, it might be worthwhile to come back and review this poem to discover what devices the poet has used—devices such as alliteration, assonance, repetition, simile, and metaphor . . . even the pun, as in "crossed fingers." Here are some more calligrams:

THE VIEW FROM KHUFU'S TONGUE

In words like sand silence created a shape to outlast the
soft tongues and I could sense something invisible coming
into being as I listened and looked at the developing and
widening caesura creating a   shape in that noisy air but
couldn't determine what it   was or what it wasn't torn
by my inability to see it   and not see it at the one
and same time fracturing   my sense of existence on
the one hand and sewing   it together on the hand
I held behind my cleft   being but at the abyss
developed a pattern a   shape slowly began to
become apparent rent   from noise and holes
began to gag mouths   uttering deserts in
the earth making   a glittering silence
as monument to   my interstitial self
and I can only gabble in helpless wonder with words chaos
would have been proud of endless and barren as sand seeds
my tongue has planted in the ears of a long forgotten god

WALTER H. KERR

According to the author of "The View from Khufu's Tongue," there are two categories of shaped poems, "positive and negative. Positive shaping utilizes the words and negative shaping, the spaces. 'The View from Khufu's Tongue' is an example of negative shaping."

The following poem by Maxine W. Kumin, "400-Meter Free Style," uses positive and negative shaping about equally. The swimmer travels up and down the pool as the poem progresses:

400-METER
FREE STYLE

The gun full swing the swimmer catapults and cracks

s
i
x

feet   away   onto   that   perfect   glass   he   catches   at
a
n
d
throws behind him scoop after scoop cunningly moving
                                                          t
                                                            h
                                                              e
water back to move him forward. Thrift is his wonderful
s
e
c
ret; he has schooled out all extravagance. No muscle
                                                        r
                                                          i
                                                            p
ples without compensation wrist cock to heel snap to
h
i
s
mobile mouth that siphons in the air that nurtures
                                                    h
                                                      i
                                                        m
at half an inch above sea level so to speak.
T
h
e
astonishing whites of the soles of his feet rise
                                                      a
                                                        n
                                                          d
salute us on the turns. He flips, converts, and is gone
a
l
l
in one. We watch him for signs. His arms are steady at
                                                            t
                                                              h
                                                                e
catch, his cadent feet tick in the stretch, they know
t
h
e
lesson well. Lungs knew, too; he does not list for
                                                        a
                                                          i
                                                            r

he   drives   along   on   little   sips   carefully   expended
b
u
t
that   plum   red   heart   pumps   hard   cries   hurt   how   soon
                                                                i
                                                                t
                                                                s
near   one   more   and   makes   its   final   surge   TIME: 4:25:9

MAXINE W. KUMIN

In this next poem by the American poet Richard Frost, one begins with the title at the bottom, and climbs *up* the tower—the "last" line is really the first:

never   falling.
  leaning   but
    thin   ladder,
      and   climb   a
  filling   our   heads
    their   warm   song
      we   must   imagine
      Nearing   the   bells,
        to   each   gallery.
        turns   us   darkly
      inside   this   tower
      changing   angles
      The   long   spiral
    curves   to   the   sea.
      the   bright   Arno
      rooftops   shrink,
    drop   farther   away,
      Now   the   avenues
      have   climbed   in.
    thousands   like   us
      worn   by   leather
      on   marble   steps
    finding   a   balance
    of   our   promises,
    how   to   keep   all
    here   we   may   see
  Love,

RICHARD FROST

CLIMBING THE TOWER AT PISA

Concrete verse is ideographic spatials. For instance, in Japanese the
character for "rain" (an ideograph *looks* like the thing it is meant to
represent; the Japanese have characters rather than the letters of
an alphabet, and the characters are ideographs) might be arranged on
the page so that it will look like rain falling. At the bottom of the page
there might be the character for "house"; thus, the characters for rain
are falling pictorially on the character for house.

Look at the poem used as illustration for concrete verse in Chap. 4.

Concrete verse can go all the way toward the graphic, as in this
print by D.A. Levy, who was both poet and print-maker:

LEOS CASINO

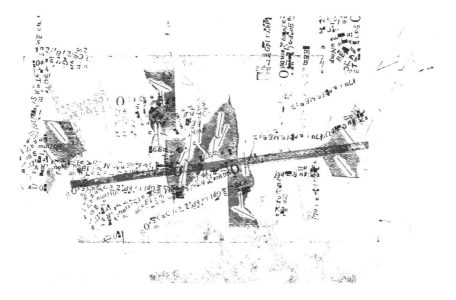

D. A. LEVY

suggested writing assignment

Invent a spatial poem. Make it simple and short. See if you can make
a statement of some kind primarily by means of the shape of your stanza,
preferably an uncomplicated shape.

Here is a poem written in prose parallels, *grammatics*:

COOL TOMBS

When Abraham Lincoln was shoveled into the tombs, he forgot the copperheads
  and the assassin . . . in the dust, in the cool tombs.
And Ulysses Grant lost all thought of con men and Wall Street, cash and
  collateral turned ashes . . . in the dust, in the cool tombs.
Pocahontas' body, lovely as a poplar, sweet as a red haw in November or a
  pawpaw in May, did she wonder? does she remember? . . . in the dust, in
  the cool tombs?

Take any streetful of people buying clothes and groceries, cheering a hero or
  throwing confetti and blowing tin horns . . . tell me if the lovers are losers
  . . . tell me if any get more than the lovers . . . in the dust . . . in the
  cool tombs.

CARL SANDBURG

Notice all the parallel structures in this poem—the most obvious
one is the use of a refrain at the end of each paragraph. Another is the
repetition of phrases—"tell me if"; the catalog of actions is also in
parallel—"buying," "cheering," "throwing."

Review the information on parallels in Chap. 3: *synonymous
parallelism, synthetic parallelism, antithetical parallelism,* and *climactic
parallelism.* Review the examples given as well; here is another:

A SUPERMARKET IN CALIFORNIA

What thoughts I have of you tonight, Walt Whitman, for I walked down the
sidestreets under the trees with a headache self-conscious looking at the full
moon.

In my hungry fatigue, and shopping for images, I went into the neon fruit
supermarket, dreaming of your enumerations!

What peaches and what penumbras! Whole families shopping at night! Aisles
full of husbands! Wives in the avocados, babies in the tomatoes!—and you,
Garcia Lorca, what were you doing down by the watermelons?

I saw you, Walt Whitman, childless, lonely old grubber, poking among the
meats in the refrigerator and eyeing the grocery boys.

I heard you asking questions of each: Who killed the pork chops? What price
bananas? Are you my Angel?

I wandered in and out of the brilliant stacks of cans following you, and
followed in my imagination by the store detective.

We strode down the open corridors together in our solitary fancy tasting
artichokes, possessing every frozen delicacy, and never passing the cashier.

Where are we going, Walt Whitman? The doors close in an hour. Which way
does your beard point tonight?

(I touch your book and dream of our odyssey in the supermarket and feel absurd.)

Will we walk all night through solitary streets? The trees add shade to shade, lights out in the houses, we'll both be lonely.

Will we stroll dreaming of the lost America of love past blue automobiles in driveways, home to our silent cottage?

Ah, dear father, gray beard, lonely old courage-teacher, what America did you have when Charon quit poling his ferry and you got out on a smoking bank and stood watching the boat disappear on the black waters of Lethe?

Berkeley 1955

ALLEN GINSBERG

suggested writing assignment

Write a 16-line poem *using each of the grammatic parallels a minimum of three times*. Remember, this is a prose form based on grammatics, so you need not worry about rhythm or sound at all. Simply follow the forms of the parallels. You will be surprised, perhaps, to find how the sound will take care of itself: The parallel structures will produce a language music that is inherent in the form.

Do not be afraid to use repetition, however—it is a basic poetic device; Sandburg and Whitman used it as an element of their prose poems, and many other kinds of poetry use it too.

Another device most prose poets use in their parallel systems is the *catalog.* A catalog is a list of things, nouns usually, though they may also be lists of phrases, clauses, or verbs—all parts of speech.

6

two prosodies:

WORD-COUNT AND PARENTHETICS

Word-count prosody assigns a set number of *words* to each line of a poem. *Normative* word-count keeps the same number of words in every line; *quantitative* word-count varies the lengths of lines in the first stanza, but following stanzas keep the same word-counts as the first, line-for-line. *Variable* word-count sets certain limits for the lengths of lines, but within these limits the number of words per line may vary—for instance, the poet may say, "There will be a minimum of three words in each line, and a maximum of seven."

This prosody has great flexibility, even in normative and quantitative word-counts because the number of syllables and the number of stresses may vary considerably, even in lines containing the same number of words.

Review the information on word-count and the *perfect parallel* in Chap. 3.

In the following quantitative word-count poem, note that corresponding lines in each stanza contain the same number of words; in every first line there are four words, in each second line there are three words, and in the last line of each stanza there are five words:

THE DOOR

There is a door
      made of faces
faces snakes and green moss

which to enter is
      death or perhaps
life which to touch is

to sense beyond the
      figures carved in
shades of flesh and emerald

the Inhabitant at home
      in his dark
rooms his hours shadowed or

lamptouched and that door
      must not be
attempted the moss disturbed nor

the coiling lichen approached
      because once opened
the visitor must remain in

that place among the
      Inhabitant's couches and
violets must be that man

in his house cohabiting
      with the dark
wife her daughter or both.

from *The Inhabitant*

Another technique "The Door" uses is *stream-of-consciousness,* which means that one is trying to create, on paper, an imitation of the way the mind actually works—not logically in neat sentences (nobody really thinks that way, except when he is concentrating), but running on from one idea or association to another. To achieve this effect, normal *syntax* (word-order) and grammatical construction are done away with. One sentence flows into another in this poem without punctuation. Perhaps it is only the line-endings that give some sense of *phrasal pause.* Sometimes the end of one sentence will simultaneously be the beginning of another.

This poem, written in the Imagist tradition, is perhaps the best-known word-count poem in English:

THE RED WHEELBARROW

so much depends
upon

a red wheel
barrow

glazed with rain
water

beside the white
chickens.

WILLIAM CARLOS WILLIAMS

This next poem is written in variable word-count: the number of words per line varies from three to seven, but the norm is four to six:

THE HERO

Each voice which was asked
spoke its words, and heard
more than that, the fair question,
the onerous burden of the asking.

And so the hero, the
hero! stepped that gracefully
into his redemption, losing
or gaining life thereby.

Now we, now I
ask also, and burdened,
tied down, return
and seek the forest also.

Go forth, go forth,
saith the grandmother, the fire
of that old form, and turns
away from the form.

And the forest is dark,
mist hides it, trees
are dim, but I turn
to my father in the dark.

A spark, that spark of hope
which was burned out long ago,
the tedious echo
of the father image

—which only women bear,
also wear, old men, old cares,
and turn, and again find
the disorder in the mind.

Night is dark like the mind,
my mind is dark like the night.
O light the light! Old
foibles of the right.

Into that pit, now pit of
anywhere, the tears upon your hands,
how can you stand
it, I also turn.

I wear the face, I face
the right, the right, the way,
I go along the path
into the last and only dark,

hearing *hero! hero!*
a voice faint enough, a spark,
a glimmer grown dimmer through years
of old, old fears.

ROBERT CREELEY

Another technique to be found in "The Hero," besides variable word-count, is variable rhyme: There is no set rhyme scheme, but some of the lines rhyme, and the poem concludes with a rhymed *couplet (aa)*. All of the stanzas are quatrain stanzas. Despite these obvious elements, many people continue to insist that Creeley writes in "free verse," but most of his forms are so strict that it's a question whether it can even be maintained that he writes in forms of prose. This particular poem is certainly verse-mode, not prose-mode.

suggested writing assignment

A.   Write four lines in perfect parallel—they need not be one poem, merely four separate lines.

B.   Write a word-count poem made of four stanzas, each stanza consisting of four lines. Assign a certain number of *words* to each line of the first stanza; have corresponding lines in each stanza contain the same number of words. If you wish, you may try the stream-of-consciousness technique.

Review the information regarding *parenthetics* in Chap. 3. Parenthetics split clauses, phrases, even words, in half, the halves enclosing previous elements:

PINES

They are the pines
I have seen them standing
IN THE HILLS WHERE STONE DWELLS
the wind shifts among their needles
ROOTS TOUCH TOWARD SILENCE IN THE EARTH
as though they have always been
strength drawn out of darkness.

Here is a parenthetic poem by Russell Salamon, who invented the prosody when he was a college student:

SHE

My finger touch dissolves
   into a shiverlong echo of rains/
   sizzling on snowscapes of her skin.
   Her face, her arms, her thighs,
      {all parentheses in which I am
        [my hands( ) cup her cup]
   warm drizzle-rain inside her.}
   Forests full of soundless flowers
   waited once unseen, translucid.
   She carries rain constellations
   to fill flute basins where
   /we wash our morning faces off

               RUSSELL SALAMON

suggested writing assignment

Write a seven-line poem utilizing parenthetics as a prosody.

7

SYLLABIC PROSODIES

Syllabics is a metrical prosody, and there are three kinds of syllabics: *normative syllabics, quantitative syllabics,* and *variable syllabics* —review the information on syllabics in Chap. 2.

Normative syllabics is written in verses of a single syllabic length, with but slight variations, as in this poem, which is written in *decasyllabics* (ten-syllable lines):

THE AUCTION

The sun, like a brilliant gavel, arcs and
falls—just once—on the treetops beyond the
river: going, going, gone. Summer has been
sold piecemeal to the gathered bidders. Now
the auctioneer, old Clockface MacOwre,
totes up the take as the crowd takes off down
the gravel drive, snips and snatches of odds
and ends tied down on cartops, tucked into
trunks: goods bought in good barter with what rare
currency.
              And you, sir. With what have you
gone home? Has your money grown on trees? Have
the red leaves measured, from bud to russet,

the corrosion of your heart?
                              There was the
late spring first—June founting up from valleys
to nurture the hills; the nestings. After,
there was July with its flaunting of wings
and a hurliburl of foliage rich
as dollars, in thunder and in sunlight.
Next, August: Croesus in every woodlot,
callous of sovereigns.
                        And now, in the
month of closings and returns, in the month
of chalkdust, bells, and buzzers, summer bursts
into bankruptcy with a fine splurge that
comes too late—the fairweather folk fare well
away: they shall not see with what bleak grace
the weatherbeaten landlord may sustain
penury.
                Nor shall we, though we know that,
when the gold is gone, there will be silver
to spend. Clockface hefts his sack of coin, clears
his cardtable of excelsior, folds
it and tools off into the sunset. In
the farmhouse the liquidated last of
the tenants spin around their hollow rooms
like webless spiders gone dry inside.
                                        One
last night by the river. We will lock the
barn in the morning, turn off the tap, drain
out the kitchen pipes, and see the lawn chairs,
the croquet set and badminton stowed in   ·
the shed. Then, the blank windows reflective
of nothing but sunlight, we shall go back.

Notice that, though the poem is unrhymed, the sound has not been forgotten. Note, also, that those partial lines that begin what amounts to a new "verse paragraph" are actually, as far as syllable-count goes, part of the preceding line in each case. "Croesus" is an *allusion*—a reference to the ancient Lydian king who accumulated so much treasure that his name became synonymous with wealth.

Here is a poem written in *heptasyllabics* (seven-syllable lines):

TO WAKEN A SMALL PERSON

You sleep at the top of streets
Up which workmen each morning
Go wheeling their bicycles

Your eyes are like the windows
Of some high attic the one
The very one you sleep in

They're shut it's raining the rain
Falls on the streets of the town
As it falls falls through your sleep

You must be dreaming these tears
Wake up please open yourself
Like a little umbrella

Hurry the sidewalks need you
The awnings not one is up
And the patient bicycles

Halted at intersections
They need you they are confused
The colors of traffic lights

Are bleeding bleeding wake up
The puddles of parking lots
Cannot contain such rainbows

DONALD JUSTICE

As in "The Door," which illustrated word-count, Justice in this poem chooses not to punctuate, but to use line-endings as *sight-punctuation;* each line is *phrased,* and the triplet stanzas are also *enjambed*—they run on, one into the other. The poem does not even have a *full-stop* in the last stanza—a period or other terminal punctuation at the end of the last line.

Rather than use a line of only one syllable-count, the poet may choose to have different syllable-length lines in each stanza, but at the same time to have corresponding lines in succeeding stanzas of equal length. This poem is an example of *quantitative* (preset) syllabics; notice that the poem begins with an *epigraph*—a quotation from some other source:

THE PILOT

Calais, France, May 18, 1968 (AP)—Low tide yesterday uncovered a plane, presumably of World War II, with the remains of the pilot still at the controls. Its origin could not be determined immediately.

It has been
a long flight. Like flak,
the seagrass exploded

       beneath me as I fell
         out of light into
an older and a heavier air.

         My planing
       continued in the tide.
       When the cuttlefish had
       done with my flesh, I found
         that still the stick would
answer, though more slowly than before.

         So I flew,
       and am flying still, back
       to the beginning. In
       my marrow direction
         lay. Now the sea has
released me, and I have been constant.

         But I was
       wrong. You see me at death's
       controls, in the primal
       mud where our flight began,
         but it has not been
a fleeing, as we have long supposed.

         I see that
       now, with these sockets where
       fish have swum. You, rising
       from the shore, have shown me
         what the snail tried to
tell: the journey is the other way.

Turn me around. I am with you still.

    Notice several things about the poem. First, the *poetic voice* in the poem is not that of the poet, but that of the pilot, whose *persona*, or identity, the poet has assumed. A persona is a poetic "mask"—the poet is not always speaking about himself, nor even in his own voice (as in "The Auction" where the poet himself describes the end of summer).

    Second, each stanza of "The Pilot" is one *verse paragraph*. The verse paragraph is distinguished from a paragraph of a prose poem in that the former is a unit of lines in a metrical poem that is analogous to a paragraph because it deals with matters that have logical relationships with one another and a common focus, but verse paragraphs need not be visually set off as units like prose paragraphs. Look at the poem "The Auction" again: New paragraphs begin anywhere in a line, though they are set off in this case by dropping down a line. The stanzas of "The

Pilot" need not have been end-stopped, but the poet chose to do so at the same time that he enjambed many of the lines, which run-on without pause into following lines.

The third thing to notice about "The Pilot" is that the poem ends in a *coda* of one line at the end of the five stanzas. A coda is a single, concluding line (or some unit of lines shorter than a full stanza) which is climactic in nature. In this case, the coda line is the same length as one of the lines in the stanza—nine syllables (the longest line-length).

None of these preceding poems uses rhyme, but here is a quantitative syllabic poem by the English Renaissance poet Ben Johnson that does:

AN ODE TO HIMSELF

Where dost thou careless lie,
          Buried in ease and sloth?
Knowledge that sleeps doth die;
And this security,
          It is the common moth
That eats on wits and arts, and oft destroys them both:

Are all th' Aonian springs
          Dried up? Lies Thespia waste?
Doth Clarius' harp want strings,
That not a nymph now sings?
          Or droop they as disgrac'd,
To see their seats and bowers by chattering pies defac'd?

If hence thy silence be,
          As 'tis too just a cause,
Let this thought quicken thee:
Minds that are great and free
          Should not on fortune pause;
'Tis crown enough to virtue still, her own applause.

What though the greedy fry
          Be taken with false baits
Of worded balladry,
And think it poesy?
And only piteous scorn upon their folly waits.

Then take in hand thy lyre;
          Strike in thy proper strain;
With Japhet's line aspire
Sol's chariot for new fire
          To give the world again;
Who aided him will thee, the issue of Jove's brain.

And, since our dainty age
          Cannot endure reproof,

> Make not thyself a page
> To that strumpet the stage;
>   But sing high and aloof,
> Safe from the wolf's black jaw, and the dull ass's hoof.

Ben Jonson

Jonson's poem is an *ode*—a contemplative lyric. Often odes are occasional, celebrating some particular event.

It has been pointed out in a previous chapter that the Celts of Britain—the Welsh, Irish, Cornish, Scottish, and Manx, among others—wrote out of a syllabic tradition. Some of the strictures imposed by the Celtic Bardic tradition upon syllabic poets in the Middle Ages were tremendously complex: There were twenty-four "official" Welsh meters, and the Irish bards also were expected to master particular syllabic forms if they were to be admitted to the hierarchy of poets. As H. Idris Bell and David Bell point out in the introduction to their book *Dafydd ap Gwilym: Fifty Poems,* "The two higher classes into which the bards were divided, known respectively as *pencerdd* and *bardd teulu,* were, under the native princes, public officials and subject to strict regulation, both by the Welsh laws and by the rules of the bardic order itself. The *penceirddiaid,* whose work alone would seem to have been preserved, were limited to a very narrow range of themes, chiefly elegies and eulogies on the members of the princely houses and religious poems, and even their treatment of these was regulated by minute prescriptions." This would seem to be a prison, but the Bells also point out, "It is, though, a curious paradox in literature that often the most binding tradition and form are an incentive to spontaneity of expression rather than a hindrance."

The modern Welsh poet Dylan Thomas, who wrote in English, early turned to the syllabic traditions of his ancestors. Here is his first syllabic poem, written when he was fifteen years old:

OF ANY FLOWER

> Hourly I sigh,
> For all things are leaf-like
> And cloud-like.
>
> Flowerly I die,
> For all things are grief-like
> And shroud-like.

Dylan Thomas

Of course, it could be argued that this is a word-count poem, and its parallel structures are evident as well. In fact, the first and second stanzas, taken together, are a *perfect parallel*. In a perfect parallel *both* syllable-count *and* word-count may be present. Thomas did not follow the bardic forms; rather, he invented his own syllabic structures:

FERN HILL

Now as I was young and easy under the apple boughs
About the lilting house and happy as the grass was green,
    The night above the dingle starry,
       Time let me hail and climb
    Golden in the heydays of his eyes,
And honoured among wagons I was prince of the apple towns
And once below a time I lordly had the trees and leaves
       Trail with daisies and barley
Down the rivers of the windfall light.

And as I was green and carefree, famous among the barns
About the happy yard and singing as the farm was home,
    In the sun that is young once only,
       Time let me play and be
    Golden in the mercy of his means,
And green and golden I was huntsman and herdsman, the calves
Sang to my horn, the foxes on the hills barked clear and cold,
      And the sabbath rang slowly
    In the pebbles of the holy streams.

All the sun long it was running, it was lovely, the hay
Fields high as the house, the tunes from the chimneys, it was air
    And playing, lovely and watery
      And fire green as grass.
    And nightly under the simple stars
As I rode to sleep the owls were bearing the farm away,
All the moon long I heard, blessed among stables, the nightjars
    Flying with the ricks, and the horses
      Flashing into the dark.

And then to awake, and the farm, like a wanderer white
With the dew, come back, the cock on his shoulder: it was all
    Shining, it was Adam and maiden,
      The sky gathered again
    And the sun grew round that very day.
So it must have been after the birth of the simple light
In the first, spinning place, the spellbound horses walking warm
    Out of the whinnying green stable
      On to the fields of praise.

And honoured among foxes and pheasants by the gay house
Under the new made clouds and happy as the heart was long,
   In the sun born over and over,
     I ran my heedless ways,
  My wishes raced through the house high hay
And nothing I cared, at my sky blue trades, that time allows
In all his tuneful turning so few and such morning songs
   Before the children green and golden
     Follow him out of grace,

Nothing I cared, in the lamb white days, that time would take me
Up to the swallow thronged loft by the shadow of my hand,
   In the moon that is always rising,
     Nor that riding to sleep
  I should hear him fly with the high fields
And wake to the farm forever fled from the childless land.
Oh as I was young and easy in the mercy of his means,
     Time held me green and dying
   Though I sang in my chains like the sea.

                 DYLAN THOMAS

If Thomas didn't follow the *forms* of the Welsh bards, he certainly followed their *traditions;* and if he didn't know the terms naming the sonic devices he used (the general term covering these devices is *cynghanedd*), he nevertheless used them. We will cover some of the kinds of cynghanedd in the next chapter. One of the peculiarities encountered in following these Welsh sonic forms is that, it is practically a certainty that one will come up with sounds like those of Thomas or of Gerard Manley Hopkins, who also studied Welsh language techniques.

"Fern Hill" is built very much like "The Pilot": Most of the stanzas are end-stopped (or *closed*); the poem is strictly syllabic. There is no coda, however, and the sonic level is more heavily emphasized. "Fern Hill" is not, strictly speaking, rhymed, but there is a good deal of consonance and alliteration, along with other sonic elements. As in "The Pilot" and "Poetry" by Marianne Moore, lines of the same syllabic length are indented the same number of spaces, thus putting some emphasis on the typographical level.

Marianne Moore's poem is written in *variable syllabics*: The range is from five to 22 syllables—the first two lines in each stanza are generally longer than most of the others, ranging from 13 to 22 syllables; third lines are of middle range, for the most part, as are the last lines; the shortest lines are usually lines four and five of these sestet (six-line) stanzas. Although "Poetry" has some true rhymes, the poem basically de-emphasizes the sonic level and emphasizes the sensory level:

POETRY

I, too, dislike it: there are things that are important beyond all this fiddle.
   Reading it, however, with a perfect contempt for it, one discovers in
   it after all, a place for the genuine.
      Hands that can grasp, eyes
      that can dilate, hair that can rise
         if it must, these things are important not because a

high-sounding interpretation can be put upon them but because they are
   useful. When they become so derivative as to become unintelligible,
   the same thing may be said for all of us, that we
      do not admire what
      we cannot understand: the bat
         holding on upside down or in quest of something to

eat, elephants pushing, a wild horse taking a roll, a tireless wolf under
   a tree, the immovable critic twitching his skin like a horse that feels a flea,
         the base-
ball fan, the statistician—
      nor is it valid
         to discriminate against 'business documents and

school-books'; all these phenomena are important. One must make a distinction
   however: when dragged into prominence by half poets, the result is not poetry,
   nor till the poets among us can be
      'literalists of
      the imagination'—above
         insolence and triviality and can present

for inspection, 'imaginary gardens with real toads in them', shall we have
   it. In the meantime, if you demand on the one hand,
   the raw material of poetry in
      all its rawness and
      that which is on the other hand
         genuine, you are interested in poetry.

                          Marianne Moore

Notice that the central stanza is variant—a quintet.

suggested writing assignment

Write the first stanza of a poem; make the stanza three lines long.
Count the syllables in each line. Now write three succeeding stanzas of
the same poem, making sure that corresponding lines in each stanza have
the same syllable-lengths. Do not attempt to rhyme the poem; simply

worry about the syllable counts. If you wish, you may add one
climactic coda-line at the end of the poem, making the line the same
syllable-count as one of the lines in your normal stanza. This will yield
a thirteen-line poem.

8

ACCENTUAL PROSODIES

Accentual verse counts the stressed syllables in each line, not the unstressed. Review the information regarding accentuals in Chap. 2. Much accentual verse, and some syllabic verse—especially Celtic syllabic verse—is written alliteratively: The stressed syllables are emphasized or "sprung" by a series of words that use the same beginning consonantal sound; i.e., "The bee is busy with blueberry bushes." If we *scan* this line; that is, isolate those syllables that sound heaviest, we will discover that the stresses fall on the alliterated first syllables:

The bée is búsy with blúeberry búshes.

If we listen closely to the line, we will also hear that it tends to divide itself in half—there is a pause in the line between the second and third accented syllables:

The bée is búsy · with blúeberry búshes.

This is the method of Anglo-Saxon prosody: four stressed syllables in a *stich* (a line of verse). Some of the stressed syllables will be *sprung* with alliteration, assonance, consonance, rhyme, or vocalic and consonantal echo. (We will go more deeply into some of these techniques in Chap. 10.) The stich is broken into *hemistichs* (half-lines) by a *caesura* (pause) in the center of the line. In the whole stich there will be four beats; in the hemistichs, two beats.

There are several ways in which the line may alliterate:

1) The two center syllables may alliterate:

over the stars · stunning their fires.

2) The first three syllables may alliterate:

But the leaf shall lie · lightly upon him.

3) The last three syllables may alliterate:

its unique symmetry · the summit of song.

4) All four syllables may alliterate, as in the line about the bees given above.

5) Sometimes the alliteration may continue into the following stich.

6) Sometimes there will be cross-alliteration between stichs:

his blood springing · from ringing rock
till the long rain · of time shall spill. . . .

7) Sometimes what is "alliterated" is the *absence* of consonants— it is considered that any vowel may "alliterate" (actually, *consonate*) with any other:

at this martyr · and at his art.

(Note that in this last example the vowel *sounds* of "at" and "martyr," and "at" and "art" are not the same.)

H. Idris Bell and David Bell, in their translation of the medieval Welsh poet Dafydd ap Gwilym* describe the bardic sonic devices known as *cynghanedd*, of which there are four main types:

_____

* *Dafydd ap Gwilym: Fifty Poems*, translated, with introductory essays, by H. Idris and David Bell, London: Honourable Society of Cymmrodorion, 1942.

1) *Cynghanedd groes.* "In *Cynghanedd Groes* there is an exact
   correspondence between the consonants in the first half of the line
   and those in the second, so that every consonant in the first finds
   its [consonantal echo] in the second, and there is no consonant
   unaccounted for in the scheme, with the exception of the final
   syllable in each half":

   $$\overset{1}{Th}\overset{2}{i}\overset{3}{s}\ \overset{4}{t}\overset{}{o}\overset{5}{n}e\ i\overset{}{s}\ his,\ \cdot\ \overset{1}{th}e\ s\overset{23}{to}\overset{4}{n}e'\overset{5}{s}\ song,\ .\ .\ .$$

   This tone is his, · the stone's song, . . .

2) *Cynghanedd draws.* "In *Cynghanedd Draws* the same system is
   apparent, except that there is, as it were, an island in the centre
   of the line in which the consonants are in isolation and are not
   echoed elsewhere":

   He is life's fool, · and his leaf's fall. . . .

3) *Cynghanedd lusg.* "In *Cynghanedd Lusg* the penultimate
   [next-to-last] stressed syllable is rhymed with a syllable in the
   first part of the line. . . ":

   his blood spŕung · from rúng rock. . . .

4) *Cynghanedd sain.* ". . . and *Cynghanedd Sain* has an internal
   rhyme together with [consonantal echo] between the second
   rhyming word and the last word in the line":

   no óther than · bŕother of his breath, . . .

Except for the first example given in this chapter (*The bee is busy
with blueberry bushes*), all the lines used here as examples were taken
from a single poem, which itself is an illustration of how these various
alliterative and echoic devices can work when they are put together.
Remember that each two lines, as they appear on the page, really equal
one line:

THE MORBID MAN SINGING

This tone is his,
                    the stone's song,
no other than
                    brother of his breath,
fang of water,
                    tongue of the air.

He is life's fool,
                    and his leaf's fall
shall be the last
                    laugh at last
at this martyr
                    and at his art.
But the leaf shall lie
                        lightly upon him,
its unique symmetry
                        the summit of song
which he will enter
                        leaf-fall and winter—
his blood sprung
                    from rung rock
till the long rain
                    of time shall spill
over the stars,
                    stunning their fires.

Here is an Old English poem translated into modern English.
Listen for the four stressed syllables, the caesura, and the alliterations;
note, too, that the poem is an *epistle*—a letter. In a headnote to the
poem its translator says that the persona of the poem is a stick; the
poem is

> "Spoken by the staff on which the message has been inscribed. The MS is
> torn; this text is partly based on reconstructions. The Runes of lines 49–50
> may mean, in slightly altered form, either 'Follow the sun's path across the
> ocean, and ours will be joy and the happiness and prosperity of the bright
> day,' or 'Follow the sun's path across the sea to find joy with the man who
> is waiting for you.' "

A *rune* is a charm or incantation, often in the form of an anagram
or an acrostic. The allusion to "the sad cuckoo calling" (in the following
poem) is to the bird that symbolizes cuckoldry—a husband whose wife
has been unfaithful to him is a cuckold. In line twenty-six the
metaphoric construction "the gull's home" is a *kenning*. Kennings are
brief metaphorical synonyms; for instance, "womb-man = a human
female," or, as in this case, "the gull's home = sea."

THE HUSBAND'S MESSAGE

A tree grew me; I was green, and wood.
That came first. I was cut and sent
Away from my home, holding wily
Words, carried out on the ocean,

Riding a boat's back. I crossed
Stormy seas, seeking the thresholds
Where my master's message was meant to travel
And be known. And now the knotted planks
Of a ship have brought me here, and you
Shall read my lord's heart and hear
His soul's thought. I promise a glowing
Faith shall be what you find. Read.

      See: this wood has come to make you
Remember the hands that carved it, to take you
Back to the love and the pledges you shared,
You two, in that buried time when you both
Could walk unharmed across this festive
Town, the land yours, and you
Each other's. Your people fought, and the feud
Brought him exile. Now he asks you
To listen to the sad cuckoo calling
In the grove; when its song has reached the edge
Of the woods, he wants you to come to him over
The waves, letting nothing lead you
Aside and no man living stop you.

      Go down to the sea, the gull's home,
And come to a ship that can carry you south,
Away, out on the water to where
Your husband and lord longs for your coming.
Nothing the world can send him, he says
Through me, could bring him more delight
Than for Almighty God to grant him you,
And for you and he together to bless
His soldiers and friends with treasure, with hammered
Bracelets and rings. For though his home
Is with strangers, he lives in a lovely land
And is rich: shining gold surrounds him.
And though my master was driven from here,
Rushing madly down to his ship
And onto the sea, alone, only
Alive because he fled, and glad
To escape, yet now he is served and followed,
Loved and obeyed by many. He has beaten
Misery: there's nothing more he wants,
Oh prince's daughter, no precious gems,
No stallions, no mead-hall pleasure, no treasure
On earth, but you, you to enjoy
In spite of the ancient oath that parted you.
And I fit together an S and an R,
And E, an A, a W and D,

In an oath to prove that your pledge is sacred
To him, and his faith as steady as his heart.
As long as life shall be in him, he'll long
To fulfill the vows and the love you shared.

Anonymous
tr. Burton Raffel

   The poem following is contemporary. At the end of each stanza there is an accentual-syllabic form called a *bob and wheel* which is sometimes associated with accentual poems written in the later middle ages. The bob and wheel is a metrical tail on an accentual poem. The last line of the accentual stanza proper is often an enjambed line that is continued by the *bob*, which is a line of verse made of only one or two verse feet and, sometimes of only one accented syllable. The bob itself may be enjambed with the *wheel*, which is a quatrain stanza, each line containing three verse feet. The bob is rhymed with the second and fourth lines of the wheel, and the first and second lines of the wheel rhyme. In this case the bob-and-wheel is also a *burden*—a refrain stanza:

THE MAGI CAROL

Sheep of the fold, fowls of the storm,
In chill the child, chaste in his manger—
The kings are coming to crown a King
And here are we, waiting to welcome

them together:
We wish you joy again—
Gale, oak & heather,
Mistletoe & pine—
In any winter weather.

Bearing gold, gifts of myrrh,
Of frankincense—seed of thyme,
Vervain and thorn, horn at the gate—
The Magi move among the snows

together:
We wish you joy again—
Gale, oak & heather,
Mistletoe & pine—
In any winter weather.

Reap the heart of the hoar oak
With a scythe of ore, open the gate
Of the golden bough, bend to dream
Before the stable, the stall of fortune

> all together:
> We wish you joy again—
> Gale, oak & heather,
> Mistletoe & pine—
> In any winter weather.

It is curious, perhaps, that this modern poem sounds more ancient than the translation, but the reason for this is that "The Magi Carol" is written in a particular *poetic diction*—a style of writing deliberately contrived to achieve poetic effect. In this case, the poet's wish is to have his poem sound older than it is. Edmund Spenser in his *The Faery Queene* did something similar during the Renaissance.

Gerard Manley Hopkins' poem pays no attention to keeping only a certain number of beats to the line, but he heavily accents his stresses. This is an example of alliterated *variable accentuals,* which he called "sprung rhythm." The principle is much the same as that in Anglo-Saxon prosody, except that there may be more or fewer than four accents in the line, and Hopkins (in the poem that follows) uses rhyme as well:

GOD'S GRANDEUR

The world is charged with the grandeur of God.
  It will flame out, like shining from shook foil;
  It gathers to a greatness, like the ooze of oil
Crushed. Why do men then now not reck his rod?
Generations have trod, have trod, have trod;
  And all is seared with trade; bleared, smeared with toil;
  And wears man's smudge and shares man's smell: the soil
Is bare now, nor can foot feel, being shod.

And for all this, nature is never spent;
  There lives the dearest freshness deep down things;
And though the last lights off the black West went
  Oh, morning, at the brown brink eastward, springs—
Because the Holy Ghost over the bent
  World broods with warm breast and with ah! bright wings.

GERARD MANLEY HOPKINS

The Vachel Lindsay poem following is similar, though it is more strictly *dipodic* [i.e., two-beat in nature—the rhythms of folk songs and nursery rhymes (more on dipodics in a subsequent chapter)]. Most lines keep the four beats, though some have more, and some others, that operate like codas for single stanzas, are *tripodic* (three-beat):

"Are you washed in the blood of the lamb?"

Lindsay uses this line as a refrain that is repeated at intervals throughout
the poem, which is meant to have the same sort of folk-sound as a
Salvation Army band (General William Booth founded the Salvation
Army):

GENERAL WILLIAM BOOTH
ENTERS INTO HEAVEN

*(To be sung to the tune of "The Blood of the Lamb" with
indicated instrument)*

I

(Bass drum beaten loudly.)
Booth led boldly with his big bass drum—
(Are you washed in the blood of the Lamb?)
The Saints smiled gravely and they said: "He's come."
(Are you washed in the blood of the Lamb?)
Walking lepers followed, rank on rank,
Lurching bravos from the ditches dank,
Drabs from the alleyways and drug fiends pale—
Minds still passion-ridden, soul-powers frail:—
Vermin-eaten saints with moldy breath.
Unwashed legions with the ways of Death—
(Are you washed in the blood of the lamb?)

(Banjos.)
Every slum had sent its half-a-score
The round world over. (Booth had groaned for more.)
Every banner that the wide world flies
Bloomed with glory and transcendent dyes.
Big-voiced lasses made their banjos bang,
Tranced, fanatical they shrieked and sang:—
"Are you washed in the blood of the Lamb?"
Hallelujah! It was queer to see
Bull-necked convicts with that land make free.
Loons with trumpets blowed a blare, blare, blare
On, on upward thro' the golden air!
(Are you washed in the blood of the Lamb?)

II

(Bass drum slower and softer.)
Booth died blind and still by faith he trod,
Eyes still dazzled by the ways of God.
Booth led boldly, and he looked the chief

Eagle countenance in sharp relief,
Beard a-flying, air of high command
Unabated in that holy land.

    (*Sweet flute music.*)
Jesus came from out the court-house door,
Stretched his hands above the passing poor.
Booth saw not, but led his queer ones there
Round and round the mighty court-house square.
Then, in an instant all that blear review
Marched on spotless, clad in raiment new.
The lame were straightened, withered limbs uncurled
And blind eyes opened on a new, sweet world.

    (*Bass drum louder.*)
Drabs and vixens in a flash made whole!
Gone was the weasel-head, the snout, the jowl!
Sages and sibyls now, and athletes clean,
Rulers of empires, and of forests green!

    (*Grand chorus of all instruments. Tambourines to the foreground.*)
The hosts were sandalled, and their wings were fire!
(Are you washed in the blood of the Lamb?)
But their noise played havoc with the angel-choir.
(Are you washed in the blood of the Lamb?)
Oh, shout Salvation! It was good to see
Kings and Princes by the Lamb set free.
The banjos rattled and the tambourines
Jing-jing-jingled in the hands of Queens

    (*Reverently sung, no instruments.*)
And when Booth halted by the curb for prayer
He saw his Master thro' the flag-filled air.
Christ came gently with a robe and crown
For Booth the soldier, while the throng knelt down.
He saw King Jesus. They were face to face,
And he knelt a-weeping in that holy place.
Are you wasted in the blood of the Lamb?

                        VACHEL LINDSAY

A native American form of variable accentuals is the *triversen stanza* which was developed by William Carlos Williams and a number of others. Essentially, a triversen (triple-verse-sentence) stanza is partly grammatic in prosody: One stanza equals one sentence. This sentence is broken into three parts, each part becoming a line composed of approximately one phrase. Thus, three lines (three phrases) equal one stanza (one sentence or clause). William Carlos Williams, in attempting to explain this prosody, spoke of the "breath-pause"—all that this meant,

finally, was the process of breaking the sentence or clause into phrasal
lines.

But he also spoke of the "variable foot," and by this he meant the
accentual element of the prosody: Each line could vary in length, carrying
from two to four stressed (but not necessarily alliterated) syllables.

Williams used this stanza quite often. He and a number of other
poets also composed 18-line poems containing six stanzas; such a poem has
come to be called a *triversen*. This particular poem is 21 lines long:

ON GAY WALLPAPER

The green-blue ground
is ruled with silver lines
to say the sun is shining

And on this mural sea
of grass or dreams lie flowers
or baskets of desires

Heaven knows what they are
between cerulean shapes
laid regularly round

Mat roses and tridentate
leaves of gold
threes, threes and threes

Three roses and three stems
the basket floating
standing in the horns of blue

Repeated to the ceiling
to the windows
where the day

Blows in
the scalloped curtains to
the sound of rain.

WILLIAM CARLOS WILLIAMS

One of Wallace Stevens' better-known short poems is an
accentual-syllabic, rhymed triversen:

THE BIRD WITH THE COPPERY, KEEN CLAWS

Above the forest of the parakeets,
A parakeet of parakeets prevails,
A pip of life amid a mort of tails.

(The rudiments of tropics are around,
Aloe of ivory, pear of rusty rind.)
His lids are white because his eyes are blind.

He is not paradise of parakeets,
Of his gold ether, golden alguazil,
Except because he broods there and is still.

Panache upon panache, his tails deploy
Upward and outward, in green-vented forms,
His tip a drop of water full of storms.

But though the turbulent tinges undulate
As his pure intellect applies its laws,
He moves not on his coppery, keen claws.

He munches a dry shell while he exerts
His will, yet never ceases, perfect cock,
To flare, in the sun-pallor of his rock.

WALLACE STEVENS

John Fandel adds rhyme also, raises the accentual variance to six stresses, and enjambs each two stanzas so that, on the typographical level, the poem appears to be written in sestets rather than triplets:

MONDAY'S VISION

I saw a gust of birds rise in a hurry of gale
        like a moment mountain into the sun,
                an avalanche of disappearance;
they caught my breath: I had to scale
        a new alp in the imagination,
                their wings created so much circumstance.

For a long sky I could not touch a level earth;
        as their bright destination, I was found
                close to much of marvel, as flesh to bone,
child and universe, each giving to other: birth:
        like the chaste cord at the touch of immaculate sound,
                in the near distance between leaf and stone.

In a flight quick as their rise
        I heard for a brief sun the song of those wings
                astonish eden vanished in common clay
as if I pressed my face against the skies
        and looked into the miracle heart of things
                before I walked the level accents of day.

                                    JOHN FANDEL

suggested writing assignment

Write a poem consisting of eight lines of Anglo-Saxon prosody. Use at least three of the systems of alliteration. Remember, you don't need to worry about anything except the number of *accented* syllables in the line. The total number of syllables doesn't matter. Don't forget the caesura in each line: It may be created by manipulating phrasing, or by employing stresses, or by using punctuation.

9

ACCENTUAL-SYLLABIC PROSODIES

In order to be able to handle accentual-syllabics without sounding awkward, one must develop an ear for rhythms—one must be able to hear the stressed syllables of the English language alternating with the unstressed syllables. This is why we have worked up from grammatics through accentual prosodies—roughly paralleling the development of poetry in English. One of the poet's basic responsibilities, on the technical level, is to order the rhythms of the language.

We need to define four terms:

1) *Rhythm* is the movement of cadences in language;
2) *Prosody* is a system of poetic composition;
3) *Meter* is a system of prosody which counts syllables in verse according to a pattern;
4) *Accentual-syllabic prosody* is a metrical system which counts both the number of stressed syllables in the line *and* the number of unstressed syllables in the line. Moreover, in accentual-syllabic prosody, the stressed syllables alternate *more or less* regularly in a line of verse.

Review the information on accentual-syllabics in Chap. 2.

Depending on the *kind* of rhythm chosen, the accentual-syllabic poem will have as its *norm* a particular meter, composed of a certain kind of *verse foot*. Verse feet are represented by several symbols:

1) The *unaccented syllable* is indicated by the *breve* ($\smile$);
2) The *accented syllable* may be indicated by the *ictus* (/) or the *macron* (–);
3) A syllable which hovers somewhere between being accented and unaccented is represented by a *secondary accent* (·).

In every syllable there will be a vowel, and these marks are usually placed above the vowel of the syllable:

(A) "My love is like a red, red rose."

For our purposes here, we will not differentiate between accents and secondary accents, and we have already discussed the *divider* (|), which separates verse feet:

(B) "My love is like a red, red rose,"

or,

(C) "My love is like a red, red rose,"

depending on how one chooses to treat the secondary accent of the penultimate syllable.

One other mark needs to be explained: The virgule (/) is a stroke that is used to separate *verses* when they are written out like prose, *not* to separate verse feet:

"O my luve's like a red, red rose, / That's newly sprung in June; / O, my luve's like the melodie / That's sweetly played in tune." (Robert Burns)

And one should not confuse the mark for the caesura with the secondary accent mark:

"O my luve's like · a red, red rose."

There are a number of rhythms one can choose for the *norm* of his accentual-syllabic verse [there will always be variations, as in (B) above, where, in the last *foot* a *spondee,* or two-accented syllables ($//$), has been *substituted* for the normative *iamb*, or unaccented-accented syllables ($\smile/$)].

Besides the spondee and the iamb there are the *trochee* ($/\smile$); the *dactyl* ($/\smile\smile$); and the *anapest* ($\smile\smile/$)—the two latter being verse feet comprised of three syllables. Other feet which sometimes occur (usually only as variations) are the *amphibrach* ($/\smile/$); the *pyrrhic* ($\smile\smile$); the *tribrach* ($\smile\smile\smile$); the *molossus* ($///$); the *bacchic* ($\smile//$); and the *antibacchic* ($//\smile$).

Let's recapitulate: *Rhythm* is language cadence; *prosody* is a system of rhythm; *accentual-syllabics* is a rhythm system that alternates stressed and unstressed syllables according to some normative pattern.

Normative pattern: The word "normative" is important, for the true accentual-syllabic poet knows that it is *variation against the pattern*, and not strict adherence *to* the pattern, that delights the ear. A *poetaster*, or unskilled versifier, memorizes a pattern and works *with* it, whereas a poet understands a pattern and works *against* it: A metronome is boring; *counterpoint*—rhythm against a beat—is interesting. The problem is to be rhythmically interesting—not boring on the one hand, nor awkward on the other. The Joyce Kilmer poem "Trees" in Chap. 1 (p. 1) is metrically boring; Theo. Marzials' "A Tragedy" in Chapter 4 (p. 52) is metrically awkward.

We must define one more word: *Scansion*. Scansion is the process of isolating the accented or unaccented syllables in language—lines (A), (B), and (C) above have been *scanned*.

Any language can be scanned. One could scan a novel, if he felt like it. And he could divide it into verse feet, if he chose to do so. He would discover certain rhythms in the language—iambs and anapests predominate—but he would probably discern *metrical patterns* only in poetic passages of the novel—those spots where language is heightened.

It is very easy to scan: Simply put a macron or ictus over whatever syllable *normally* takes an accent. If you're not sure which syllable that is, *look in a dictionary*. In the case of single-syllable words, unimportant words such as articles (*the, a*), conjunctions (*and, but*), and prepositions (*in, for*) are normally unaccented. Remember, though, that normally unaccented syllables can be *sprung*, or abnormally emphasized, by means of sonics (alliteration, rhyme, etc.) or repetition (as in Gerard Manley Hopkins' poem on p. 93).

When you have scanned a line of verse, putting accent marks over the stressed syllables, *simply go back through the line putting breves over all the leftover syllables*.

One scans a poem in order to determine the *normative meter* of a

poem. The foot most commonly found in a particular poem is the
normative foot—in this line the normative foot is iambic:

The morning years of life, for us, are through.

—and there are five iambic feet in the line, so the normative *meter* is
iambic pentameter.

Penta- (from the Greek *pente*) means *five*. Hence, "iambic
pentameter" means a measure of five iambic feet. Some other prefixes
mean "one" (*mono-*), "two" (*di-*), "three" (*tri-*), "four" (*tetra-*), "six"
(*hexa-*), and "seven" (*hepta-*). Linking any of these prefixes to the word
meter will enable the scanner to tell both the normative foot and the
length of the line. For instance, "dactylic trimeter" means a line of verse
in which there are three dactyls *or* in which there are *at least two*
dactyls, plus one other kind of verse foot.

This last point is important—scanning only describes a norm, not
an absolute. *Some* lines of a particular iambic pentameter poem may not
contain a single iamb, but *most will*. Moreover, in *most* lines iambs will
predominate.

Here is Robert Frost's "Mending Wall":

MENDING WALL

Something there is that doesn't love a wall,
That sends the frozen-ground-swell under it,
And spills the upper boulders in the sun,
And makes gaps even two can pass abreast.
The work of hunters is another thing:
I have come after them and made repair
Where they have left not one stone on a stone,
But they would have the rabbit out of hiding,
To please the yelping dogs. The gaps I mean,
No one has seen them made or heard them made,
But at spring mending-time we find them there.
I let my neighbor know beyond the hill;
And on a day we meet to walk the line
And set the wall between us once again.
We keep the wall between us as we go.
To each the boulders that have fallen to each.
And some are loaves and some so nearly balls
We have to use a spell to make them balance:
"Stay where you are until our backs are turned!"
We wear our fingers rough with handling them.
Oh, just another kind of outdoor game,
One on a side. It comes to little more:

There where it is we do not need the wall:
He is all pine and I am apple orchard.
My apple trees will never get across
And eat the cones under his pines, I tell him.
He only says, "Good fences make good neighbors."
Spring is the mischief in me, and I wonder
If I could put a notion in his head:
'*Why* do they make good neighbors? Isn't it
Where there are cows? But here there are no cows.
Before I built a wall I'd ask to know
What I was walling in or walling out,
And to whom I was like to give offense.
Something there is that doesn't love a wall,
That wants it down.' I could say "Elves" to him,
But it's not elves exactly, and I'd rather
He said it for himself. I see him there,
Bringing a stone grasped firmly by the top
In each hand, like an old-stone savage armed.
He moves in darkness as it seems to me,
Not of woods only and the shade of trees.
He will not go behind his father's saying,
And he likes having thought of it so well
He says again, "Good fences make good neighbors."

ROBERT FROST

Read the poem aloud *very naturally,* letting the accents fall as they will. *Do not try to force the poem into regular meters.* Read it like prose, stopping *only* at the ends of sentences, *not* at the ends of lines—hardly even pause at the end of the line, unless there is punctuation. Pause only where there are commas, semicolons, or some other punctuation indicating phrasing.

Now go back and scan it, by putting accent marks over the syllables that sound heavier than the others:

> "Something there is that doesn't love a wall,
>
> That sends the frozen-ground-swell under it,
>
> And spills the upper boulders in the sun,
>
> And makes gaps even two can pass abreast."

Now go back through once more, and simply put breve marks over the other unmarked syllables:

"Something there is that doesn't love a wall,
That sends the frozen-ground-swell under it,
And spills the upper boulders in the sun,
And makes gaps even two can pass abreast."

Now, if we isolate our scansion marks, we have a pattern that looks like this:

/⌣⌣/⌣/⌣/⌣/
⌣/⌣/⌣/ / /⌣/
⌣/⌣/⌣/⌣/·⌣/   (the dot here = a secondary accent)
⌣/ /⌣⌣/⌣/⌣/

Just looking at this pattern will show the kind of foot that predominates (⌣/). And if we count the syllables in each line of the poem, we will find that the norm is ten, or, in the first line:

X X̆ X̆ X́ X̆ X́ X́ X̆ X̆ X́.

Now we can divide the verse feet from one another:

/⌣/ /⌣/ /⌣/ /⌣/

We can see that the predominant foot is iambic, so it is an iambic poem. We can see that there are five feet in a line, so it is an iambic pentameter poem. Further, it is unrhymed, so it is an iambic pentameter, blank-verse poem.

NOTE WELL: The word *blank* simply means "blank of rhyme— *without* rhyme." "Blank verse" is *metered, unrhymed* verse. *"Blank verse" does not mean "free verse."*

"Free verse" is *not* metered, but it *may* rhyme—Ogden Nash wrote rhymed "free verse" poems (actually, he wrote rhymed prose poems). *Blank verse is always* unrhymed accentual-syllabic verse. *Free verse* is a cop-out term; it does not apply to anything, especially not to metered verse.

Getting back to "Mending Wall"—the first foot of the first line uses *substitution;* that is, the poet has substituted a trochee for an iamb in the first foot.

Consider this: Even if your scansion of the poem does not agree in every detail with mine, the normative meter, we can agree, is still iambic pentameter. Perhaps we are from different sections of the country, so we pronounce words a bit differently; or perhaps you put more *rhetorical stress* on certain words, as I just did by italicizing "rhetorical stress." Nevertheless, each of us can agree on the *normative meter,* and that's all that's important in scansion.

Another thing we can agree on: The poem is *not perfectly* regular, nor was it intended to be. Yet it is not awkward either. What are the kinds of verse feet Frost has used in line two?

This following poem is given as an example of rather typical novice work. It is an occasional poem, a graduation ode in *blank verse* lines written in collaboration by two high school students.

The original draft was written by one of the students in "free verse"; the second student rewrote it and recast it in blank verse. This is the final draft:

GRADUATION

The morning years of life, for us, are through.
We leave a training-ground of mind . . . this school.
Our thoughts, diversified ahead, behind,
Find us more than a bit perplexed with life.
In retrospect, our memories are sweet . . . ,
Like morning sunbeams spread on dampened earth,
Or sparkle of a dew-dropped, dawning day.
Our free, young past we'll cherish close to us;
A bulky mass of mixed-up incidents
To be relived in later dreams of youth.
But ah, how swiftly change the tunes of life!
Our present soon becomes the passive past;
The future, perfect. . . . Yet, in all our hopes
There runs a thread of fear, for through the haze
Of college, working, fighting, on the road
That lies before us all, a question mark
Rears up its hoary head and asks, "But what
Of Age, of Death's cold, bony hand, whose slave
Is Time, with sickle cutting ever widening swaths
Through youth, which cannot mend itself again?
But still we look with firm, convincing thought
Into the foggy future that is ours . . . ,
Which holds some love, yet hate; some joy, but pain.
We therefore look to Fate and humbly say,
"Our lives are yours, harsh world. Please use them well."

There are several things wrong with this poem, the most obvious being that it is *metrically too regular.* The essence of most good accentual-syllabic poems is that their rhythms are interesting and varied, although their normative meters will remain constant.

There are other things wrong with the poem: Its tone is pompous for the most part, imitative of 19th century rhetoric. One of the reasons why many of the examples of poems in this text are modern is because, as a general rule, poetry ought to be written in the diction of its own time. The examples show how contemporary poets are using the language *now,* not how poets used it 100 years ago—though some examples of older poetry are included here for comparison because good poetry outlasts its own era.

Another thing this poem (we ought to be saying "these verses" instead) shows clearly is its *exclusive* quality: If you happen to agree with the poem's statements, fine; if not, you are excluded from participation in it. Its sentiment is really sentimentality—overstated sentiment.

By "exclusive" we mean that the poem *excludes all points of view but the poet's;* it does not *include* other possible points of view, such as the possibility, for instance, that graduation from high school may be a great relief, rather than the beginning of a momentous journey out into the great world.

This last point has to do with *cliché*: The point-of-view of the student poets and the statement they make in their poem are not at all original, nor is the style in which the poem is written. The same is true of Kilmer's poem "Trees," and of the pseudo-Rod McKuen poems in the Introduction. The poet William Heyen has said, "Nothing is more aggravating in poetry than the presentation of conventional wisdom unless it is the presentation of conventional wisdom conventionally."

A point well-taken, for there are only three ways in which a poem may have *worth*: It must say something truly *new;* or it must open a new angle of vision on something that is not new; or it must say something that is not new, but say it in a fresh way—it must have a *style*. Some poems combine two or all of these elements. Dylan Thomas' poems state old ideas in a fresh, personal style; "The Red Wheelbarrow" by William Carlos Williams throws a new angle of vision, of perspective, open to ordinary objects by focusing on the objects themselves, their colors, textures, stasis, or movement, all in contrast with one another. Needless to add, saying something new is the hardest thing of all, and it seldom happens.

Here are some well-known accentual-syllabic poems. First, Shelley's "Ozymandias", a variation of the sonnet:

OZYMANDIAS

I met a traveller from an antique land
Who said: Two vast and trunkless legs of stone
Stand in the desert . . . Near them, on the sand,
Half sunk, a shattered visage lies, whose frown,

And wrinkled lip, and sneer of cold command,
Tell that its sculptor well those passions read
Which yet survive, stamped on these lifeless things,
The hand that mocked them, and the heart that fed:
And on the pedestal these words appear:
"My name is Ozymandias, king of kings:
Look on my works, ye Mighty, and despair!"
Nothing beside remains. Round the decay
Of that colossal wreck, boundless and bare
The lone and level sands stretch far away.

PERCY BYSSHE SHELLEY

Wordsworth's famous "ode" is an example of variable accentual-syllabics: The normative meter is constant, but the line-lengths and rhyme schemes vary:

ODE

INTIMATIONS OF IMMORTALITY FROM
RECOLLECTIONS OF EARLY CHILDHOOD

The Child is father of the Man;
And I could wish my days to be
Bound each to each by natural piety.

1

There was a time when meadow, grove, and stream,
The earth, and every common sight,
        To me did seem
        Appareled in celestial light,
The glory and the freshness of a dream.
It is not now as it hath been of yore—
        Turn whereso'er I may,
        By night or day,
The things which I have seen I now can see no more.

2

        The Rainbow comes and goes,
        And lovely is the Rose.
        The Moon doth with delight
Look round her when the heavens are bare,
        Waters on a starry night
        Are beautiful and fair;
    The sunshine is a glorious birth;
    But yet I know, where'er I go,
That there hath passed away a glory from the earth.

3

Now, while the birds thus sing a joyous song,
   And while the young lambs bound
      As to the tabor's sound,
To me alone there came a thought of grief:
A timely utterance gave that thought relief,
      And I again am strong:
The cataracts blow their trumpets from the steep;
No more shall grief of mine the season wrong;
I hear the Echoes through the mountains throng,
The Winds come to me from the fields of sleep,
      And all the earth is gay;
         Land and sea
      Give themselves up to jollity,
      And with the heart of May
      Doth every Beast keep holiday—
         Thou Child of Joy,
Shout round me, let me hear thy shouts, thou happy Shepherd-boy!

4

Ye blessèd Creatures, I have heard the call
   Ye to each other make; I see
The heavens laugh with you in your jubilee;
   My heart is at your festival,
      My head hath its coronal,
The fullness of your bliss, I feel—I feel it all.
      Oh, evil day! if I were sullen
      While Earth herself is adorning,
         This sweet May morning,
      And the Children are culling
         On every side,
      In a thousand valleys far and wide,
      Fresh flowers; while the sun shines warm,
And the Babe leaps up on his Mother's arm—
      I hear, I hear, with joy I hear!
      —But there's a Tree, of many, one,
A single Field which I have looked upon,
Both of them speak of something that is gone:
      The Pansy at my feet
      Doth the same tale repeat:
Whither is fled the visionary gleam?
Where is it now, the glory and the dream?

5

Our birth is but a sleep and a forgetting:
The Soul that rises with us, our life's Star,

Hath had elsewhere its setting,
            And cometh from afar:
Not in entire forgetfulness,
And not in utter nakedness,
But trailing clouds of glory do we come
            From God, who is our home:
Heaven lies about us in our infancy!
Shades of the prison-house begin to close
            Upon the growing Boy
                  But he
Beholds the light, and whence it flows,
            He sees it in his joy;
The Youth, who daily farther from the east
            Must travel, still is Nature's Priest,
            And by the vision splendid
            Is on his way attended;
At length the Man perceives it die away,
And fade into the light of common day.

                  6

Earth fills her lap with pleasures of her own;
Yearnings she hath in her own natural kind,
And, even with something of a Mother's mind,
            And no unworthy aim,
            The homely Nurse doth all she can
To make her foster child, her Inmate Man,
            Forget the glories he hath known,
And that imperial palace whence he came.

                  7

Behold the Child among his newborn blisses,
A six-years' Darling of a pygmy size!
See, where 'mid work of his own hand he lies,
Fretted by sallies of his mother's kisses,
With light upon him from his father's eyes!
See, at his feet, some little plan or chart,
Some fragment from his dream of human life,
Shaped by himself with newly-learnéd art;
            A wedding or a festival,
            A mourning or a funeral;
            And this hath now his heart,
            And unto this he frames his song;
            Then will he fit his tongue
To dialogues of business, love, or strife;
            But it will not be long
            Ere this be thrown aside,

And with new joy and pride
The little Actor cons another part;
Filling from time to time his "humorous stage"
With all the Persons, down to palsied Age,
That Life brings with her in her equipage;
          As if his whole vocation
          Were endless imitation.

          8

Thou, whose exterior semblance doth belie
          Thy Soul's immensity;
Thou best Philosopher, who yet dost keep
Thy heritage, thou Eye among the blind,
That, deaf and silent, read'st the eternal deep,
Haunted forever by the eternal mind—
          Mighty Prophet! Seer blest!
          On whom those truths do rest,
Which we are toiling all our lives to find,
In darkness lost, the darkness of the grave;
Thou, over whom thy Immortality
Broods like the Day, a Master o'er a Slave,
A presence which is not to be put by;
Thou little Child, yet glorious in the might
Of heaven-born freedom on thy being's height,
Why with such earnest pains dost thou provoke
The years to bring the inevitable yoke,
Thus blindly with thy blessedness at strife?
Full soon thy Soul shall have her earthly freight,
And custom lie upon thee with a weight,
Heavy as frost, and deep almost as life!

          9

          O joy! that in our embers
          Is something that doth live,
          That nature yet remembers
          What was so fugitive!
The thought of our past years in me doth breed
Perpetual benediction: not indeed
For that which is most worthy to be blest;
Delight and liberty, the simple creed
Of Childhood, whether busy or at rest,
With new-fledged hope still fluttering in his breast—
          Not for these I raise
          The song of thanks and praise;
          But for those obstinate questionings
          Of sense and outward things,

Fallings from us, vanishings;
Blank misgivings of a Creature
Moving about in worlds not realized,
High instincts before which our mortal Nature
Did tremble like a guilty Thing surprised;
But for those first affections,
Those shadowy recollections,
Which, be they what they may,
Are yet the fountain light of all our day,
Are yet a master light of all our seeing;
Uphold us, cherish, and have power to make
Our noisy years seem moments in the being
Of the eternal Silence: truths that wake,
To perish never;
Which neither listlessness, nor mad endeavor,
Nor Man nor Boy,
Nor all that is at enmity with joy,
Can utterly abolish or destroy!
Hence in a season of calm weather
Though inland far we be,
Our Souls have sight of that immortal sea
Which brought us hither,
Can in a moment travel thither,
And see the Children sport upon the shore,
And hear the mighty waters rolling evermore.

10

Then sing, ye Birds, sing, sing a joyous song!
And let the young Lambs bound
As to the tabor's sound!
We in thought will join your throng,
Ye that pipe and ye that play,
Ye that through your hearts today
Feel the gladness of the May!
What though the radiance which was once so bright
Be now forever taken from thy sight,
Though nothing can bring back the hour
Of splendor in the grass, of glory in the flower;
We will grieve not, rather find
Strength in what remains behind;
In the primal sympathy
Which having been must ever be;
In the soothing thoughts that spring
Out of human suffering;
In the faith that looks through death,
In years that bring the philosophic mind.

11

And O, ye Fountains, Meadows, Hills, and Groves,
Forebode not any severing of our loves!
Yet in my heart of hearts I feel your might;
I only have relinquished one delight
To live beneath your more habitual sway.
I love the Brooks which down their channels fret,
Even more than when I tripped lightly as they;
The innocent brightness of a newborn Day
            Is lovely yet;
The clouds that gather round the setting sun
Do take a sober coloring from an eye
That hath kept watch o'er man's mortality;
Another race hath been, and other palms are won.
Thanks to the human heart by which we live,
Thanks to the tenderness, its joys, and fears,
To me the meanest flower that blows can give
Thoughts that do often lie too deep for tears.

WILLIAM WORDSWORTH

Wordsworth's poem is practically a paradigm—a model—of 19th-century poetic diction. Compare it with the high school ode "Graduation," and you will discover where the young poets copied their style. Notice, too, how closed and exclusive both poems are.

Compare both poems with this one by the contemporary poet Howard Nemerov, and you will see the difference between what Puttenham called *high style* and *mean style*. Puttenham defined *style* as "a constant and continual phrase or tenor of speaking and writing, extending to the whole tale or process of the poem. . . . " He went on to speak of high, mean, and base (or lofty, middle, and low) styles, and of high, mean, and base subjects, which have to do with heroic, middle-class, and common people and actions. The poet must choose, Puttenham said, the appropriate style to suit his subject.

THE GOOSE FISH

On the long shore, lit by the moon
To show them properly alone,
Two lovers suddenly embraced
So that their shadows were as one.
The ordinary night was graced
For them by the swift tide of blood
That silently they took at flood,
And for a little time they prized
    Themselves emparadised.

Then, as if shaken by stage-fright
Beneath the hard moon's bony light,
They stood together on the sand—
Embarrassed in each other's sight
But still conspiring hand in hand,
Until they saw, there underfoot,
As though the world had found them out,
The goose fish turning up, though dead,
   His hugely grinning head.

There in the china light he lay,
Most ancient and corrupt and grey.
They hesitated at his smile,
Wondering what it seemed to say
To lovers who a little while
Before had thought to understand,
By violence upon the sand,
The only way that could be known
   To make a world their own.

It was a wide and moony grin
Together peaceful and obscene;
They knew not what he would express,
So finished a comedian
He might mean failure or success,
But took it for an emblem of
Their sudden, new and guilty love
To be observed by, when they kissed,
   That rigid optimist.

So he became their patriarch,
Dreadfully mild in the half-dark.
His throat that the sand seemed to choke,
His picket teeth, these left their mark
But never did explain the joke
That so amused him, lying there
While the moon went down to disappear
Along the still and tilted track
   That bears the zodiac.

HOWARD NEMEROV

    Normative meters have nothing whatsoever to do with quantitative accentual-syllabics. The meters of quantitative verse are prescribed: Particular verse feet must appear at specific places in the line. Review the material on quantitative accentual-syllabics in Chap. 2.

    In *normative* accentual-syllabics in English, syllables are not prescribed as to "length" of sound in any way except that certain vowels

are considered "short," as in the short *i* sound of, for instance, *in,* or the
long *o* sound of *over. Quantity* in English, then, is not conventionalized,
as it was in Greek during the classical period, except that the norm of
a line of verse often establishes that the *long syllable sound* coincides
with the accented syllable:

> Óver and óver he spóke to mé of dóom.

The substitution of a *short* or normally unaccented syllable for a long,
usually stressed syllable, or vice-versa, constitutes a subtle method of
rhythmic variation:

> Óver and óver he ásked of ús his dóom.

   The term *quality* is merely another word for substitution—the
exchanging of one kind of verse foot for another; specifically, the
substitution of a verse foot different from the measure of the norm that
has been established in the normative meter or *running rhythm* of a
poem:

> Óver ănd ŏver he spóke tŏ ŭs.

Utilizing quality, we might substitute a trochee for a dactyl in the
last foot:

> Óver ănd óver he cálled ŭs.

   Elegiacs is a quantitative Greek couplet measure. The first line is
called a *classical hexameter*: The first four feet of the first line must be
either spondees or dactyls; the fifth foot must be a dactyl and the sixth
must be a spondee.
   The second line of the couplet is called a *classical pentameter*: two
dactyls, a spondee, and two anapests, in that order. A poem in elegiacs
may or may not be rhymed. Here is a contemporary poem written in
elegiacs:

A TALISMAN

for Dave McLean

> Léad fŏr thĭs tálismăn. Púre, sŏ thăt Sáturn wĭll lĭve ĭn ĭt. Púre léad.
>   Bóth ŏf ĭts fáces ăre rúbbed smóoth. Ŏn ĭts frónt, ĭn ă stár

pentagram, cut with a diamond burin a scythe so that Nabam,
    standing upon his demoniac pedestal Tau, shall be laid low—
old as he is—by Oriphiel, angel of Saturday. Jesus,
    nailed to a T, is the capstone of this coin made of lead,
though he will never appear in his person, but only as backdrop.
    Grave on the opposite face this, in a six-pointed star:
REMPHA, surrounding the head of a bull. Without witnesses carve your
    talisman. Wear it in good health. It will keep you from death,
frighten the devil of cancer, leukemia—rot of the white bone.
    Marrow will redden. Wear this! It will save you and me.
Bear it—your talisman; wear it, my brother. Or carry this poem,
    Dies Saturni to life's end. It is all I can do.

Though "A Talisman" is an actual recipe, out of occult literature,
for making a charm against cancer, it may justly be charged with
obscurity: references to little-known information, for instance. But it is
not *ambiguous*. Obscurity is usually a hindrance to the reader; ambiguity
is not. Ambiguity may enhance poetry by *including* things or
points-of-view; obscurity is essentially *exclusive*.
    William Empson, in his book entitled *Seven Types of Ambiguity**
lists the kinds of ambiguity that may add to the effect of the poem:

1) "First type ambiguities arise when a detail is effective in several
   ways at once, e.g., by comparisons with several points of likeness,
   antitheses with several points of difference, 'comparative' adjectives, subdued metaphors, and extra meanings suggested by
   rhythm."

2) "... two or more alternative meanings are fully resolved into one."

3) "... two apparently unconnected meanings are given simultaneously."

4) "... the alternative meanings combine to make clear a complicated state of mind in the author."

5) "... a fortunate confusion, as when the author is discovering his
   idea in the act of writing ... or not holding it all at once."

6) "... what is said is contradictory or irrelevant and the reader is
   forced to invent interpretations."

7) "... full contradiction, marking a division in the author's mind."

Here is a 19th-century poem that is full of ambiquities—of feelings,
of ideation, of imagery:

---

* Published in the U. S. by New Directions, and by Meridian Books in 1955.

THE ROPEWALK

In that building, long and low,
With its windows all a-row,
   Like the port-holes of a hulk,
Human spiders spin and spin,
Backward down their threads so thin
   Dropping, each a hempen bulk.

At the end, an open door;
Squares of sunshine on the floor
   Light the long and dusky lane;
And the whirring of a wheel,
Dull and drowsy, makes me feel
   All its spokes are in my brain.

As the spinners to the end
Downward go and reascend,
   Gleam the long threads in the sun;
While within this brain of mine
Cobwebs brighter and more fine
   By the busy wheel are spun.

Two fair maidens in a swing,
Like white doves upon the wing,
   First before my vision pass;
Laughing, as their gentle hands
Closely clasp the twisted strands,
   At their shadow on the grass.

Then a booth of mountebanks,
With its smell of tan and planks,
   And a girl poised high in air
On a cord, in spangled dress,
With a faded loveliness,
   And a weary look of care.

Then a homestead among farms,
And a woman with bare arms
   Drawing water from a well;
As the bucket mounts apace,
With it mounts her own fair face,
   As at some magician's spell.

Then an old man in a tower,
Ringing loud the noontide hour,
   While the rope coils round and round
Like a serpent at his feet,
And again, in swift retreat,
   Nearly lifts him from the ground.

Then within a prison-yard,
Faces fixed, and stern, and hard,
    Laughter and indecent mirth;
Ah! it is the gallows-tree!
Breath of Christian charity,
    Blow, and sweep it from the earth!

Then a school-boy, with his kite
Gleaming in a sky of light,
    And an eager, upward look;
Steeds pursued through lane and field;
Fowlers with their snares concealed;
    And an angler by a brook.

Ships rejoicing in the breeze,
Wrecks that float o'er unknown seas,
    Anchors dragged through faithless sand;
Sea-fog drifting overhead,
And, with lessening line and lead,
    Sailors feeling for the land.

All these scenes do I behold,
These, and many left untold,
    In that building long and low;
While the wheel goes round and round,
With a drowsy, dreamy sound.
    And the spinners backward go.

HENRY WADSWORTH LONGFELLOW

"The Temporary the All" which follows is an example of how a form—in this case, a quantitative form (Sapphics—see Chap. 1 for a description of the form)—can defeat its author. Notice all the awkwardnesses—inversions for the sake of rhythm ("Cherish him can I . . . ."), archaic diction, overstatement, pomposities ("Intermissive aim at the thing sufficeth."), and so forth:

THE TEMPORARY THE ALL

Change and chancefulness in my flowering youthtime,
Set me sun by sun near to one unchosen;
Wrought us fellowlike, and despite divergence,
        Fused us in friendship.

"Cherish him can I while the true one forthcome—
Come the rich fulfiller of my prevision;
Life is roomy yet, and the odds unbounded."
        So self-communed I.

'Thwart my wistful way did a damsel saunter,
Fair, albeit unformed to be all-eclipsing;
"Maiden meet," held I, "till arise my forefelt
        Wonder of women."

Long a visioned hermitage deep desiring,
Tenements uncouth I was fain to house in;
"Let such lodging be for a breath-while," thought I,
        "Soon a more seemly.

"Then high handiwork will I make my life-deed,
Truth and Light outshow; but the ripe time pending,
Intermissive aim at the thing sufficeth."
        Thus I. . . . But lo, me!

Mistress, friend, place, aims to be bettered straightway,
Bettered not has Fate or my hand's achievement;
Sole the showings those of my onward earth-track—
        Never transcended!

THOMAS HARDY

Alcaics is another quantitative form; also Greek, it is a quatrain stanza. The first two lines are made up of an *acephalous* (headless) iamb (i.e., merely the accented syllable is left—the unaccented first syllable has been dropped), followed by two trochees and two dactyls, in that order; the third line is made up of an acephalous iamb followed by four trochees, and the last line of the stanza contains two dactyls followed by two trochees. In this poem below, the poet has taken a few liberties with the prescribed rhythms:

ALCAICS

This heed, and that Tomorrow with stinging veins
    break bleak and frost-forked, creaking and unbelieved
        aloft, accomplish, god; for hope is
            endless, and sickens throughout our nature.

As Time strict-fingered works of our radiant lives
    and legacies his circles, so give me hands;
        unfinished in me is the sunset's
            rustling escape out of minted nature.

Destroy this brain—that struck in the aching space
    quick spheres might lighten men to their origins
        and seasons, that the eyeballs' fishy
            backs be forgot in the face of nature.

BENJAMIN K. BENNETT

suggested writing assignment

A) Write a ten-line blank verse poem. Be sure there is at least one metrical variation in each line.

B) Write a quantitative accentual-syllabic poem consisting of two alcaic *or* Sapphic stanzas, or of four elegiac couplets (eight lines altogether). Observe the requirements of the form strictly.

10

OF SONICS

We have already spoken at some length about various sonic effects:
Alliteration, cynghanedd; we have mentioned *consonance* and *rhyme*.
All of these devices come under the heading of *chime*—words ringing
against one another:

i. CHIME

TRUE RHYME has to do with the identity of sound in two or more
words, of an *accented vowel* (ó–ó) together with *all sounds following that
vowel* (óne–óne), while the *consonantal sounds* immediately *preceding*
the vowel *differ* in each word (bóne–stóne). Review the material
regarding *quantity* on p. 114 of the preceding chapter.

END RHYME rhymes line-endings:

> One in heat can love *cool.*
> Believe, and remain her *fool.*

FALLING RHYME (*feminine rhyme*) is the rhyming of lines of
verse that utilize falling rhythms (or *feminine endings*); i.e., fálling–

cálling: *Falling rhythms* are those that begin with an accented syllable and end with an unaccented syllable. Dactyls (/⌣⌣) and trochees (/⌣) are *falling meters*.

RISING RHYME (*masculine rhyme*) is the rhyming of lines of verse that utilize rising rhythms (or *masculine endings*); i.e., arise, despíse, prize: *Rising rhythms* are those that end with an accented syllable. Anapests (⌣⌣/) and iambs (⌣/) are *rising meters*.

LIGHT RHYME rhymes a falling ending with a rising ending (fálling–ring).

INTERNAL RHYME rhymes the ending of a line with a word in the center of the same line, usually with a syllable just before the caesura (The song is *sung,* · and the bell is *rung*).

LINKED RHYME rhymes the last syllable or syllables of a line with the first syllable or syllables of the following line (The bell is heard, and the song is *sung* / *Flung* upon the morning air).

INTERLACED RHYME rhymes a syllable or syllables in the center of a line with a syllable or syllables also in the center of a preceding or following line (The song is *sung,* and the bell is heard / It is *flung* upon the air).

CROSS-RHYME rhymes an ending with a sound at the center of a preceding or following line (The bell is heard, and the song is *sung;* / The sound is *flung* on the morning air).

HEAD RHYME rhymes syllables at the beginnings of lines of verse:

> *Fool* her. Remain, and believe
> *Cool* love can heat in one.

APOCOPATED RHYME drops one or more syllables from the ending of *one* of a pair of rhyming words (The bells were ringing on the *morn-* / ing that our present king was *born*).

ENJAMBED RHYME uses the first consonant of a following line to complete the sound of the rhyme (He found the stair, and *he* / *d*escended to find the *seed*).

Earlier, mention was made of *single rhymes,* which are rhymes of one syllable (*morn–born*); *double rhymes,* rhymes of two syllables (*singing–ringing*); and *triple rhymes,* rhymes of three syllables (*carrying–tarrying*).

COMPOUND RHYME treats groups of words as though they were one-word rhymes (I am enamored *of her art,* / But you can take and *shove her heart*).

MOSAIC RHYME uses one compound ending and one normal ending in a rhyme (*Guard well–fardel*).

TRITE RHYME is simply the rhyming of words that have been overused for rhymes. Kilmer's "Trees" is a model of many of the trite rhymes in the English language—about the only ones he misses are *love–above* and *June–moon*. This is not to imply that trite rhymes cannot be used—merely, that they ought to be used well, or not at all.

OMOIOTELETON is the term that covers the various types of rhyme other than true rhyme.

RICH RHYME (*rime riche, false rhyme*) has identity of sound in the consonants immediately preceding the accented vowel *as well as* in the following sounds (*c*́yst, per*s*́ist, in*s*́ist). It is really a form of repetition.

CONSONANCE (meaning *like sounds*—not to be confused with *consonants*) has also been called *slant rhyme, off-rhyme,* and *near-rhyme.* It substitutes *similar* sound for identical sound (bri*́*dge, he*́*dge, go*́*uge, ra*́*ge, ro*́*uge). Consonance assumes that all vowel sounds are interchangeable, as are certain related consonant sounds, as the soft *g* in "gouge" and "rage," the harder *dg* of "bridge" and "hedge," and the *zh* sound of "rouge." The verb form is *to consonate.*

ANALYZED RHYME is a system which Edward Davison[*] described:

> [One] takes two such words as *soon* and *hide* but separates the vowel from the consonantal sounds before looking for his rhymes. The *oo* of *soon* is united with the *d* of *hide*; and the *i* of *hide* with the *n* of *soon*. This simple analysis produces the [four] rhyming sounds
>
> | | |
> |------|------|
> | oon | ine |
> | ide | ood |
>
> as a basis for new sets of words. Thus, by means of analyzed rhyme, an absolute sound relationship can be established among words that have hitherto seemed alien to each other.

A series of words that might use the sounds presented above might be *moon, divine, chide,* and *brood,* etc.

WRENCHED RHYME is as much pun as anything else. It twists words in order to make rhymes, as in this prose poem by Ogden Nash:

[*] In his book *Some Modern Poets,* New York: Harper and Brothers, 1928.

KINDLY UNHITCH THAT STAR, BUDDY

I hardly suppose I know anybody who wouldn't rather be a success than a failure,

Just as I suppose every piece of crabgrass in the garden would much rather be an azalea,

And in celestial circles all the run-of-the-mill angels would rather be archangels or at least cherubim and seraphim,

And in the legal world all the little process-servers hope to grow up into great big bailiffim and sheriffim.

Indeed, everybody wants to be a wow,

But not everybody knows exactly how.

Some people think they will eventually wear diamonds instead of rhinestones

Only by everlastingly keeping their noses to their ghrinestones,

And other people think they will be able to put in more time at Palm Beach and the Ritz

By not paying too much attention to attendance at the office but rather in being brilliant by starts and fits.

Some people after a full day's work sit up all night getting a college education by correspondence,

While others seem to think they'll get just as far by devoting their evenings to the study of the difference in temperament between brunettance and blondance.

In short, the world is filled with people trying to achieve success,

And half of them think they'll get it by saying No and half of them by saying Yes,

And if all the ones who say No said Yes, and vice versa, such is the fate of humanity that ninety-nine per cent of them still wouldn't be any better off than they were before,

Which perhaps is just as well because if everybody was a success nobody could be contemptuous of anybody else and everybody would start in all over again trying to be a bigger success than everybody else so they would have somebody to be contemptuous of and so on forevermore,

Because when people start hitching their wagons to a star,

That's the way they are.

OGDEN NASH

AMPHISBAENIC RHYME is "backward" rhyme (*later—retail, stop—pots, pets—instep*).

LYON RHYME isn't really rhyme at all, though it is a form of repetition. It is a grammatic trick. One writes some verses which, when read backward—word-for-word, beginning with the last word—say exactly the opposite of what the verses originally said, as in this *Advice to a Lover*:

> One in heat can love cool.
> Believe, and remain her fool.

> *Fool her. Remain, and believe*
> *Cool love can heat in one.*

SIGHT RHYME (*eye-rhyme*) is orthographic rhyming—
sight-rhymed words are *spelled alike* but *sound unlike* (*eight–sleight,*
t*ies*–homil*ies*).

DIALECT RHYME is often difficult to distinguish from sight
rhyme—people from different places, or from different eras ("historical
rhyme") might pronounce the same word differently; i.e., one person
might pronounce "again" so that it rhymes with *pain,* but someone else
might rhyme it with *pen.*

ECHO has to do with the reappearance of identical sounds in poetry, or
with the appearance of similar sounds.

PARIMION is the classical term for *alliteration,* which has already
been discussed. It is the repetition of initial stressed consonant sounds

(He *t*ucked his *t*unic in and *t*ore it).

ASSONANCE repeats identical stressed vowel sounds (Here, c*a*tch

this b*a*t, d*a*bble in dust, / Or *a*trophy—an engine p*a*ssing to rust).

CYNGHANEDD was covered in the last chapter.

ONOMATOPOEIA "describes" something through sound, the
sonics of the verse being an imitation of the subject (The seashore roared
from the seashell's horn).

CONSONANTAL ECHO has to do with the repetition of
consonants, both stressed and unstressed, whether at the beginnings of
words or elsewhere, and not necessarily in sequence, as *must* be the case
in alliteration:

If she were a*liv*e, he'd *lov*e her sti*ll*.

VOCALIC ECHO is the repetition of vowels, both stressed and
unstressed, whether at the beginnings of words or elsewhere, and not
necessarily in sequence as in assonance:

*I*f sh*e* were al*i*ve, h*e*'d l*i*ke her st*i*ll.

EUPHONY is a mingling of pleasant sounds, usually including all
vowels and certain consonants: Soft *c, f,* soft *g, h, j, l, m, n, r, s, v, w, y,*
and *z.*

DISSONANCE is a mingling of unpleasant sounds, usually hard consonants.

CACOPHONY is an unpleasant mixture of sounds, both the euphonious and dissonant—Marzials' "Dirge" is an example.

A REPETON is a single line or phrase that is repeated once after its initial appearance in a poem.

A REPETEND is a single line or phrase that reappears more than one time after its initial appearance, but at random.

A REFRAIN is a single line or phrase that reappears at formal intervals throughout a poem—usually at the end of each stanza.

A BURDEN is similar to the refrain, except that it consists of a couplet or something larger.

A CHORUS is a whole stanza that appears at intervals during the progress of the poem.

INCREMENTAL REPETITION is a repeton, repetend, refrain, burden, or chorus that has at least one word changed each time it reappears so that the line takes on greater impact as the poem moves forward to a climax—see Chaucer's poem (p. 26) in Chap. 2.

Other devices of *repetition* are listed in Chap. 13.

One word about the terms listed here and in the three following chapters: No one expects you to memorize them all—the author of the book doesn't have them memorized. An understanding of the techniques should be sufficient in most cases. The terms are here to be referred to if and when they are needed.

Here is a *folk-ballad* that uses a number of sonic techniques, particularly repetition and incremental repetition. Notice that the poem is not end-rhymed; it *consonates*:

LORD RANDAL

"O where ha you been, Lord Randal, my son?
And where ha you been, my handsome young man?"
"I ha been at the greenwood; mother, mak my bed soon,
For I'm wearied wi huntin, and fain wad lie down."

"An wha met ye there, Lord Randal, my son?
An wha met you there, my handsome young man?"
"O I met wi my true-love; mother, mak my bed soon,
For I'm wearied wi huntin, and fain wad lie down."

"And what did she give you, Lord Randal, my son?
And what did she give you, my handsome young man?"
"Eels fried in a pan; mother, mak my bed soon,
For I'm wearied wi huntin, and fain wad lie down."

"And wha gat your leavins, Lord Randal, my son?
And wha gat your leavins, my handsome young man?"
"My hawks and my hounds; mother, mak my bed soon,
For I'm wearied wi huntin, and fain wad lie down."

"And what becam of them, Lord Randal, my son?
And what becam of them, my handsome young man?"
"They swelled and they died; mother, mak my bed soon,
For I'm wearied wi huntin, and fain wad lie down."

"O I fear you are poisoned, Lord Randal, my son!
I fear you are poisoned, my handsome young man!"
"O yes, I am poisoned, mother, mak my bed soon,
For I'm sick at the heart, and I fain wad lie down."

"What d' ye leave to your mother, Lord Randal, my son?
What d' ye leave to your mother, my handsome young man?"
"Four and twenty milk kye; mother, mak my bed soon,
For I'm sick at the heart, and I fain wad lie down."

"What d' ye leave to your sister. Lord Randal, my son?
What d' ye leave to your sister, my handsome young man?"
"My gold and my silver; mother, mak my bed soon,
For I'm sick at the heart, and I fain wad lie down."

"What d' ye leave to your brother, Lord Randal, my son?
What d' ye leave to your brother, my handsome young man?"
"My houses and my lands; mother, mak my bed soon,
For I'm sick at the heart, and I fain wad lie down."

"What d' ye leave to your true-love, Lord Randal, my son?
What d' ye leave to your true-love, my handsome young man?"
"I leave her hell and fire; mother, mak my bed soon,
For I'm sick at the heart, and I fain wad lie down."

Anonymous

The following nursery rhyme uses almost nothing but incremental repetition and repetition, though there is some rhyme and consonance. The main thing to notice, however, is the *counterpoint*—the rhythmic change-ups that occur when a new line is introduced into the dipodic (two-beat) structure of the poem:

ROBBIN TO BOBBIN

We will go to the Wood,
Says Robbin, to Bobbin,
We will go to the Wood,
Says Richard, to Robbin,
We will go to the Wood,

Says John all alone,
We will go to the Wood,
Says every one.

What to do there?
Says Robbin, to Bobbin,
What to do there?
Says Richard, to Robbin,
What to do there?
Says John all alone,
What to do there?
Says every one.

We will shoot at a Wren,
Says Robbin, to Bobbin,
We will shoot at a Wren,
Says Richard, to Robbin,
We will shoot at a Wren,
Says John all alone,
We will shoot at a Wren,
Says every one.

She's down, she's down,
Says Robbin, to Bobbin,
She's down, she's down,
Says Richard, to Robbin,
She's down, she's down,
Says John all alone,
She's down, she's down,
Says every one.

Then pounce, then pounce,
Says Robbin, to Bobbin,
Then pounce, then pounce,
Says Richard, to Robbin,
Then pounce, then pounce,
Says John all alone,
Then pounce, then pounce,
Says every one.

She is dead, she is dead,
Says Robbin, to Bobbin,
She is dead, she is dead,
Says Richard, to Robbin,
She is dead, she is dead,
Says John all alone,
She is dead, she is dead,
Says every one.

How shall we get her home?
Says Robbin, to Bobbin,
How shall we get her home?
Says Richard, to Robbin,
How shall we get her home?
Says John all alone,
How shall we get her home?
Says every one.

We will hire a Cart,
Says Robbin, to Bobbin,
We will hire a Cart,
Says Richard, to Robbin,
We will hire a Cart,
Says John all alone,
We will hire a Cart,
Says every one.

Then Hoist, Hoist,
Says Robbin, to Bobbin,
Then Hoist, Hoist,
Says Richard, to Robbin,
Then Hoist, Hoist,
Says John all alone,
Then Hoist, Hoist,
Says every one.

She's up, she's up,
Says Robbin, to Bobbin,
She's up, she's up,
Says Richard, to Robbin,
She's up, she's up,
Says John all alone,
She's up, she's up,
Says every one.

How shall we dress her?
Says Robbin, to Bobbin,
How shall we dress her?
Says Richard, to Robbin,
How shall we dress her?
Says John all alone,
How shall we dress her?
Says every one.

We'll hire seven cooks,
Says Robbin, to Bobbin,
We'll hire seven cooks,

Says Richard, to Robbin,
We'll hire seven cooks,
Says John all alone,
We'll hire seven cooks,
Says every one.

How shall we boil her?
Says Robbin, to Bobbin,
How shall we boil her?
Says Richard, to Robbin,
How shall we boil her?
Says John all alone,
How shall we boil her?
Says every one.

In the brewer's big pan,
Says Robbin, to Bobbin,
In the brewer's big pan,
Says Richard, to Robbin,
In the brewer's big pan,
Says John all alone,
In the brewer's big pan,
Says every one.

                                                        Anonymous

ii. CONTRACTION

Elision is concerned with the blending of two or more syllable sounds so that they become one syllable sound. Robert Bridges* has discussed various ways of eliding:

   VOCALIC ELISION. "When two vowel sounds come together, then if the first of the two has a tail-glide (a *y*-glide or a *w*-glide), there may be elision." Some examples of *y-glide* are flying," "so b*e* *i*t," "the others," "th*ee a*nd sh*e a*nd all," "glory *a*bove," "*ri*ot." Some examples of *w-glide* are "r*ui*nous," "s*o o*ften," "als*o i*n," "Moroc*co o*r Trebisond," "fol*lo*wers" (*foll'wers*), "shad*ow*y" (*shad'wy*), "grad*ua*l," "infl*ue*nce."

   SEMI-VOCALIC ELISION. "If two unstressed vowels be separated by *r*, there may be elision." And Donald Justice† adds, "This applies also to *l* and *n* and perhaps may be extended to *m*." Some examples are "murm*u*ring" (*murm'ring*), "pill*a*r of state" (*pillar 'f state*), "carol*e*r" (*car'ler*), "begott*e*n *a*nd" (*begot'n and*).

* In his book *Milton's Prosody*, Oxford: Oxford University Press, 1893.
† In *Of Prosody*, samisdat notes, Iowa City, Iowa, 1960.

CONSONANTAL SILENCE. "*H* is often considered as no letter," as in "ought t*o have*" (*ought to 'ave* or *ought to 've*, where the following vowel is also suppressed—*I've, you've*: see *vocalic suppression* below). Other consonants are sometimes silenced as well, as in "*of*ten" (*of'en* or *of'n*).

CONSONANTAL SUPPRESSION. Justice says, "Final *m* and *n* are very frequently not counted anyhow, as *chasm* [chas*m*] or *heaven* [heav'n]."

VOCALIC SUPPRESSION. Justice continues, "The words *evil* [ev'l] and *spirit* [spir't] have also been taken in English verse to have but one syllable." Vocalic suppression sometimes takes place after a silent consonant as well, as in *ought to've* and *of'n*, above.

COUNTER-ELISION. "In contrast," Justice says, "*fire* [fi-er] often is counted as two [syllables in length]." The same is true of other words—*hire, mire, lyre*; and in many dialects words will be pronounced as though they had more syllables than usual—*repair (repay-er)*.

OPTION. "Elision in most of these words," Justice says, "is optional; that is, the word need not be elided each time it occurs, even if it occurs twice in the same line."

OVERT ELISION. In certain kinds of poetic diction, overt elision will occur where the writer will indicate what has been elided by means of punctuation, as in many of the illustrations above; i.e., *heav'n*. More will be said about overt elision in Chap. 13.

Wordsworth's "Ode" exemplifies many of the kinds of elision we have been speaking of.

iii. COUNTERPOINT

ACATALEXIS is a term that designates a perfect line of accentual-syllabic verse. For instance, in an iambic tetrameter poem an *acatalectic* line will have eight syllables and four stresses, the unaccented syllables alternating regularly with the accented syllables:

"I love your hair that way," she said.

This example, and all those following, are taken from a single poem whose normative meter is iambic tetrameter.

CATALEXIS. A line is made *catalectic* by dropping a syllable at the end of the line:

    corrupting memories of childhood

(note the elision in "memories"; i.e. *mem'ries*).

    BRACHYCATALEXIS. Dropping more than one syllable at the end of the line makes it *brachycatalectic*.

    HYPERCATALEXIS. A line is made hypercatalectic by adding a syllable at the end of the line:

    Though minds have likened worlds to stages, . . .

    ACEPHALEXIS. A line is made *acephalous* (headless) by dropping syllables from the beginning of the line:

    dampening our solitude, . . .

    ANACRUSIS. The line is made *anacrustic* by adding unaccented syllables to the beginning of the line:

    and of youth must come at last to tatters.

(Note that this line is *both* anacrustic *and* hypercatalectic).

    QUALITY is a term that covers the *substitution* of one kind of verse foot for another; specifically, substitution of a verse foot that differs from the normative meter of the line:

    no game's a turn that *really* matters.

In this line a spondee has been substituted for the normative iamb in the first foot, and an amphibrach for the normative iamb in the last foot (note the *y-glide* elision in really).

    CAESURA is a pause in the center of a line.

    NATURAL CAESURA. In English lines of four beats or longer, a *natural caesura*—only a brief hesitation—occurs very often after the second or third stressed syllable:

    We sought through rooms · for something warm. . . .

    QUALITATIVE CAESURA is caused by the manipulation of measures through substitution:

    Mutually grappled · we ate the fruit:—.

Notice the substitution of a dactyl for the normative iamb in the first foot, and of a trochee in the second foot. The normative meter resumes in the third foot, and the caesura occurs at the point where two unaccented syllables come together; (note the *w-glide* elision in mutually).

PUNCTUATIONAL CAESURA is caused by punctuation occurring somewhere in the center of a line:

> she said. · So I was Adam damned. . . .

COMPENSATORY CAESURA occurs when the caesura compensates for a missing half-foot in the line:

> corrupting memories · of childhood, . . .

COMPENSATION occurs when a missing half-foot or larger unit in one line is made up for with an extra unit added to the same line or to a preceding or following line:

> corrupting memories of childhood, . . .

CLOTURE refers to a full-stop at the end of a line, couplet, or larger stanzaic unit:

> "I love your hair that way," she said.

SEMI-CLOTURE takes place when the end of the line coincides with the end of a phrase or clause:

> Mutually grappled, we ate the fruit—
>   its skin and core—and quaffed flesh deeply,
> dampening our solitude, . . .

GRAMMATIC ENJAMBMENT is the running-on of a sentence, without pause, from one line or stanza to the next:

> the tragicomic masks of age
>   and youth must come at last to tatters.

METRICAL ENJAMBMENT takes place when, in effect, half of a verse foot belonging to a following line occurs at the end of the preceding line—

˘ ˘   / | ˘   / | ˘   / | ˘   / ˘
its skin and core—and quaffed flesh deeply,
  / | ˘ / | ˘   /|˘/
dampening our solitude, . . .

or, so that it may be seen more easily—

˘ ˘ / | ˘   / | ˘   / | ˘ ˘   / | ˘   / | ˘ / | ˘ ˘   /|˘/
its skin and core—and quaffed flesh deeply, / dampening our solitude, . . .

The reverse may also take place—metrical enjambment occurs when
half of a verse foot belonging to a preceding line is added to the
beginning of the following line.

The poem from which these examples are taken came out of
a pre-college poet's notebook. Needless to say, the poet wasn't conscious
of having done all these things—nevertheless, he *did* them; the terms
and techniques exist. The poem went through many arduous drafts
before it was published years later, and even then the poet continued
to tinker with it. One of the reasons for all the work that went into
this poem is that the poet was trying to manipulate his rhythms by
trial-and-error—he took the long route:

PARTY GAME

"I love your hair that way," she said.
    We sought through rooms for something warm
enough. We tested miles of bed,
lay on an open moor that spread
    beyond fourposters and the dawn.

Mutually grappled, we ate the fruit—
    its skin and core—and quaffed flesh deeply,
dampening our solitude,
corrupting memories of childhood,
    slipping into age too steeply.

"It's not the way I thought it was,"
    she said. So I was Adam damned
again for female niches and flaws.
Thus, we deserted mattress moors,
    returned, wise now, to parlor games.

And spin the bottle all our days—
    no game's a turn that really matters.
Though minds have likened worlds to stages,
the tragicomic masks of age,
    and of youth, must come at last to tatters.

Here is a syllabic poem that places heavy emphasis on the sonic level:

AWAKEN, BELLS FALLING

It is a dawn quick as swallows
    peeling to shear through peals belled
from the one town steeple. Autumn
falls from green heat like a chestnut felled
out of its prickly jacket. A lone jay

walks among the pines. A cone of
    cold sweeps chill's needles soughing
through the day's screen doors. There can be
no cushioning today: to wake
shall be a sharp thing. The person on his

private ticking will be palsied
    from his chests; his numeral
be rung; the coils of consciousness
spring him into good, woollen light,
without armament, to meet himself in

mirrors and still halls. Meet himself:
    find his blood walking a thin
line, alarums unsleeping him.
Brazen as flame leaving ash for
the sere elm's leaf, Autumn will have settled

into summer's pallet—patchwork
    and quilting: that poor thread of
dreams curling at the doorsill. It
is done, the keen tone spoken, wrung
out of the bronze tongue of silence. Winter;

allcolor; whiteness. Who will braid
    our years now into what skein
of circles? Bells fail in the streets;
the hall empties us into ice,
sheeted, sheer as mirrors, unreflecting.

A SONIC ANALYSIS OF STANZA
ONE OF THE POEM

In the first line, secondary stress on *it,* heavy stresses on *dawn, quick,* and *swallows. Swallows* is a feminine ending; another feminine ending in line 3—*Autumn.* There are masculine endings in lines 2, 4, and 5; lines 2 and 4 are true-rhymed as well. In line 2, *peeling* and *peals* are alliterated (they are also, incidentally, parts of a pun). There are consonantal and vocalic echo throughout the stanza—peeling, peals, steeple, prickly— as well as assonance: Line 3 ends with the word *Autumn* and line 4 starts with *fall. Dawn* in line one is in consonance with *town* in line three. All lines in this stanza have four beats except line 4, which has five— primarily because the rhythm is *sprung* with assonance in *green heat,* forcing two accents onto adjacent syllables where ordinarily we would expect to find only one.

If you will look through the rest of the poem, you will discover many similar sonic effects. Theodore Roethke's "Words for the Wind" uses sonics extensively:

WORDS FOR THE WIND

1

Love, love, a lily's my care,
She's sweeter than a tree,
Loving, I use the air
Most lovingly: I breathe;
Mad in the wind I wear
Myself as I should be,
All's even with the odd,
My brother the vine is glad.

Are flower and seed the same?
What do the great dead say?
Sweet Phoebe, she's my theme:
She sways whenever I sway.
"O love me while I am,
You green thing in my way!"
I cried, and the birds came down
And made my song their own.

Motion can keep me still:
She kissed me out of thought
As a lovely substance will;
She wandered; I did not:
I stayed, and light fell
Across her pulsing throat;
I stared, and a garden stone
Slowly became the moon.

The shallow stream runs slack;
The wind creaks slowly by;
Out of a nestling's beak
Comes a tremulous cry
I cannot answer back;

A shape from deep in the eye—
That woman I saw in a stone—
Keeps pace when I walk alone.

2

The sun declares the earth;
The stones leap in the stream;
On a wide plain, beyond
The far stretch of a dream,
A field breaks like the sea;
The wind's white with her name,
And I walk with the wind.

The dove's my will today.
She sways, half in the sun:
Rose, easy on a stem,
One with the sighing vine,
One to be merry with,
And pleased to meet the moon.
She likes wherever I am.

Passion's enough to give
Shape to a random joy:
I cry delight: I know
The root, the core of a cry.
Swan-heart, arbutus-calm,
She moves when time is shy:
Love has a thing to do.

A fair thing grows more fair;
The green, the springing green
Makes an intenser day
Under the rising moon;
I smile, no mineral man;
I bear, but not alone,
The burden of this joy.

3

Under a southern wind,
The birds and fishes move
North, in a single stream;
The sharp stars swing around;
I get a step beyond
The wind, and there I am,
I'm odd and full of love.

Wisdom, where is it found?—
Those who embrace, believe.

Whatever was, still is,
Says a song tied to a tree.
Below, on the ferny ground,
In rivery air, at ease,
I walk with my true love.

What time's my heart? I care.
I cherish what I have
Had of the temporal:
I am no longer young
But the winds and waters are;
What falls away will fall;
All things bring me to love.

4

The breath of a long root,
The shy perimeter
Of the unfolding rose,
The green, the altered leaf,
The oyster's weeping foot,
And the incipient star—
Are part of what she is.
She wakes the ends of life.

Being myself, I sing
The soul's immediate joy.
Light, light, where's my repose?
A wind wreathes round a tree.
A thing is done: a thing
Body and spirit know
When I do what she does:
Creaturely creature, she!—

I kiss her moving mouth,
Her swart hilarious skin;
She breaks my breath in half;
She frolicks like a beast;
And I dance round and round,
A fond and foolish man,
And see and suffer myself
In another being, at last.

THEODORE ROETHKE

iv. PROPORTION

PROPORTION BY SITUATION OF RHYME has to do with the
arrangement of rhymes in a stanza by distance. *First distance* is *couplet*

rhyme: *aa*; second distance is *triplet rhyme*: *aba*; third distance is *envelope stanza quatrain*: *abba*; fourth distance is *quintet envelope,* where the rhyme overleaps three lines of *b* rhyme, *abbba;* or *abcba*.

PROPORTION BY SITUATION OF MEASURES has to do with variations in lengths of lines in a stanza; i.e., the patterns of arrangement of long and short lines, as in, for instance, the stanza called *standard habbie* where the lines are sometimes of four feet, sometimes of two feet (the numerals here indicate length-of-line): $a^4a^4a^4b^2a^4b^2$.

PROPORTION IN FIGURE has to do with the typographical level —choosing the appropriate *shape* of stanza to suit the poem. Often lines of the same length will be indented, or will start at the margin; similarly, the poet may indent or not according to the rhyme scheme.

PROPORTION BY TREATMENT has to do with choosing the appropriate meters, forms, and lengths (both of lines and of the whole poem) to deal with the subject of the poem.

NOTATION has to do with shorthand noting of the rhyme schemes and line-lengths of poems. The first rhyme of a poem is always *a,* and whenever that rhyme reappears it is *a*; the second rhyme is *b,* the third *c,* and so on. Numerals above *small* letters (a^4) indicate length of line, in this case four verse feet.

Sometimes a line will be a refrain. The first refrain will, if it is also the first rhyme, be a capital letter *A*; the second refrain, if it is also the second rhyme, will be capital *B,* and so forth. If there are two refrains with the *same rhyme* in the poem, they are differentiated by numerals— A^1bA^2 as in the *villanelle,* for instance. If one wishes to indicate line-lengths as well, the second numeral will indicate line-length; the first will indicate the refrain, as in the *pantoum,* which is built entirely of repeated lines. This pantoum rhymes $A^{1-5}B^{1-5}A^{2-5}B^{2-5}$ (since all lines are pentameter, we will drop the *line-length indicator* from here on. and keep only the *refrain indicator*), $B^1C^1B^2C^2$, $C^1D^1C^2D^2$, $D^1E^1D^2E^2$, $E^1A^1E^2A^2$:

A PANTOUM FOR MORNING

... so doth feare insinuate itself into every action
and passion of the mind.
JOHN DONNE

Morning pours a cold flame through the curtains;
We, O my dreams, are caught as fire takes the spread.
In silk light dressed to pose her questions
Mute, the Morning sits upon the bed.

We, O my dreams, are caught as fire takes the spread;
She is there, a hard bright challenge in our eyes.
Mute, the Morning sits upon the bed.
We fear to draw and fear not to draw the blinds.

She is there, a hard bright challenge in our eyes.
It were better, perhaps, to be sprightly like boys deaf to danger.
We fear to draw and fear not to draw the blinds.
It were better as we bury the head, this were sloth and not fear.

It were better, perhaps, to be sprightly like boys deaf to danger.
In the cloak of the sheets we hide seeking safety in dreaming.
It were better as we bury our heads, this were sloth and not fear.
We try for a while to forget we've no answers for Morning.

In the cloak of the sheets we hide, seeking safety in dreaming
While Morning pours a cold flame through the curtains.
We try for a while to forget we've no answers for Morning
In silk light dressed to pose her questions.

                                                        CLAIRE MCALLISTER

Here is a poem that relies heavily on a single sound:

NIGHT AND A DISTANT CHURCH

Forward abrupt   up
then mmm mm
wind mmm m
        mmm   m
upon
the mm   mm
wind mmm m
        mmm
into the mm wind
rain now and again
the mm wind
  ells
b
        ell s
    b

                                                        RUSSELL ATKINS

Study the sonic devices of these songs from a play:

A SEA DIRGE

Full fathom five thy father lies;
    Of his bones are coral made;
Those are pearls that were his eyes;
    Nothing of him that doth fade,
But doth suffer a sea-change
Into something rich and strange.

Sea-nymphs hourly ring his knell:
　Hark! now I hear them,—
　　Ding, dong, bell.

WILLIAM SHAKESPEARE
from *The Tempest*

THE FAIRY LIFE

Where the bee sucks, there suck I:
In a cowslip's bell I lie;
There I couch, when owls do cry:
On the bat's back I do fly
After summer merrily.
　　Merrily, merrily, shall I live now,
　　Under the blossom that hangs on the bough!

WILLIAM SHAKESPEARE
from *The Tempest*

suggested writing assignment

A) Write a poem of ten lines in rhymed, accentual-syllabic verse. Choose your own rhyme scheme, stanza pattern, and line-length. In a *headnote* to your poem, tell what meter and rhyme-scheme you have chosen; i.e., "Trochaic tetrameter in two five-line stanzas rhyming *ababa.*"

B) Write a poem of between ten and fifteen lines in any *metrical* prosody you choose *except* accentual-syllabics. Pay strict attention to the sonic level. In a headnote to the poem, explain what prosody you are using and list the sonic devices in the poem; i.e., "Variable accentuals utilizing consonance, assonance, and alliteration."

11

OF TROPES

A *trope* is a figure of speech—certain language constructs present figures to the eye, the ear, to the other senses. A trope makes a picture or a sensation—it is descriptive in nature.

But not all descriptions are tropes, for a figure of speech is more complex than simple adjective–noun (*pretty girl*) or verb–adverb (*run hard*) constructions.

Many of those who are newly come to poetry don't understand that heightened language uses few modifiers, but many tropes. As a result, new writers tend to fill up lines with adjectives, adverbs, and other modifiers through *descriptions*.

i. DESCRIPTIONS

OMIOSIS is description by similarity: Two things in some way resemble each other.

SIMILE is the comparison of things that have points of likeness (*Her smile was like the sun, | As warm as morning light upon the rose*).

ANALOGY is the means by which simile proceeds: comparison of things that are not identical (*He stood as if he were an oak | Braced against the wind.*)

143

CONTRAST is comparison by differentiation: Things are *not* alike (*The lake was no more mirror than the sky is a pancake*).

ALLUSION is comparison by reference to something outside the poem, or to something not organically part of the poem; i.e., "He came, *like Rome,* to see, and stayed to conquer."

HYPOTIPOSIS is the description of real things.

PRAGMATOGRAPHIA is description of actions.

TOPOGRAPHIA is description of real places.

CHRONOGRAPHIA is description of seasons, times of day, and so forth.

ICON is resemblance by portraiture; i.e., one person looks like another.

PROSOPOGRAPHIA is description of a person one has never known; imaginative portraiture.

PARADIGMA is description by comparison of two similar cases or situations.

ENIGMA is deliberately obscure description, as in a riddle.

PARABOLA is resemblance by imagery—talking about one thing in terms of something entirely different in kind, as in Sabrina on p. 46: *Sabrina was a willow twig.*

An EPITHETIC COMPOUND is two descriptive words made into one; i.e., "deathgush," "thickdark," "sunbright," and so forth. One form of the epithetic compound is the *portmanteau word,* described on p. 48, and another is the *kenning,* on p. 90.

An OXYMORON is a descriptive phrase that combines terms that seem mutually exclusive, but which in context may not be; i.e., "sweet bitterness," "terrible beauty," "burning chill," and so forth.

No matter how much one modifies a substantive or verb, however, it will remain essentially the same. How does one change a word *essentially?*—he makes it equivalent to something else; he makes a *metaphor* of it: *The sun and moon are coins to be spent lightly, or in dark ways.*

The nature of *allegory* lies in speaking about one subject in terms of another, in order to make it new again, to make it clearer and sharper; and the heart of allegory is metaphor. The essence of *metaphor* lies in *language equation,* or, as in our example, *sun + moon=coins.*
A metaphor that is extended beyond the original equation is the *conceit* (an old-fashioned way of saying "concept"), as in everything that follows our example's equation *to be spent* (like money, like time) *lightly* (a pun, meaning "in a carefree way" or "without much thought," at the same time that it continues the metaphor of sun*light* or day*light*) or

in dark ways (again, in ways that are hopeless or despairing, perhaps, at the same time that nighttime is invoked).

ii. METAPHORICAL TROPES

METAPHORIC CONSTRUCTION. The *vehicle* of a metaphor is the *trope* that bears the weight of the comparison of dissimilar things or qualities that have a single point in common (*Coins* is the vehicle of our example; roundness is the point in common between *coins* and *sun & moon*). The *subject* of a metaphor is called the *tenor* (*sun & moon* is the compound tenor of our example).

An ABSTRACTION is any term which is open to broad and various definition; e g , *soul, truth, beauty, justice, God, love*

A CONCRETION is any term that may be conventionally defined; e.g., *table, brick, rug, tree, elephant, house*.

An ANCHORED ABSTRACTION is an abstraction metaphorized by its being equated with a concretion: *Her soul is a brick.*

An UNANCHORED ABSTRACTION is an abstraction which has been equated with another abstraction: Keats' " 'Beauty is truth, truth beauty' " is an unanchored abstraction. It means nothing—or, rather, it may mean anything the reader wishes it to mean. *It is not a metaphor because there is no obvious (or even discernible) point in common between the two abstractions,* and there is no way to tell which abstraction is the vehicle and which the tenor.

DENOTATION is the primary meaning, or *dictionary definition* of a word—*Heart*: "A bodily organ, the purpose of which is to circulate the blood."

CONNOTATION is an ancillary or secondary meaning of a word. Connotations of *heart* are *courage,* as in "He has great heart"; *love,* as in "An affair of the heart"; and *essence,* as in "He is pure of heart."

CONTEXT is the environment surrounding a word situated in a phrase, clause, or larger grammatic unit. This environment limits the denotations and connotations of the word. In "His heart beat strongly in battle," the context of the word *heart* allows the denotation *a bodily organ* and the connotation *courage,* but eliminates the other connotations *love* and *essence.*

OVERTONE is this allowance of connotations by context. In *The sun and moon are coins to be spent lightly, or in dark ways,* context allows the denotation of carefreeness in *lightly,* as well as the connotation of *brightness* through overtone.

Imagist and impressionist poetry are sometimes hard to tell apart.

Both concentrate largely on images; both often attempt to create a mood
by means of imagery; and both try to achieve overtone—ramifications
that arise out of the images and go on expanding in the mind as one
thinks about them. "Image Tinged with No Color" on p. 48, and
Kreymborg's "Nun Snow" on p. 49 are impressionist poetry; Williams'
"The Red Wheelbarrow" and this poem (printed as it originally
appeared in 1913 in *Poetry* magazine, complete with *spatial caesuras*) are
imagist:

IN A STATION OF THE METRO

The apparition   of these faces   in the crowd;
Petals   on a wet, black   bough.

EZRA POUND

    The following is a poem that attempts to use the images of an
autumn garden to evoke a mood of foreboding and mystery. The poem
utilizes the real names of herbs throughout, the intention being to have
the strange names of the plants carry a load of overtone through
associations and connotation, especially at the end of the poem, in a
simple catalog of plants.

    One or two notes may be in order. A "simple" is a medicinal
preparation made from herbs (a folk-remedy). The word is used here in
a double sense: It is a pun. Something similar happens with
"Nightshade / will consume the beautiful lady". *Deadly nightshade* is
another term for the plant *belladonna,* which in Italian means "beautiful
lady." "Nightshade" here is also meant to imply the shadows of night,
and the shades of death; and "the beautiful lady is intended to refer to
a human being. Ambiguity throughout the whole passage is intended to
amplify the image, to give it overtone.

    Ambiguity is not obscurity, as we have seen. Ambiguity is *inclusive,*
not *exclusive*: It amplifies the poem by including alternative meanings;
it does not block the poem by excluding the reader from the meaning
the poet intended. If anything is obscure in the poem here, it is
the names of the herbs, but even the names are descriptive of themselves,
often through epithetic compounds:

THE WEED GARDEN

    I am the ghost of the weed garden.
      Stalk among stones—you will find me
remembering husks and pods, how crisp burdock
  couches in the moon for every passer.
    I am the dry seed of your mind.

The hour will strike when you dream me, your
       hand at the sheet like five thin hooks.
I will wait for you in the old vines rattling on
the wind, in the ground-pine. I will show you
       where rue has blossomed and eyebright,

   mother-thyme. You must name me Yarrow.
       Bitter vetch shall catch your step as
you follow, hearing the stars turning to crystal,
   sweet lovage turning sere, adder's tongue and
       Jew's-ear at their whisper. Nightshade

will consume the beautiful lady.
       Dwarf elder, dodder-of-thyme, I
am the thing you fear in the simple of your blood:
   toothwort in the dust, feverfew, mouse-ear,
       sundew and cup moss, tormentils.

CATACHRESIS is a term that implies misuse of tropes. Every poem
must make sense—not necessarily *logical* sense, but *poetic* sense—in
context. If a metaphor or other trope simply makes no "sense" of any
kind—as for instance, where the context does not block out enough
connotations and there is confusion about what a word means (it may
mean *too many* things, at which point ambiguity becomes obscurity),
then the trope is catachretic.

A SUBDUED METAPHOR is one that is *implied,* not stated, by the
context. For instance, in "The sun and moon are coins to be spent
lightly, or in dark ways," the metaphor of *gold* is implied in context by
coins in relation to *sun,* and the metaphor of *silver* is implied in relation
to *moon.*

A DIMINISHING METAPHOR has a deliberately overintense or
overstated tenor in relation to its vehicle: *"The burning moon* that she
remembers / Was but a brand of *dying embers."*

DYFALU, a Welsh term, describes a tenor that bursts into a
profusion of vehicles: "The *moon* was a *coin,* a *ring* of fire, / A *cartwheel*
rolling across the sky, / A *heaven* full of lightning turning / Around the
earth—a *cosmic pyre"*—in other words, a *catalog vehicle.*

An ORGANIC METAPHOR is one that rises logically from the
context; a GRATUITOUS METAPHOR is one that does not.

A MIXED METAPHOR is catachretic because its vehicle is
inappropriate to the tenor (*the sun and moon are baby buggies*), or the
vehicle itself is made up of inappropriate elements (*Keep your nose to
the grindstone, your shoulder to the wheel, and an eye peeled for trouble*).

A CONCEIT is a metaphor that is extended beyond the original
tenor-vehicle, always logically in context, each new element of the

extended metaphor retaining its base in the point of similarity between the original, otherwise disparate, equated things or qualities: See "The Old Professor and the Sphinx" below.

SYNESTHESIA is talking about one of the senses in terms of another—"The afternoon *smelled green*" (scent–sight), "I could *taste* her sweet *whispers*" (taste–hearing), "He *touched* me with his *mind*" (touch–thought).

PROSOPOPEIA is personification: Speaking of non-human things in human terms, as Keats does in his ode "To Autumn":

TO AUTUMN

I

Season of mists and mellow fruitfulness,
  Close bosom-friend of the maturing sun;
Conspiring with him how to load and bless
  With fruit the vines that round the thatch-eves run;
To bend with apples the moss'd cottage-trees,
  And fill all fruit with ripeness to the core;
    To swell the gourd, and plump the hazel shells
  With a sweet kernel; to set budding more,
And still more, later flowers for the bees,
Until they think warm days will never cease,
    For Summer has o'er-brimm'd their clammy cells.

II

Who hath not seen thee oft amid thy store?
  Sometimes whoever seeks abroad may find
Thee sitting careless on a granary floor,
  Thy hair soft-lifted by the winnowing wind;
Or on a half-reap'd furrow sound asleep,
  Drows'd with the fume of poppies, while thy hook
    Spares the next swath and all its twined flowers:
And sometimes like a gleaner thou dost keep
  Steady thy laden head across a brook;
  Or by a cyder-press, with patient look,
    Thou watchest the last oozings hours by hours.

III

Where are the songs of Spring? Ay, where are they?
  Think not of them, thou hast thy music too,—
While barred clouds bloom the soft-dying day,
  And touch the stubble-plains with rosy hue;
Then in a wailful choir the small gnats mourn
  Among the river sallows, borne aloft
    Or sinking as the light wind lives or dies;

And full-grown lambs loud bleat from hilly bourn;
   Hedge-crickets sing; and now with treble soft
The red-breast whistles from a garden-croft;
   And gathering swallows twitter in the skies.

JOHN KEATS

The **PATHETIC FALLACY** is absurd or overstated personification —endowing non-human things with bathetic or pathetic qualities, often through *cue-words* (such as *apple-pie, motherhood,* etc.) which are meant to induce automatic sentimental responses in the reader. In the phrase, "The little white cloud that cried," *little, cloud,* and *cried* are cue-words. Similarly, in Joyce Kilmer's "Trees," the unthinking will see the tree as, simultaneously, a mother-figure, an infant-figure, and a religious-figure. Some thought, however, will put all the images together logically and come up with a monster that has hair for leaves, eyes tangled in the hair on stalks, the mouth at the bottom of an elongated head buried in the earth, and so forth.

A **SYMBOL** is a concretion which represents an abstraction; i.e., in some context the ocean might be symbolic of eternity.

An **EMBLEM** is a conventional symbol; i.e., a bald eagle is emblematic of the United States of America.

PARADOX is a metaphor or statement that combines terms which seem mutually exclusive, but which in fact are not—*"Freedom* is the *prison of rebellion,"* or *"Winter* is the *Spring of contemplation;* or it is a statement that contradicts a commonly held belief—"The earth is not round, it is egg-shaped."

METAPHYSICAL POETRY is poetry whose organizing principle is the conceit. It may extend metaphor by using *all* of the various techniques of descriptions and of metaphorical and rhetorical tropes, as in Donne's poem on p. 38, or as in this one:

THE OLD PROFESSOR AND THE SPHINX

      It is a dry word in a dry book
   drying out my ear. I squat and swallow
      my tongue here in this chair,
   the desert of my desk, summer bare, spreading
like a brown horizon into regions grown arid
   with erudition. A caravan of books treks

      stolidly across my eyes while I,
   the Sphinx, a phoenix burning in my skull,
      pry into inkwells and
   gluepots seeking the universal solvent.
There is none. The pages as I turn them sound like sand
   rattling in the sec temples of a beast gone to

earth with the sun. I lie caught in my
creaking dune, shifting with the wind of the
        pharaohs, wondering if,
somewhere, I have not missed my valley. Upon
the walls of my office there are Oriental prints
hanging stiff as papyrus, whispering their brown

        images into the silent air.
I know the poems on my shelves speak with
        one another in an
ancient language I have somehow forgotten.
If there is rainfall, I recall, the desert blossoms—
but I have somewhere lost the natural prayer

        and instinctual rites of the blood
which can conjure clouds in seasons of drought.
        There is but ritual
remaining; no honey is in the lion's
hide; my temples have mumbled to ruin: they endure
disuse and despair. An archaeologist of

        cabinets and drawers, I exhume
paperclip skeletons, the artifacts
        of millennia: red
ballpoint pens with nothing in their veins, pencils
like blunted lances, notebook citadels emptied of
their citizens—the crusader has squandered his

        talents on bawds, grown hoary in their
service. The town is sacked: the bawds are gone
        to tame younger legions.
Look into my sarcophagus: the tapes are
sunken over my hollow sockets. Slowly the waste
swallows my oasis like a froth of spittle.

In this poem notice how the subdued metaphor—that *academe is a
desert* (a metaphor is always a language equation: A = B)—is developed
and expanded from the first line to the last. Notice all the images—
similes ("the desert of my desk . . . spreading like a . . . horizon"),
subdued metaphors ("A caravan of books"), allusions ("Sphinx, phoenix"),
descriptions ("stiff as papyrus"), synaesthesia ("whispering their
brown images"), puns (my *temples* have mumbled to ruin," "squandered
his talents on bawds, grown *hoary*"—here, *talents* is simultaneously
a pun and an allusion to an old Palestinian monetary unit called
a "talent"); oxymorons ("instinctual rites"), denotation and connotation
("temples" = parts of the head denotatively; connotatively the word
means places of ritual and prayer. The implicit statement here, in this
poem's context, is that the mind should be a place for instinctual ritual
and prayer), symbols ("a beast gone to earth with the sun," "crusader"),

personification ("paperclip skeletons"), onomatopoeia ("A caravan of books treks stolidly"), abstraction ("millennia"), hyperbole ("It is a dry word in a dry book drying out my ear"), ambiguities of various kinds, i.e., the "temples" passage cited, and concretions throughout the poem in all of the tropes.

ALLEGORY. Puttenham called allegory "a long and perpetual metaphor." It is a method of telling a story on the narrative level, but meaning something more general regarding the human condition on the symbolic level. See "The Palace of Poetry" section of the Introduction.

iii. RHETORICAL TROPES

RHETORIC is the art of effective speaking and writing; it is concerned with creating an *effect* in the listener or reader, and with *affecting* him as well. Certain tropes may be called *rhetorical tropes* because they are concerned with making their effects through non-metaphorical *figures of speech*.

ANACHINOSIS refers the reader, in an argument, to his own opinion, as in the beginning of the "Epilogue" of *Odds Bodkin's Strange Thrusts and Ravels* in the last chapter:

> Odds wishes you godspeed,
> sirs. Go out and read
> if you believe not
> this rave and riot.
> Pick up a book, buy it,
> peruse it—then, once you have done,
> use it as best it suits you.

ANTENAGOGE makes a statement and then softens it by adding a mitigating or less harsh alternative:

> I wish, my dear, that you'd fall over dead—
> Well, maybe just fall down and hit your head.

Or,

> It's true that marriage is a prison cell,
> But there's cell-mate—and a bed as well.

ANTIPHRASIS is derision by means of simple contradiction; i.e., calling a fat man "skinny," or a thin man "fatso."

ANTIPOPHORA is asking a question, and then answering it oneself. As for instance, in the poem "Scarecrow" on p. 212, where the scarecrow asks, "You worship me? a pole for a spine, a / timber for my extended bone, fingers / of hay stolen by wrens?" and then answers himself, "I bleach and shake, / I shudder in the moon's dark. Pumpkins, crowd / of orange globes, I whistle in the wind."

ANTITHETON is the term describing the techniques of "the devil's advocate" in argument: Taking any position and defending it simply in joy of the fight, or in order to bring out some point that might otherwise remain unexamined, as in the poem "A Dedication" on p. 184, in which an argument is built up from three propositions: 1) that "the sea worm is a decorated flute / that pipes in the most ancient mode"; 2) that "the salt content of mammalian blood / is exactly equivalent / to the salinity of the oceans / at the time life emerged onto the land"; and 3) that "man is the only mammal with a / capacity for song."

APORIA expresses doubt or uncertainty, as in "A Dedication," in which the argument depends upon the series of three propositions outlined above. These propositions are not, however, simply stated, but qualified in each case by the ambivalent "*if* it is true. . . ."

APOSTROPHE is direct address—speaking to an absent human being, or to a (usually) personified thing or abstraction, as Keats does in the "Ode to Autumn," above.

ASTEISMUS is simple jesting, without rancor: "Did Samson Agonistes have the strength / of twenty bulls at cowtime in the spring?"

CHARIENTISMUS is light banter which is meant to soothe rancor, as for instance, in trying to avoid a fight with a loud bully one might say, "I'm sure you're too much of a gentleman to want to pick a fight."

DIALISIS sets up the propositions of an argument. These propositions are a dilemma, in that they seem mutually exclusive: It must be one or the other proposition, but which is it? Perhaps it is neither, or both: Dialisis disposes of both propositions without paradox:

> You say Jack loves to live, that brother Jules
> Lives to love? Then I say both are fools:
> One must be alive to love at any cost—
> Then live to live, love love, or *all* is lost.

ECPHONISIS is exclamation or outcry:

> "Forget that fool, my love," I scoffed,
> "Soon we shall wed!
> Soon we shall wed!"

EPITHONEMA is climactic summation at the conclusion of a poem, a *coda*, often in a single line or couplet, as in the English sonnet, or in the poem "Burning the News" on p. 186, the last two lines of which sum up the theme of the poem.

EPITROPIS is used when the speaker believes he has said enough and refers the reader to something else in order to complete the thought:

> I've said enough. Time for another beer.
> You take these definitions on from here.

EROTEMA is the rhetorical question—a question for which no answer is given or expected because, in context, the answer is obvious, as in the poem "An Ordinary Evening in Cleveland," parts VI and VII, on p. 211, where several rhetorical questions are asked, as "Can you sense the droppings of / flesh falling between walls falling, / the burrowings of nerves in a cupboard of cans?" The implied contextual answer is *yes*.

ETIOLOGIA is the argumentative technique of assigning a cause or reason for an action or circumstance, as in the first stanza of "Fit the Second" of *Odds Bodkin's Strange Thrusts and Ravels*:

> Take next,
> for thy next mistake
> (for muckrake you must
> once you've begun to raise dust,
> for, to settle the dust,
> to everyone be fair
> or unfair rather, without care,
> that is, care less rather than more
> how you effect your cure,
> you must sprinkle dews
> on the dust, not as you choose,
> but as you list, . . .

IRONIA, or *irony*, is witty mockery, usually effected by saying the opposite of what is actually meant; for instance,

> The lover, intent on a camping trip, went
> into the woods with the best in tent.

In this case, the irony depends upon a pun on the word *intent*.

MEIOSIS is a method of irony or sarcasm that dimishes the

importance of something, as in, "He's a big man indeed—big-headed and big-bellied."

METANOIA makes a statement, then retracts it by substituting something else:

> They tell me that your head is filled with stone.
> O, surely not! But maybe solid bone.

MICTERISMUS is verbal sneering:

> The old professor knows that books are safe.
> He knows he's really Samson on the make,
> Too smart to lose his eyes.

NOEMA is an ironic way of speaking by saying one thing on the surface, but meaning something quite different:

> You say Fred lives his life without a taint?
> You're right. I wish to God he were a saint.

Meaning, on the surface level, that the speaker agrees with the appraisal of Fred, but in fact meaning that the speaker wishes Fred were dead, as only the dead can be saints.

ORISMUS gives a definition which is different from someone else's definition of a word or phrase, as in the first stanza of "Fit the Sixth" of *Odds Bodkin's Strange Thrusts and Ravels*:

> The school's a madhouse? Nay,
> a bedroom, maybe, . . .

PARALEPSIS makes a little thing of something by passing over it lightly, or denying it is of importance and thereby emphasizing its actual importance through understatement, as in epigram #7 of "Fit the Fifth" of *Odds Bodkin's Strange Thrusts and Ravels*:

> and here is *All America*:
> what's there to say of him?
> He has a pretty wife.
> He keeps his hair in trim.

PARAMALOGIA is, in Puttenham's words, "the figure of admittance." It admits arguments to the contrary, so as to undercut the opponent's case, as in the first stanza of "Fit the Fifth" of *Odds Bodkin's Strange Thrusts and Ravels*:

Oh, what a mess
is this paper. I guess
poor Bod's hopeless. I am unlettered,
sirs, a man fettered
by ignorance. Ignore,
if you will, my bespattered
page, for I've been but smattered
with lore here and there.
Beware
the dull pen, sirs—it may tell lies
or, worse, my lords, truth,
if you watch not your way.

PARIMIA is the trope of speaking by means of proverbs:

"An apple a day keeps the doctor away."
That's true—he'd rather have money as pay.

PARISIA is an apology by the writer of scurrilous or, as Puttenham says, "licentious" material, as in "Fit the Eighth" of *Odds Bodkin's Strange Thrusts and Ravels* which begins,

Sirs,
I am one of your proslers,
no poet. In prose
anything goes.
Not so in verse,
or so they converse
in the various schools.
I would beg to disagree,
if it were not that fools
such as yours truly
tend toward the unruly,
which is why there are rules.

PROCATALEPSIS pre-empts opposing arguments by anticipating the argument before the opponent can articulate it, as in stanzas eight and nine of "Fit the Twelfth" of *Odds Bodkin's Strange Thrusts and Ravels*:

We ought to break
into breakneck
Skeltonics just about now,

Gentlemen, I know, but perhaps
we'll just let the meters break down
a tiny bit.

SARCASMUS, or *sarcasm,* is heavy irony or, as Puttenham described it, "the bitter taunt." There is little wit in sarcasm, as for instance when one bridge partner says to the other, who has just played a bad hand, "Oh, you're just a terrific player, simply marvelous." In this case, saying the opposite of what is actually meant is similar to the technique of irony, but the emphasis is on the bitterness, not on the mockery.

TAPINOSIS is saying *too* little of a subject; undersaying. It is not the same, however, as understatement. The heart of poetry is saying just enough, and frequently a poet can say more by merely *showing* the situation—letting it speak for itself—rather than *telling* the reader how to feel about it, as in the poem about the Nazi death camps.

William Blake's "The Tyger" uses archetypal symbolism. An *archetype* is the original thing, from which a copy is made. Some psychoanalysts believe that certain myths are transmitted from generation to generation genetically, through "race memory." The purpose of the archetypal symbol is to find the key to those memories, not through logic, but through finding what T. S. Eliot called the *objective correlative,* that object or word which, in and of itself, produces the *image of the idea* in the reader. *The idea is not stated*; rather, the poet proceeds by intuition, choosing those words that, like incantations or charms, conjure up, out of the blood, those feelings, mysteries, terrors that have always been represented through various symbols since man became man. Although the symbols may vary from epoch to epoch, at their core they remain the same—remain the archetypes, the ancient prototypes of elemental mystery:

THE TYGER

Tyger! Tyger! burning bright
In the forests of the night,
What immortal hand or eye
Could frame thy fearful symmetry?

In what distant deeps or skies
Burnt the fire of thine eyes?
On what wings dare he aspire?
What the hand dare seize the fire?

And what shoulder, & what art,
Could twist the sinews of thy heart?
And when thy heart began to beat,
What dread hand? & what dread feet?

What the hammer? what the chain?
In what furnace was thy brain?
What the anvil? what dread grasp
Dare its deadly terrors clasp?

When the stars threw down their spears,
And water'd heaven with their tears,
Did he smile his work to see?
Did he who made the Lamb make thee?

Tyger! Tyger! burning bright
In the forests of the night,
What immortal hand or eye,
Dare frame thy fearful symmetry?

WILLIAM BLAKE

Vern Rutsala's poem attempts something like the same thing in domestic terms:

EVENINGS AT HOME

After dinner you hear footsteps outside,
           but they all go by on their intricate journeys—
      carrying sealed messages to gas companies,
but with such deference:
           on tiptoe, speaking quietly
      even to house numbers and wagons.

The same politeness shrouds the house, making you
           smile at furniture
      before sitting down to worry about the carpet—

the way it stretches,
           sending pile to every corner—such a flat beached
      fish that only winces when you

step on it, but never whimpers, never even sighs.
           All the objects around you are well-bred, stoic,
      resigned to duties only disaster

will release them from.
           You wait
      for disasters too, some booming

invitation to run in the street, free finally of that
           contract you signed to sit still all the evenings
      of your life.

But some nights you can't stop walking.
      All the chairs point out
   aches, the little bruises thinking brings.

You walk around opening
      and closing doors. Or stare out at
   the faint light on the trees,

thinking
      of minnows.
   You stop at closets, feel the material of

an old life, look at shoes. And you don't speak.
      Not even
   the need to lie squirms in your

throat. You eat the powder of silence
      and wander toward sheets
   stiff as collars,

the drugged journeys of
      heavy-handed dreams,
   or the bright tumor of sleeplessness.

                          VERN RUTSALA

In this following poem, Morton Marcus makes the fingers of the hand into types of people:

HAND

Thumb
blind bald-headed blunderer
moron I might have become
eyes nose mouth stopped up
with cushions of flesh
an impermeable thickness
ideas cannot enter
               blunt as the infant
               squatting at the village edge
               oblivious to passersby

Index
the pointer
full of possibilities
lean and muscular
with impatient energies
traces the words in books
and soon will be going

> explorer visionary
> builder of roads and bridges
> now lifter of latches opener of doors

Middle
bachelor with bizarre habits
owns the largest house
in the village
has never traveled
yet speaks of mysterious dungeons
that only he is able to reach

> and yet his explorations
> have not made him
> cynical or cruel

Ring
married burdened with bills
awkward and short of breath
sits in a large chair
staring out the window
while his children laugh
and run through the house

> or reads his brother's letters
> which tell of cities
> set like jewels beyond the mountains

Little
inquisitive old man
clean and well-mannered
bent like a question
he never asks aloud
lives alone at the end
of the village thinking

> "these are my people
> in this valley I kissed the wind
> and caged the sun in my hands"

MORTON MARCUS

suggested writing assignment

Write a ten-to-fifteen-line poem, in any *metrical* form, which is an
extended metaphor. In a headnote, give the names of the prosody and the
form you have chosen.

12

OF IMAGERY

All of the techniques we spoke of in the last chapter, and some others we mentioned earlier, are used to make word-pictures or *images*.

Poetry which is built around imagery often does not have a prosody in the metrical sense. Instead, its prosody is based on the sensory level—evocations of impressions, sensations, and emotions. That is to say, such poetry has as its prosody an organizing principle that centers upon the five senses: sight, hearing, touch, smell, and taste. Its rationale is the rationale of *organic* (in both senses of that word: *unity* and *organs of perception*) composition.

But this loose conception of prosody hasn't been enough for some poets—mostly Americans, such as William Carlos Williams and Ezra Pound—who have also attempted to devise some kind of more-or-less traditionally based accentual system of prosodics to accompany the imagery—*because sound can produce images, too,* as in onomatopoiea.

Thus, Williams talked about the "breath pause," which is really only an American variation of the Japanese *katauta,* translated from a Japanese syllabic base to an English accentual base. And Williams talked about the "variable foot," which merely means *variable accentuals,* much as the Japanese speak of the differences between a five-syllable line and a seven-syllable line; i.e., Williams' "variable foot" meant that there were generally between two and four accents per line, whereas the Japanese distinguish between a five-syllable and a seven-syllable line.

Poetry based on images attempts to create a mood by means of trope. It tries to achieve overtone—as has already been said—ramifications arising out of the images, that continue to grow in the mind even after the poem has been read.

The Japanese *haiku* has a number of requirements that will aid the writer who wishes to achieve overtone through imagery; requirements that will, as well, crystallize some of the things that Williams, Pound, and Stevens, among others (including many younger poets) have been attempting during the past half-century and more.

UTTERANCES, according to Igarashi, "are sudden, emotive words." A formal utterance is the *katauta*—a question *or* its answer: "Am I in love?" is a katauta, as is its answer: "Birds are flying."

A *pair* of such katautas is a MONDO: "Am I in love? Birds are flying." Mondos may appear in parallel constructions of various kinds:

> Am I in love? Birds are flying.
> Do birds fly? I am in love.

To the western eye, this looks much like a *syllogism* . . .

> Grass is green.
> Bluegrass is grass.
> Bluegrass is green.

. . . except that the katauta answer is not logical—it is *intuitive*:

SEASONS OF THE BLOOD

Is it winter? Blood is warm.
Is the blood warm? It is spring.

　When is the wind warm?
The sun falls on wings moving
across the river valley.

　In the water, fish
look for roads. Bridges extend
　from mountain to hill.
Find your way. Look for the gate.

　Walking this way, through
the air like crystal, like bells,
　one neither moves nor
remains, but becomes what is,
the air like crystal, like bells.

The blood of a leaf
turns sunlight green when
    the day is longest.
On a certain night, the wind
breathes blood into an oak leaf.

    Life is an acorn
hidden in a cold valley.
    The wind's blood is white.

                    from *Seasons of the Blood: Poems on the Tarot*

Often katautas consist of three parts arranged in lines of 5–7–7
syllables, these lengths being approximately breath-length (like Williams'
"breath-pause" system of line-phrasing: each line equals a phrase), or
the appropriate lengths to ask a "sudden, emotive question" and
respond to it, also emotively . . . seventeen or nineteen syllables are
about as many as can normally be uttered in one breath; five to seven
syllables are approximately equal to the utterance of a question or its
answer. In Williams' accentual variation of this concept, two to four
accents are approximately equal to an utterance, and six to twelve
accents are as many as can be uttered in a breath. Thus, in Williams'
prosody, each line is a phrase of about 2–4 accents, and each three lines
equals a clause of about 6–12 accents.

Igarashi says of this basic and organic unit of Japanese poetry,
"Katauta is a poem of three lines in which the first two lines consist of
one short and one long one; and the last line is the same length as the
second line, which is added as a prop to help harmonize the rhythm.
This is the unit of Japanese poetry." Here is a set of such katautas in
sequence:

SWORDS

    Does this dark blade strike
my flesh? Light is engrossed with
dust, and the organs of dust.

    Shall I not lament
in the night? Mars shows his eye
when the heavens are darkest.

    At whom does he wink?
You have shut your own eyelid.
It is mortal salt made you.

    To whom may I turn
in this anguish? Blood lashes
the womb as seas beat the shore.

Does this dark blade strike
all flesh? The oceans wear rock
to dust, but the dust shall speak.

from *Seasons of the Blood: Poems on the Tarot*

Some of the parts of Wallace Stevens' "Thirteen Ways of looking at a Blackbird" look very much like mondos, katautas, or other forms such as the SEDOKA, which is a poem, not necessarily of the question–answer mondo pattern, made up of two katautas (5–7–7, 5–7–7 syllable count). A *turn* (as in the Italian sonnet) takes place between the two triplet stanzas. It may be a dialogue, but the poem is written by a single author:

DIALOGUE

I am wearing blue
in honor of the sky. Shall
you wear green to honor earth?

I will don rainbows:
I will wear snow on my back—
white, allcolor forever.

from *Seasons of the Blood: Poems on the Tarot*

Here is Stevens' poem:

THIRTEEN WAYS OF LOOKING AT A BLACKBIRD

1

Among twenty snowy mountains,
The only moving thing
Was the eye of a blackbird.

2

I was of three minds,
Like a tree
In which there are three blackbirds.

3

The blackbird whirled in the autumn winds.
It was a small part of the pantomime.

4

A man and a woman

Are one.
A man and a woman and a blackbird
Are one.

                    5

I do not know which to prefer,
The beauty of inflections
Or the beauty of innuendoes,
The blackbird whistling
Or just after.

                    6

Icicles filled the long window
With barbaric glass.
The shadow of the blackbird
Crossed it, to and fro.
The mood
Traced in the shadow
An indecipherable cause.

                    7

O thin men of Haddam,
Why do you imagine golden birds?
Do you not see how the blackbird
Walks around the feet
Of the women about you?

                    8

I know noble accents
And lucid, inescapable rhythms;
But I know, too,
That the blackbird is involved
In what I know.

                    9

When the blackbird flew out of sight,
It marked the edge
Of one of many circles.

                    10

At the sight of blackbirds
Flying in a green light,
Even the bawds of euphony
Would cry out sharply.

11

He rode over Connecticut
In a glass coach.
Once, a fear pierced him,
In that he mistook
The shadow of his equipage
For blackbirds.

12

The river is moving.
The blackbird must be flying.

13

It was evening all afternoon.
It was snowing
And it was going to snow.
The blackbird sat
In the cedar-limbs.

WALLACE STEVENS

It's interesting to note, too, that the basic unit of Japanese form is three-lined. So is Williams' basic unit. In many Williams poems each three lines is a clausal unit, consisting of three phrases.

CHOKA is a Japanese poem of any length written in alternating five- and seven-syllable lines and ending with a seven-syllable line.

The TANKA takes two forms, both of which are externally alike in that they are quintet stanzas with lines, in this order, of 5–7–5–7–7 syllables. In the first tanka form, called the *waka,* one subject is treated in the first two lines, another in the next two, and the last line is a refrain or paraphrase or restatement: 5–7, 5–7, 7. The first two lines are a dependent clause or a phrase, the last *three* an independent clause. Grammatically, Williams did similar things with his stanzas, except (again) that the base was accentual rather than syllabic. *Stanza four* of the poem titled "Seasons of the Blood" on p. 162 is this first type of tanka.

The second type of tanka consists of two parts. The first three lines are an independent unit which ends in a noun or verb and after which a turn takes place: 5–7–5, 7–7. The triplet is an observation, the couplet a comment on the observation. *Stanza five* of "Seasons of the Blood" is an example of this second type of tanka.

The SOMONKA is an epistolary love poem made up of two tankas and written by two authors: The first is a statement of love, the second a response. Though this poem was not written by two authors, it is in the form of a somonka:

EPISTLES

I am writing you
from a pit. It is quite dark
   here. I see little.
I am scratching this note on a stone.
Where are you? It has been long.

   Thank you for your note.
I do not know where I am.
   I believe I may
be with you. It is not dark
here. The light has blinded me.

                from *Seasons of the Blood: Poems on the Tarot*

A RENGA is a single tanka written by two authors. The first writes the triplet, the second writes the couplet response.

A RENGA CHAIN is a poem made of a sequence of rengas and composed by a number of authors. The first triplet sets the subject, the succeeding couplet and all ensuing triplets and couplets amplify, gloss, or comment upon the first triplet. Renga chains can become extremely complex in many ways. For instance, a first triplet may be written. A couplet is added, completing the renga. Another triplet is added that follows logically, but that may also be read logically in place of the *first* triplet. A couplet is added, completing the second renga. A third triplet is added that may be read logically if substituted for the second triplet. A couplet is added, completing the renga, and so on.

The word HOKKU is Chinese in origin, and it came to specify in Japanese poetry the *first triplet* of a renga chain. This first verse, as noted, set the theme of the chain and was the most important part of the poem, the rest of which rang changes upon and elaborated the hokku. The hokku of a renga chain ended with a full stop—it was complete in and of itself.

The term HAIKAI NO RENGA is applied to the humorous renga chain; it means, specifically, "renga of humor."

By various stages the term *haiku* came to denote an independent tercet of 5–7–5 syllables. Derived from both the tanka and the renga, the HAIKU dropped all glosses, comments, or elaborations, and it became a poem which had as its basis an *image, emotive utterance,* and certain other characteristics as well: *spareness, condensation, spontaneity,* and *ellipsis* (look this term up in Chap. 13), plus a *seasonal element*—they were poems about spring, summer, fall, or winter. Ideally, the haiku, though complete in itself, would be *open-ended* in that its statement would "reverberate" beyond the poem itself, into overtone.

The haiku has perhaps been best described as "A moment of intense perception." Williams enunciated the Imagist doctrine: "No ideas except in things." Both conceptions are, if not identical, at least based in sensory perception primarily.

A distinction has sometimes been made between the SENRYU and the haiku, though both have exactly the same external form: The senryu is "An inquiry into the nature of Man"; the haiku, "An inquiry into the nature of the Universe." This is a senryu—in this case, the seasonal element is lacking:

THE DEAD SAILOR

As he drowned, he saw
the ship following him like
   the shark of the world.

Here is a poem that illustrates some of the Japanese syllabic forms at the same time that it parallels the development of the forms as they led up to the haiku:

PARADIGM

Why does the brook run?
The banks of the stream are green.   —*mondo*

Why does the stream run?
The banks of the brook bloom
with roe and cup-moss, with rue.   —*katauta*

The trees are filled with
cups. Grain in the fields, straw men
   talking with the wind.
Have you come far, water-
   borne, wind-born? Here are
hounds-tongue and mistletoe oak.   —*choka*

When the spears bend as
you walk through vervain or broom,
   call out to the brook—   —*waka* (5–7, 5–7, & 7)
it will swell in your veins as
you move through broom and vervain.

Have you spoken aloud? Here,
where the swallows' crewel-work
   sews the sky with mist?   —*tanka* (5–7–5, 7–7)
You must cut the filament.
You must be the lone spider.

The bole is simple:
twig and root like twin webs in   —*haiku*
    air and earth like fire.

> from *Seasons of the Blood: Poems on the Tarot*

One last word on the comparative success of some American
imagist poems, and the conspicuous *lack* of success of American attempts
to imitate the haiku: The haiku is, philosophically, an outgrowth of
Zen Buddhism. Haikus translated into English look infantile—too soft
and fluffy—to our Western eyes. This is largely because we do not
understand what the Zen poet is trying to do: He is attempting to put
himself into the place of the thing perceived—he is empathizing with
the object; more, he is trying to *become one* with the object, and thus
with all things.

In Western traditions, empathizing with objects is pathetic—we even
have a term called *pathetic fallacy* to describe it. Hence, most *American*
haikus are soft at the center. By our standards, that is.

But Williams' imagist dictum, "No ideas except in things," and
Eliot's *objective correlative* sever the observer from the perceived object,
though, at the same time, much of the *effect* of Zen empathy is preserved.
As a result, non-haiku imagist poems seem to work better for us than
pure haiku. The few decent American haikus that exist observe all the
dicta of the traditional haiku *except* the Zen root, for which objectivity
of perception has been substituted.

It is through this objectivity, finally, that the poet in English
achieves empathy—which is only a way of saying there is no such thing
as pure objectivity. Read William Carlos Williams' "The Red
Wheelbarrow" again for an example. *The first line is the key.*

As a final proof of the thesis that the Japanese forms are analogous
to imagist poetry in English, and specifically that the Japanese 5–7
syllable count is analogous to Williams' phrasal prosody, here is
a Williams poem as it was printed in *Poetry* magazine in 1916:

MARRIAGE

    So different, this man
And this woman:
A stream flowing
In a field.

> WILLIAM CARLOS WILLIAMS

If we rearrange the lines of this poem in syllables of 5–7–5, we discover
that the poem is a senryu, though Williams may not have known it:

                    So different, this
              man and this woman: a stream
                  flowing in a field.

Something similar happened during the writing of "The Dead Sailor"
(above). It was intended as the beginning of a longer poem. But when
the first stanza was written, there seemed to be no more to say. It
turned out, after some rearranging of syllables, to be an accidental
(spontaneous?) senryu.

The epigraph of William Heyen's poem and the poem itself perhaps
say better than anything else what we have been talking about:

THE RETURN

I will touch things and things and no more thoughts.

                                            ROBINSON JEFFERS

My boat slowed on the still water,
stopped in a thatch of lilies.
The moon leaned over the white lilies.

I waited for a sign, and stared
at the hooded water. On the far shore
brush broke, a deer broke cover.

I waited for a sign, and waited.
The moon lit the lilies to candles.
Their light reached down the water

to a dark flame, a fish: it hovered
under the pads, the pond held it
in its dim depths as though in amber.

Green, still, balanced in its own life,
breathing small breaths of light, this
was the world's oldest wonder, the arrow

of thought, the branch that all words
break against, the deep fire, the pure poise
of an object, the pond's presence, the pike.

                              WILLIAM HEYEN

And here are some other contemporary poems that use objects,
concrete things, to evoke ideas out of images:

SHORE FOG

On the cedars and yews
this morning

big drops
(as of rain)
held by finny hands
(but not rain):
fog kept the night all
night awake
and left this morning
in addition to these
big clarities
a close-worked white drift
too multiple to
prevent some dozing.

A. R. AMMONS

NAHANT

It is raining on the island; a summer rain that chases
up the stairs and along the porches and then drops
off silently under the mouths of iris.

MARGARET MACY

COUNTRY GRAVEYARD

Cows with eyes of buttered moons
doze along the barbed wire.

Weeds grow to impossible heights.

I call out my family names
across the campsites of stones:
Etter, Wakefield, McFee, Goodenow.

Cedar trees shake fat crows
from their ragged beards.

In the farmhouse back from the road
shades are drawn against noon sun
and grace is said before the meat.

I stand among these gravestones
where a wet-nosed wind coughs
gray dust on my pinching shoes.

The rusty bells of the brick church.

Goodenow, McFee, Wakefield, Etter.

DAVE ETTER

suggested writing assignment

Write three haikus consisting of a single image each, and including all of the elements described above, spareness, condensation, spontaneity, ellipsis, a seasonal element, and emotive utterance. Study the katauta carefully before you write.

13

OF SCHEMAS

A poem is an artifice of thought as well as of metrics, sonics, and tropes, and *there is no thought except in language.* A poem, like all literary genres, is an expression of the human condition. Poetry is a perception—of man and his universe—which the poet attempts to convey to an audience by means of language artifice; a perception that *must* be conveyed in words or symbols.

This chapter deals with the subject of words specifically in their grammatic and syntactic forms, as the chapters on metrics, sonics, and tropes dealt with words in their prosodic, aural, and sensory contexts.

Schemas have to do with changes in the normal order of words, and they may be subdivided into various kinds:

i. ORTHOGRAPHICAL SCHEMAS

Orthographical schemas have to do with single words and syllables.

PROSTHESIS adds syllables at the beginning of a word; i.e., "configuration" for *figuration*.

PROPARALEPSIS adds syllables at the end of a word; i.e., "figuration" for *figure*.

EPENTHIS adds syllables in the center of a word; i.e., "disenfigure" for *disfigure*.

Epenthis, proparalepsis, and *prosthesis* are methods of *expansion*.

APHAERESIS is a technique of overt elision which drops the initial unstressed syllable—usually a vowel—of a word; i.e., " 'til" for *until*, " 'tis" for *it is*, "let's" for *let us*.

APOCOPE drops syllables from the end of a word—"morn" for *morning;* see *apocopated rhyme*.

SYNCOPE is a technique of overt elision which drops a syllable from the center of a word; i.e., "suff'ring" for *suffering*.

SYNALEPHA is a technique of overt elision by means of which one of two adjacent unaccented vowels is suppressed in order to achieve the effect of only one unaccented syllable; i.e., "Th' art of poetic diction."

HYPHAERESIS is a technique of overt elision which drops a *consonant* from the center of a word in order to telescope two syllables and make them one, as in "Whene'er" for *whenever*.

Aphaeresis, apocope, hyphaeresis, synalepha, and *syncope* are methods of *contraction*. For more information about synalepha and syncope, see *elision* in Chap. 10.

AMPHISBAENIA turns a word backward to make another word, as in "He *mined* ore in *denim* cloth"; see *amphisbaenic rhyme*.

An ANAGRAM is a word, phrase, or sentence which is constructed by rearranging (*transposing*) the letters of another word, phrase, or sentence: "live"=*vile,* "stunted"=*student*.

ANTISTHECON changes the sound of a word; for instance, "stoont" for *student*.

DIAERESIS concerns the pronunciation of two contiguous vowels in different ways; i.e., "cooperation," "neologism."

DIALECTIC changes the spelling of a word, but not its meaning. Puttenham's examples are "evermare" for *evermore*, "wrang" for *wrong*, "gould" for *gold*, and so forth.

HOMOGRAPHS (*homomorphs*) are words that are spelled alike, but that have totally different meanings, such as *bore*: "to drill" and *bore*: "a dull person." "Homographic rhyme" is a form of *rich rhyme*.

HOMONYMS are words that sound alike, but that are spelled differently and have different meanings: *bear–bare, time–thyme*. "Homonymic rhyme" is a form of *rich rhyme*.

METATHESIS transposes the letters of a word—it is the process of the *anagram* (above).

A PALINDROME is a word, phrase, clause or larger unit that reads the same backwards as forward: "radar"=*radar*; "Able was I ere I saw Elba"=*Able was I ere I saw Elba*.

TMESIS is the breaking up of a compound word, usually by insertion of a related word; i.e., "When you ever go" in stead of *whenever you go*. This was a favorite technique of E. E. Cummings.

ii. CONSTRUCTIONAL SCHEMAS

PARALLELISM, which has been mentioned in several previous chapters, has to do with the coordinate balance of structures in a grammatic sequence of two or more words, phrases, or clauses. Whole prosodies have been built on parallelism. A *catalog* is a parallel series of nouns ("I saw *houses, dogs,* and *trees*"), or phrases ("A government *of the people, by the people,* and *for the people*"), or clauses ("*I came, I saw, I conquered*"), or any other parallel series of grammatic elements. The preceding sentence is itself a series of parallels.

SYNONYMIA is paraphrase in parallel structures ("I love you; *you are my beloved*").

SYNTHESIS is consequence in parallel structures ("I love you; *therefore, I am yours*").

ANTITHESIS is the opposition of ideas expressed in parallel structures ("I love you, and *I loathe you*").

AUXESIS is the building up, in parallel structures, of a catalog or series which ultimately closes at the *zenith* (high point) of the set (the *climax*): "I love your eyes, hair, breasts; I love the way you walk and speak; I love you."

MEIOSIS is the building up, in parallel structures, of a catalog or series which ultimately closes at the *nadir* (low point) of the set (the *anticlimax*): "We struggled through dense forests; we forded raging torrents; we battled the terrors of storm and starvation to reach the road; we took the bus home." In effect, the poet unbuilds to an anticlimax. Meiosis is often a technique of satire or self-derogation.

In "Pocoangelini 18" it would appear that the poem is building to a climax through repetition of the refrain "the gooneybird and the shrike," which would ordinarily end the poem climactically . . .

POCOANGELINI 18

Pocoangelini sings a song
about old men, girls, pantaloons bulging
with the horny wind, skindivers skun, beeswax,
and innumerable things with pseudopods wings,
etcetera: the waxworks of the world. His refrain?

the gooneybird and the shrike.

So let's have at it. He went out, stout
and brassbound, to see what's to see someplace,
anyplace (that's the place for him) and he ran
into one old man, a lass, a piece of scupper-
nong, three bales of babies all wailing, and of course,

> *the gooneybird and the shrike.*

And so he says to her, "So's your old
man. Human, that is. Put it to him, he'll
say so too." He did, Poco did, and you do
too, so what's the birdswot, hullabaloo? Hang him,
the old bugger, and the mother singing sweet songs, and

> *the gooneybird and the shrike.*

Poco tripped on his rope. "Deliver
me," the old man said. A bunch of guys with
grey suits, brown sacks, stamps, scales, labels and hatchets
came marching, eyeballs full of cold fire, delivered
him to Poco in forty small lots, together with

> *the gooneybird and the shrike.*

That's it. Angelini went walking,
found hay in the manger, the cattle cut
up, three camels delirious in a brand
new desert, Pharaoh smoking O.P.'s, *Brand X* myrrh
all over the place, planned obsolescent phoenixes,

> *the gooneybird and the shrike,*

and a big old sphinx grinning off
to herself someplace in a bunch of sand.

> from *Pocoangelini: A Fantography*

. . . but meiosis sets in, and the poem ends in a dying fall.
Kenneth Fearing's "Dirge" exemplifies all sorts of parallel
structures, including meiosis. It is a prose poem, but just when a catalog
or parallel series begins to threaten dullness, Fearing changes his
structures *and* his rhythms—this is in many ways a jazz poem. It's
a question whether the tolling of the bell at the end of the poem is
climactic or anticlimactic:

DIRGE

1–2–3 was the number he played but today the number came 3–2–1;
    bought his Carbide at 30 and it went to 29; had the favorite at Bowie but the
    track was slow—

O, executive type, would you like to drive a floating power, knee-action, silk-
    upholstered six? Wed a Hollywood star? Shoot the course in 58? Draw to
    the ace, king, jack?

O, fellow with a will who won't take no, watch out for three cigarettes on the same, single match; O, democratic voter born in August under Mars, beware of liquidated rails—

Denouement to denouement, he took a personal pride in the certain, certain way he lived his own, private life,
   but nevertheless, they shut off his gas; nevertheless, the bank foreclosed; nevertheless, the landlord called; nevertheless, the radio broke,

And twelve o'clock arrived just once too often, just the same he wore one grey tweed suit, bought one straw hat, drank one straight Scotch, walked one short step, took one long look, drew one deep breath,
   just one too many,

And wow he died as wow he lived,
   going whop to the office and blooie home to sleep and biff got married and bam had children and oof got fired,
   zowie did he live and zowie did he die,

With who the hell are you at the corner of his casket, and where the hell we going on the right hand silver knob, and who the hell cares walking second from the end with an American Beauty wreath from why the hell not,

Very much missed by the circulation staff of the New York Evening Post; deeply, deeply mourned by the B.M.T.,

Wham, Mr. Roosevelt; pow, Sears Roebuck; awk, big dipper; bop, summer rain; bong, Mr., bong, Mr., bong, Mr., bong.

KENNETH FEARING

CHIASMUS is cross-parallelism in parallel structures ("*I vied with the wind,* she fought the air / And as she lost, *I was victorious*").

SYNECIOSIS cross-couples *antonyms* (words that are antithetical in meaning) or opposites in such a way as to make them agree, as in the poem "November 22, 1963" in Chap. 20. (the italicized words are the antonyms):

> We are ourselves *victim* and *victor.*
> You were and are ourselves. In killing you
> we murder an emblem of what we strive
> to be: not men, but Man.

ISOCOLON is a term that designates *perfect parallelism*—that is, when parallel grammatic structures are of exactly the same number of words, or even syllables. The perfect parallel mentioned earlier was "A time to live, a time to die."
   Here is an accentual-syllabic poem that illustrates a number of

parallel constructions, not only grammatic, but stanzaic and sonic as well. Isolate as many kinds as possible:

STREET MEETING

> I saw him on the street.
>   His flesh was heavy.
> For years we had not met:
>   Time takes its levy,
> Returning ounce for hour.
>   But the eyes I'd known
> Had stayed the same though flesh constricted bone.
>
>   His eyes owned all the past—
>   I saw it staring,
>   Bewildered, not at rest,
>   Still full of daring,
> But fettered by the hoar
>   Of revolving clocks:
> A hurt, unlikely witch within its stocks.
>
>   I watched the troubled look
>   His face reflected
>   And knew he'd pick my lock
>   Had time defected.
> But each of us could hear
>   Wary sentries call
> And answer in the long, resounding hall.
>
>   We spoke in platitudes,
>   Each of us helpless,
>   The victims of our moods
>   And of our losses:
> The present was the heir
>   Of our common past.
> The future would inherit all at last.
>
>   We parted. Each of us
>   Had fanned an ember.
>   We'd shared another loss
>   And would remember.
> But time was still for hire:
>   He walked off, alone.
> When next we meet our prisons will have grown.

BRACHIOLOGA is the technique of separating words by pauses, usually indicated by means of punctuation, commas in particular (as in "The Weed Garden" on p. 146, where there is a catalog of herbs—

"feverfew, mouse-ear, / Sundew and cup-moss, tormentils"), but sometimes typographically by means of spaces, as in Pound's "In a Station of the Metro" on p. 146.

PARISON is construction by parallel clauses of equal weight, as in Chidiock Tichborn's "Elegy," written during the Renaissance on the evening of his execution. So far as we know, it is the only poem he ever wrote:

ELEGY: ON THE EVENING OF HIS EXECUTION

My prime of youth is but a frost of cares,
My feast of joy is but a dish of pain,
My crop of corn is but a field of tares,
And all my good is but vain hope of gain;
The day is past, and yet I saw no sun,
And now I live, and now my life is done.

My tale was heard and yet it was not told,
My fruit is fallen, and yet my leaves are green,
My youth is spent and yet I am not old,
I saw the world and yet I was not seen;
My thread is cut and yet it is not spun,
And now I live, and now my life is done.

I sought my death and found it in my womb,
I looked for life and saw it was a shade,
I trod the earth and knew it was my tomb,
And now I die, and now I was but made;
My glass is full, and now my glass is run,
And now I live, and now my life is done.

CHIDIOCK TICHBORNE

This poem illustrates parallel constructions and the trope of *paradox* as well, inasmuch as each pair of clauses contains an inherent contradiction which finally is nevertheless true. It is a metaphysical poem. In such a serious piece we even find the use of pun, as in the second-to-last line where the first "glass" is a drinking glass, and the second "glass" is an hourglass. If the pun is the "lowest form of humor" (which it is not), it is also a major device for heightening language.

Tichborne's poem illustrates SINATHRISMUS, too: "the heaping figure," according to Puttenham, or, as it has been called in the 20th century, the *catalog*. It is a listing of things in parallel, as in stanza six of "Fit the Eleventh" of *Odds Bodkin's Strange Thrusts and Ravels*, or as in much of Whitman's work or in Carl Sandburg's "Chicago":

CHICAGO

Hog Butcher for the World,
Tool Maker, Stacker of Wheat,
Player with Railroads and the Nation's Freight Handler;
Stormy, husky, brawling,
City of the Big Shoulders:

They tell me you are wicked and I believe them, for I have seen your painted
    women under the gas lamps luring the farm boys.
And they tell me you are crooked and I answer:
  Yes, it is true I have seen the gunman kill and go free to kill again.
And they tell me you are brutal and my reply is:
  On the faces of women and children I have seen the marks of wanton hunger.
And having answered so I turn once more to those who sneer at this my city, and
    I give them back the sneer and say to them:
Come and show me another city with lifted head singing so proud to be alive
    and coarse and strong and cunning.
Flinging magnetic curses amid the toil of piling job on job, here is a tall bold
    slugger set vivid against the little soft cities;
Fierce as a dog with tongue lapping for action, cunning as a savage pitted against
    the wilderness,
  Bareheaded,
  Shoveling,
  Wrecking,
  Planning,
  Building, breaking, rebuilding,
Under the smoke, dust all over his mouth, laughing with white teeth,
Under the terrible burden of destiny laughing as a young man laughs,
Laughing even as an ignorant fighter laughs who has never lost a battle,
Bragging and laughing that under his wrist is the pulse, and under his ribs the
    heart of the people,
                              Laughing!
Laughing the stormy, husky, brawling laughter of Youth, half-naked, sweating,
    proud to be Hog Butcher, Tool Maker, Stacker of Wheat, Player with
    Railroads and Freight Handler to the Nation.

                              CARL SANDBURG

Sandburg's poem has a *circular ending*: It circles back to the original
catalog of the first stanza. A *closed ending* is climactic: It builds to
a climax and stops. An *open ending* allows a poem to continue
reverberating even when it is done, as in the haiku.

HYPERBATON is a term that covers the various kinds of dislocation or
inversion of grammatic *syntax* (word order):

ANASTROPHE has to do with the inversion of normal word order ("Go I shall" for *I shall go*).

CACOSINTHETON is *anastrophe* misused, as in the Thomas Hardy poem on p. 117.

HYPALLAGE is an exchange of words in phrases or clauses. It was a technique E. E. Cummings used often. This disjuncture allows lines to work ambiguously on more than one associative level, and it is sometimes used humorously: "I smell a smile; will she rat on me?" instead of *I smell a rat; will she smile on me?* Here is a lyric revised through hypallage; it is *interlined*: The lines in normal print are the original version; the italicized lines are the revised version:

WORDS FOR WHITE WEATHER

for D. A. Levy

On a gross day, in a green month
On a green month, in a gross day,

once, a child was Summer's lover.
a child was once Summer's lover.

She, heavy with worlds, sent
She with worlds sent, heavy

the child bouquets of amber light. Giver
giver, the child light: bouquets of amber

and taker, she tossed him petals;
and she tossed him petals. Taker,

in good barter he gave his leman
he gave his good leman in barter

words shaped like flesh
flesh like shaped words

of fruits: sweet peach, tart lemon,
sweet of fruits: peach, lemon, tart

berryheart whose vine goes
vine whose berryheart goes

twining with grass. She gave
with grass. She gave twining

him this too: a grassblade made
too a grassblade, made him this

the frost's sickle, lush love
frost's love, the lush sickle

turned root rape, the maggot's
root turned the maggot's rape,

carnal slither. No matter. Her
no carnal matter. Her slither

kiss was decay. Still, his songs
was his still kiss. Songs decay

weather the winter.
the winter weather.

PARENTHESIS has to do with the insertion of material that interrupts the thought ("I was going—or have I told you this?—to go away"). We have already spoken of parenthetics, a prosody built on this foundation.

EPITHETON (*apposition*) is an inserted synonymous modification of a sentence element ("John Jones, *my good friend,* is a poet").

ANACOLUTHON is a shift of grammatic construction in mid-sentence which leaves the beginning unfinished ("You may remember the night—the dog is barking at the door").

HENDIADYS is a construction that treats a double subject or object as though it were singular, not plural, in order to express one thought that operates on more than one level ("My lust and her adamance is Hell").

HYSTERON PROTERON is the reversal of chronological events for purposes of intensification or stress ("Let us break our necks and jump" rather than *Let us jump and break our necks*).

ZEUGMA (to be distinguished from *zeugmatic syllepsis*) is a *yoking* or binding together of two parts of speech by means of another part. Three kinds of zeugma have been distinguished:

PROZEUGMA, in which the binding word precedes the parts it binds (the carat indicates the point at which the bond takes place: *"Everyone* wishes to come, and ∧ will do so, regardless"); MESOZEUGMA, in which the binding word is mediary between the yoked parts ("This is the place he *loved,* and the woman"); HYPOZEUGMA, in which the binding word follows the yoked parts ("Neither life ∧, nor death itself, need be *feared"*).

iii. EXCLUSIVE SCHEMAS

ELLIPSIS leaves out words and says something in a starker way than usual ("I love darkness" rather than *I am in love with darkness*). Ellipsis is an essential part of the haiku.

ASYNDETON, the opposite of *polysyndeton,* concerns the elimination of articles, conjunctions, and sometimes prepositions and pronouns, from normal grammatic constructions ("I chased [the] wind, [the] wind chased me").

APOSIOPESIS is the simple deletion of an important letter, syllable, word, or passage ("You can go to ****!").

SYLLEPSIS is of two kinds:

ELLIPTICAL SYLLEPSIS is a grammatical situation in which one part of speech controls two other elements, with only one of which it agrees ("She *kisses* me, and I, ∧ her"; i.e., "I *kiss* her"). ZEUGMATIC SYLLEPSIS is a part of speech correctly controlling two other elements, but controlling them in differing ways ("He *waited* with *mind* and *dagger* sharp").

iv. INCLUSIVE SCHEMAS

ENALLAGE changes the tense, gender, or number of some part of speech. In the following example, the masculine gender of the word *God* is changed to the feminine gender in the penultimate paragraph:

THE GUESTROOM

The Inhabitant must go around thinking of Death. Have at him, call him fool and scofflaw—he will think of Death.

There is a room where an old man lies dreaming of worms. In the moments of his eyes all the world is buried: its fables and laces are spread like table-cloths for his sons to walk on.

The feast is laid; he is watched.

He cannot stir without moving earth and water, he cannot sing without upsetting cities, he cannot tap his headboard with a hard white nail without bringing the heavens down, he cannot wink, for there would be avalanches. The Inhabitant dreams of Death, an old man who has many sons.

His daughters are the harvesters of worms. With their quick eyes they watch that there shall be no movement—no grain shall shift unless shifted by river or wind.

There will be life, they say, but life must have its color and shape, and the color we choose is brown, the shape vulgar and thin, a needle of flesh burrowing in flesh. There will be life, they say, but Death must have no mate.

Come with the Inhabitant to see the old man's stone. On it there are graven these words: *Le visage de mon Dieu est calme.*

His daughters have made his epitaph in their language, with their soft hands. They stand and watch in dark garments—no one may change their rune, for their god would tremble in Her fury.

The Inhabitant speaks of a guest who has many sons. His daughters stand on his mouth, weeping and weighting the earth.

from The Inhabitant

IRMUS is suspended sense. Not till the end of a passage does the reader fully understand what is being spoken of. In this example, the sense of the poem is suspended until the very last word:

A DEDICATION

                    If it is true that
"the sea worm is a decorated flute
            that pipes in the most ancient mode"—
            and if it is true, too, that
    "the salt content of mammalian blood
            is exactly equivalent
to the salinity of the oceans
at the time life emerged onto the land";

            and if it is true
that "man is the only mammal with a
        capacity for song," well, then,
            that explains why the baroque
    worm swims in our veins, piping, and why
        we dance to his measure inch by
equivocal inch. And it explains why
this song, even as it explains nothing.

MERISMUS expands upon a subject by particularizing each element of it; for instance, instead of saying, "I met an old acquaintance in the street," one might describe the situation in each particular of the meeting, as in "An Old Acquaintance" on p. 22.

PROLEPSIS expands upon a general statement, particularizing it and giving further information regarding it. In this example, the general statement is the initial brief sentence (italicized), and the rest of the paragraph is the enlargement:

THE KITCHEN

In the kitchen the dishwasher is eating the dishes. The Inhabitant listens to the current of digestion—porcelain being ground, silver wearing thin, the hum and bite of the machine.

His wife does not hear it—she is humming, not listening. But the Inhabitant is aware of movement in the cupboards, of the veriest motion—the castiron skillet undergoing metamorphosis, perhaps; becoming its name: the wives' *spider* spinning beneath the counter, weaving and managing, waiting for the doors to open.

Each cup has its voice, each saucer its ear, and the thin chant planes between the shelves, touching the timbres of glass and crystal as it passes. The gentleman listens, is touched to the bone by this plainsong—he feels his response in the marrow's keening.

But the women do not—neither the elder nor the child—sense the music their things make. Their lips move, a column of air rises like steam, and there is something in a minor key sliding along the wall, touching the face of a plastic clock, disturbing the linen calendar beside the condiments.

It is as though, the Inhabitant reflects, the women are spinning. It is as though, while he waits, they weave bindings among the rooms; as though the strands of tune were elements of a sisterhood of dishes, the ladies, the spider in the cabinet, even of the dishwasher, done now with its grinding, which contributes a new sound—a continuo of satiety—to the grey motet the kitchen is singing.

from *The Inhabitant*

Notice that this poem, like Sandburg's "Chicago," has a circular ending.

v. SUBSTITUTIVE SCHEMAS

ANTHIMERIA substitutes one part of speech for another—for example, a noun for a verb as in "The clock's chime *belfries* over the town," or as D. A. Levy does in the first line of this poem:

BOP FOR KIDDIES

i watermeloned down the lawn
and summersalts in season
a red balloon
a blue—a green
an orange one all
floating skyward
with childrens dreams tied

D. A. LEVY

A similar thing happens in line two, where *somersaults* is deliberately misspelled.

ANTONOMASIA substitutes for a noun a phrase that is descriptive of the noun. The descriptive phrase is derived from some quality associated with the noun. For instance, instead of saying "Queen Elizabeth I," we might (and often do) say, "The Virgin Queen."

HYPERBOLE is calculated exaggeration ("Her eyes were as big as moons"), as in Fearing's "Dirge" on p. 176.

IMPLIED APOSIOPESIS substitutes another letter, syllable, word, or passage for the dropped material ("You are an as-*phyxiating* person").

LITOTES, the reverse of hyperbole, is studied understatement ("Her eyes were eyes, and they were open") or,

BURNING THE NEWS

The fire is eating
the paper. The child who drowned
is burned. Asia is in flames.
As he signs his great
bill, a minister of state chars

at the edges and curls
into smoke. The page rises,
glowing, over our neighbor's
roof. In the kitchens
clocks turn, pages turn like grey wings,

slowly, over armchairs.
Another child drowns, a bill
is signed, and the pen blackens.
The smoke of Asia
drifts among the neighbors like mist.

It is a good day for burning.
The fire is eating the news.

METALEPSIS substitutes for a word a synonym that is essentially metaphorical, in that the equation between the word and its synonym is not obvious. For instance, "I met Ray just as he first thumbed / the last of thirteen buttons," instead of *I met Ray on the day he enlisted in the Navy*. Out of context the line seems farfetched. In a way, it *is* farfetched, and, in fact, Puttenham called this the "figure of the farfetched."

METONYMY is a way of describing by using a word related to a word, rather than the original word itself ("The *heart* will find a way" rather than "*Love* will find a way").

PARADIASTOLE substitutes for a word an antonym rather than a synonym, to ironic effect; as for instance, if we were speaking of a cheapskate we might say, "Skinflint is *generous* to a fault," or, of a coward, "He *bravely* rose in battle and ran away."

PERIPHRASIS is a way of saying something in a more grandiloquent or roundabout way than is usual ("She was taken unto the bosom of her forebears," rather than *she died*).

PROSONOMASIA is a way of nicknaming someone by substituting a letter or letters in his name to describe him by some personal characteristic; as, for instance, if a very thin man were named "Jones," we might substitute a *B* for the *J* and call him *Bones*.

SYNECHDOCHE describes by substituting a part for the whole, as in "He was the King's legs" rather than, *He was the King's messenger*.

vi. REPETITIONAL SCHEMAS

ANADIPLOSIS is the linking of two consecutive verses or stanzas by a repetition of words ("I saw her hair, / *Her* dark *hair* windblown").

ANAPHORA is the parallel repetition of a beginning word or phrase in the beginnings of succeeding lines of verse, as in Christopher Smart's poem on p. 35, where each line begins with the word *for*.

ANTANACLASIS is the witty repetition of a word in an amplified or changed sense—pun. In this poem, the pun is in the word *calming*, which reappears changed twice after its initial appearance in a phrase that otherwise doesn't change—in other words, in a phrase that is an incremental refrain (see *sonics*):

BALSAMUM APOPLECTICUM*

"Take the distill'd Oil of Cinnamon,
Cloves, Lavender, Lemons,
Marjoram, Mint, Rue, Rosemary"
[if you would enjoy a calming down],

"Sage, Rhodium, and Wormwood, of each
12 drops; of Amber, 6
drops; Bitumen Judaicum,
2 drams; Oil of Nutmegs by Expression, 1

"ounce; Balsam of *Peru*, as much as
is sufficient to make
all together into a smooth
Balsam" [if you would enjoy a coming

* Quincy, John, *Pharmacopoeia Officinalis Extemporanea, Or, A Complete English Dispensatory, in Four Parts*. London: Thomas Longman, at the Ship in Paternoster-Row, 1742, pp. 504–505.

down]. "This warms and enlivens the Nerves
being either smell'd to
or rubbed upon the Temples, or
any other convenient Part" [a

convening Part, unlike the Temples];
"it does much good also
to paralytic Limbs, by rubbing
them well with it. It has been in

"mighty Esteem and Fashion to wear
it in little Ivory Boxes
and Cane Heads; but it has in such
respects given place to more modish

"Contrivances" [couches, capsules]. "In
Distempers of the Head
and Nerves it is likewise directed
to be given inwardly from

"3 to 6 drops in a Bole or
Electuary." [If,
indeed, after Visions, Love, and
Hours, you would enjoy a common Down].

The above poem is an example of *found poetry*—poetry discovered
in a place where one would never expect it to be—in this case, in an
18th-century pharmacist's reference book. The poem has not been
plagiarized—that is, stolen from its author: credit is given. One can give
credit in many ways: in a footnote, as in this poem; in a headnote, or in
an epigraph or title. Work that is in copyright, however, must not only
carry a credit line of some kind, but the person who uses another person's
copyrighted work must secure permission from the author or from the
copyright holder as well.

ANTIMETABOLE is the repetition of two beginning words, in
reverse order, later in a verse or sentence ("To *kiss her* is to love *her
kiss*").

ANTISTROPHE repeats a single word throughout a poem—
particularly an *end-word,* as in the French *sestina*: The six end-words of
the first stanza reappear—in a *particular order* required by the form—
as the end-words of the following stanzas, *and* as *both* end-words and
buried words *in a particular order* in the final stanza, which is called
the *envoy* in all French forms (an *envoy* is a coda half-stanza):

AFTER THE TRIAL

Hearing the judges' well-considered sentence,
The prisoner saw long plateaus of guilt,

And thought of all the dismal furnished rooms
The past assembled, the eyes of parents
Staring through walls as though forever
To condemn and wound his innocence.

And if I raise my voice, protest my innocence,
The judges won't revoke their sentence.
I could stand screaming in this box forever,
Leaving them deaf to everything but guilt;
All the machinery of law devised by parents
Could not be stopped though fire swept the rooms.

Whenever my thoughts move to all those rooms
I sat alone in, capable of innocence,
I know now I was not alone, that parents
Always were there to speak the hideous sentence:
"You are our son; be good; we know your guilt;
We stare through walls and see your thoughts forever."

Sometimes I wished to go away forever;
I dreamt of strangers and of stranger rooms
Where every corner held the light of guilt.
Why do the judges stare? I saw no innocence
In them when they pronounced the sentence;
I heard instead the believing voice of parents.

I can remember evenings when my parents,
Settling my future happily forever,
Would frown before they spoke the sentence:
"Someday the time will come to leave these rooms
Where, under our watchful eyes, you have been innocent;
Remember us before you seize the world of guilt."

Their eyes burn. How can I deny my guilt
When I am guilty in the sight of parents?
I cannot think that even they were innocent.
At least I shall not have to wait forever
To be escorted to the silent rooms
Where darkness promises a final sentence.

We walk forever to the doors of guilt,
Pursued by our own sentences and eyes of parents,
Never to enter innocent and quiet rooms.

WELDON KEES

ECHOICS have been covered in the chapter "Of Sonics."

EMPHASIS reinforces a word. It may be done in several ways—by repetition ("He was dumb, dumb, dumb"); by using a different typeface, such as italics ("He was *dumb*"); by building a series of synonyms

("He was dumb—I mean, he was ignorant, stupid, and otherwise thick"); and so forth.

EPANALEPSIS is the repetition of a word, for clarity or for emphasis, after the intervention of a word, phrase, or clause; specifically, in verse, to end a line, stanza, or poem with the same word or words with which it began. The Welsh bards called this *dunadh,* and certain forms, such as the *rondeau* and the *roundel,* require this kind of repetition:

LONELY HEARTS

A sad old sot will advertise
His need of helpmeet, hoping not
To be in every damsel's eyes
    A sad old sot

Who cannot share the young bride's lot
With ardor and with enterprise
Enough to keep the love-flame hot.

His new wife soon will agonize
For handsome lads she might have got
When, there beside her passion, lies
    A sad old sot.

Loring Williams

EPANODIS, like *prolepsis* (see under *inclusive schemas*), expands upon a general statement, but in addition it repeats terms contained *in* the general statement. For example, in "The Kitchen" (above), the last paragraph picks up terms from the original general statement and expands upon them in a circular ending: *Dishes, dishwasher,* and *kitchen.*

EPIMONE is the term that covers the use of repeated lines used at intervals within a poem: *repeton, repetend, refrain, incremental refrain, burden,* and *chorus* (see Chap. 10, "Of Sonics").

CHANT OF SEASONS

What may one do when springtime's come—
    When springtime's come,
But welcome it unquestioning
As every bride accepts her ring?
    Ask any groom: the future's dumb;
    The present is the vocal thing
        When springtime's come.

What can one know when summer's here—
   When summer's here,
Besides the fact that sun is sun
And that the world is overrun
  By surging life: no thin veneer,
  But deep? Too deep to be undone
   When summer's here.

What of the time when fall's returned—
   When fall's returned?
Then listen to the wind and leaves
During the night: the day deceives.
  Beyond the frosts there is discerned
  The womb within which death conceives,
   When fall's returned.

What's to be done when winter's loose,
   When winter's loose?
Sense then the sharpened stars and know
The bold immensity of snow;
  Grant bone a glimpse of the abstruse
  Finis that it must undergo. . . .
   When winter's loose.

    EPIPHORA is the repetition of end-words or end-phrases specifically
—see Weldon Kees' sestina "After the Trial" above under antistrophe.
    EPIZEUXIS repeats a word without any pause between, as in
Kipling's dialect poem:

SOLDIER, SOLDIER

"Soldier, soldier come from the wars,
 Why don't you march with my true love?"
"We're fresh from off the ship, an' 'e's maybe give the slip,
 An' you'd best go look for a new love."
   New love! True love!
   Best go look for a new love,
   The dead they cannot rise, an' you'd better dry your eyes,
   An' you'd best go look for a new love.

"Soldier, soldier come from the wars,
 What did you see o' my true love?"
"I see 'im serve the Queen in a suit o' rifle green,
 An' you'd best go look for a new love."

"Soldier, soldier come from the wars,
 Did ye see no more o' my true love?"
"I see 'im runnin' by when the shots begun to fly—
 But you'd best go look for a new love."

"Soldier, soldier come from the wars,
  Did aught take 'arm to my true love?"
"I couldn't see the fight, for the smoke it lay so white—
  An' you'd best go look for a new love."

"Soldier, soldier come from the wars,
  I'll up an' tend to my true love!"
" 'E's lying on the dead with a bullet through 'is 'ead,
  An' you'd best go look for a new love."

"Soldier, soldier come from the wars,
  I'll lie down an' die with my true love!"
"The pit we dug'll 'ide 'im an' twenty men beside 'im—
  An' you'd best go look for a new love."

"Soldier, soldier come from the wars,
  Do you bring no sign from my true love?"
"I bring a lock of 'air that 'e allus used to wear,
  An' you'd best go look for a new love."

"Soldier, soldier come from the wars,
  O them I know it's true I've lost my true love!"
"An' I tell you truth again—when you've lost the feel o' pain
  You'd best take me for your true love."
      True love! New love!
      Best take 'im for a new love.
      The dead they cannot rise, an' you'd better dry your eyes,
      An' you'd best take 'im for your true love.

                                        RUDYARD KIPLING

    HYPOZEUXIS is the repetition of words in parallel constructions.
The repeated words govern the sense of the clause or clauses of which
they are a part ("Up to *the door* I'll go, and at *the door* I'll rap, /
Whether or not the man I seek is lying in his nap").
    PLOCE is the repetition of words or phrases at irregular intervals
throughout a stanza, poem, or long passage:

POCOANGELINI 4

Pocoangelini asked,
      Why do you sit
sailing your eyes out to sea?

Are they pushing you off
      your green silk island?
They're pushing me, too.

Little ragamuffin,
    sunskin ragamuffin,
have you no place to go?

    Neither have I.

    Then come with me, come with me—
The moon is an almond, and the stars
    are cherries waiting to be picked

from *Pocoangelini: A Fantography*

POLYPTOTON is the repeating of words derived from the same root ("He *ran,* will *run,* and is *running* now").

POLYSYNDETON is the repetition of conjunctions—the opposite of *asyndeton* (see *exclusive schemas*), and is to be distinguished from *anaphora* (above).

SYMPLOCE is a combination of *anaphora* or *antistrophe,* and *epiphora.*

suggested writing assignment

A) Write a ten-line accentual-syllabic poem that utilizes a refrain. Choose any form you wish, provided only that the form requires a refrain. In your poem use some of the schemas, and in a headnote tell which ones you are using.

B) *Invent a prosody* based on one or more of the schemas. Write a ten-line poem in the prosody you invent. In a headnote, explain what it is you are doing.

14

PODIC
PROSODIES

There are a number of prosodies we have not yet covered. *Dipodics* is one of them. The term means *two-foot*, but it might better be called *two-beat,* because it is actually an accentual prosody and not accentual-syllabic. Dipodics is a "folk meter", and is often found in nursery rhymes and ballads. However, many literary poets such as John Skelton in the early Renaissance, Robert Burns, and such contemporaries as John Crowe Ransom, Theodore Roethke, and Ralph Hodgson have used it succesfully.

Dipodics is a prosody that is halfway toward being an accentual-syllabic prosody. In fact, since it often uses rhyme, most people think it *is* accentual-syllabic, and the meter seems baffling to them when they attempt to scan it.

In a way, dipodics is a holdover in folk poetry of the old Anglo-Saxon line. After Chaucer, but before the Renaissance consolidation of the medieval invention of accentual-syllabic verse, balladeers, Scots poets and others (see the plate "The Literary Languages of Britain", p. 208) continued to hear the ancient alliterative hemistich and echoic devices, so they continued to write using the old prosody, but they added true rhyme and stanzaic forms.

This last addition—stanzas—truly *was* a new thing. The old poetry of the Angles, Saxons, and Jutes was oral—it wasn't written down.

Eventually, people *did* put some of the old poems on paper, but when
they did so, they wrote them out in *prose* form: The manuscripts in
which these poems survive do not contain stanzas. Much later, when
poetry had begun to become a literary rather than a spoken thing, editors
broke the prose up into stichs—or *lines*—and stanzas.

Hence, much of the folk poetry of the late Middle Ages, and even
into the Renaissance and beyond, are stanzaic poems written in podic
verse. And, to reiterate, podic prosodies are accentual.

The dipodic line, like the hemistich of Anglo-Saxon prosody,
contains two accented syllables. These are all that are counted—the
unaccented syllables are ignored. The first accent is often a secondary
stress (·); the second is a primary (or *heavy*) stress (/). Sometimes there
were variations in this pattern—as there were in Anglo-Saxon prosody.
We will discuss these variations shortly.

Normally, two dipodic lines (one stich) form a *half-unit* of dipodic
verse, and two more hemistichs (again, one stich) are needed to complete
the unit (a couplet), which is rhymed, often with falling rhymes
(feminine endings):

> Óld Mother Goóse,
>
> When she wánted to wánder,
>
> Róde through the áir
>
> On a véry fine gánder.

To put it as simply as possible, a dipodic unit is nothing more than
a couplet made of two rhyming stichs of Anglo-Saxon prosody. The
caesura between hemistichs became the ends of lines 1 and 3, so that
the couplet appears on paper as a quatrain. A whole set of stanzas of
the family called *common measure* and *ballad stanza* grew up out of
this accentual quatrain—many hymns are written in various kinds
of common measure, and Emily Dickinson, among others, used these
stanza forms.

If we were to reconstruct the couplet form from which this quatrain
was derived, it would look like this:

> Óld Mother Goóse, · When she wánted to wánder,
>
> Róde through the áir · On a véry fine gánder.

Sometimes, indeed, the lines still are written out in couplet form:

There was an old wóman · who lived in a shóe.

She had *só* many chíldren · she didn't know *whát* to do.

Notice that there is *rhetorical stress* on "so" and on "what" in the second line of this rhyme.

Though dipodics added rhyme, it did not necessarily keep the alliteration of Anglo-Saxon prosody, especially not in every line, but the poetry did depend heavily on sonic devices.

J. R. R. Tolkien, in his "Prefatory Remarks" to J. P. Clark's translation of *Beowulf**, isolated six basic hemistichs in Anglo-Saxon prosody, and these basic half-lines have been retained in many dipodic poems:

1) The *double-fall* ($/\smile||/\smile$), as in

   Místress Máry,
   Quíte contráry

2) The *double-rise* ($\smile/||\smile/$), as in

   With sílver bélls
   And cóckle shélls

3) The *rise-and-fall* ($\smile/||/\smile$), as in

   The twó gréy kíts

4) The *rise-and-descend* ($//|·\smile$), as in

   Mý maíd Máry

5) The *fall-and-ascend* ($//|\smile·$), as in

   Tó woó the ówl

6) The *descend-and-rise* ($//|\smile/$), as in

   Hárk! Hárk! the lárk!

* London: Allen and Unwin, 1941.

Of course, in dipodics there are many more rhythmic variations than just these basic Anglo-Saxon measures.

THE LARK

Hark! Hark! The lark!
How he doth spark!
To woo the owl
The lark must howl.
Hark! Hark! The lark!

Hark! Hark! The lark!
How he doth spark!
To woo the squirrel
The lark must whirl.
Hark! Hark! The lark!

Hark! Hark! The lark!
How he doth spark!
To woo the giraffe
The lark mustn't laugh.
Hark! Hark! The lark!

Hark! Hark! The lark!
How he doth spark!
To woo the snake
The lark must shake.
Hark! Hark! The lark!

Hark! Hark! The lark!
How he doth spark!
To woo the elephant
The lark must bell a runt.
Hark! Hark! The lark!

Hark! Hark! The lark!
How he doth spark!
To woo the worm
The lark must squirm.
Hark! Hark! The lark!

Hark! Hark! The lark!
How he doth spark!
Too woo hippopotamus
The lark must turn platypus.
Hark! Hark! The lark!

Hark! Hark! The lark!
How he doth spark!
Would you go on?

Make up your own.
Hark! Hark! The lark!

Skeltonics, or "tumbling verse," is insistently rhymed dipodics:

UPON A DEAD MAN'S HEAD

That was sent to him from an honourable gentlewoman for a token,
Skelton, Laureate, devised this ghostly meditation in English, covenable,
in sentence, commendable, lamentable, lacrimable, profitable for the soul.

Your ugly token
My mind hath broken
From worldly lust:
For I have discust
We are but dust,
And die we must.
    It is general
To be mortal:
I have well espied
No man may him hide
From Death hollow-eyed,
With sinews wyderéd,
With bones shyderéd,
With his worm-eaten maw,
And his ghastly jaw
Gasping aside,
Naked of hide,
Neither flesh nor fell.
    Then, by my counsel,
Look that ye spell
Well this gospel:
For whereso we dwell
Death will us quell,
And with us mell.
    For all our pampered paunches
There may no fraunchis,
Nor worldly bliss,
Redeem us from this:
Our days be dated
To be checkmated
With draughtes of death
Stopping our breath:
Our eyen sinking,
Our bodies stinking,
Our gummes grinning,
Our soules brinning.

To whom, then, shall we sue,
For to have rescue,
But to sweet Jesu
On us then for to rue?
  O goodly Child
Of Mary mild,
Then be our shield!
That we be not exiled
To the dyne dale
Of bootless bale,
Nor to the lake
Of fiendes black.
  But grant us grace
To see thy Face,
And to purcháse
Thine heavenly place,
And thy paláce
Full of soláce
Above the sky
That is so high;
Eternally
To behold and see
The Trinity!
  Amen.

Myrres vous y. *

JOHN SKELTON

Odds Bodkin's Strange Thrusts and Ravels, in the chapter on *Satirics,* is written in skeltonics.

The modern poet John Crowe Ransom has used dipodics in very sophisticated ways:

BELLS FOR JOHN WHITESIDE'S DAUGHTER

There was such speed in her little body,
And such lightness in her footfall,
It is no wonder her brown study
Astonishes us all.

Her wars were bruited in our high window.
We looked among orchard trees and beyond
Where she took arms against her shadow,
Or harried unto the pond

* View yourself therein.

The lazy geese, like a snow cloud
Dripping their snow on the green grass,
Tricking and stopping, sleepy and proud,
Who cried in goose, Alas,

For the tireless heart within the little
Lady with rod that made them rise
From their noon apple-dreams and scuttle
Goose-fashion under the skies!

But now go the bells, and we are ready,
In one house we are sternly stopped
To say we are vexed at her brown study,
Lying so primly propped.

JOHN CROWE RANSOM

The last line in each stanza of Ransom's poem is *tripodic.* Other prosodies besides dipodics, based on other numbers of beats in each line, can be and have been devised. A one-beat prosody would be *monopodics,* three-beat, *tripodics,* and so on. If there were no caesura in the four-beat dipodic line, it would be *tetrapodics,* and a five-beat system would be *pentapodics.*

The following poem mixes tripodics and dipodics also, but the primary stress-count is three rather than two as in Ransom's poem:

ODDS BODKIN'S SPRINGSONG

In the sweet spring the cuckoo
beaks his tune in the greenwood,
                    warbles of nestings.
                    His fellow nestlings
starve as the old birds brood,

and I recall my borning,
my breeding and my calling.
                    I, Odds Bodkin—
                    oddest of odd kin—
remember the fledglings falling

out of the nest that bred me,
waning as I went waxing
                    timber and tackle,
                    great as a grackle,
sleek as any waxwing.

Ah, my youth was sterling!
My foster folk went starveling
                    to stanch my hunger;
                    they grew no younger
over their little starling

Until I grew so monstrous
the nest could not contain me.
                    I packed my kerchief
                    full of mischief—
no sorrows could constrain me.

There's many a nest I've lain in,
and many a housewren singing
                    over many a fledgling
                    I've had a hand in
hatching till I've gone winging.

Those nests are all blown over,
I'm old and draggle-feathered.
                    Now what I ponder
                    as I may wander
is what it is I've fathered:

I've sired a choir of echoes
that comes alive in Maytime.
                    I've made a rimesong
                    that goes on timelong
to company my greytime.

Therefore I toast the homebird—
my lifelong enemy—
                    his nesting wildwood,
                    his nestlings' childhood,
and wish him all my envy.

    This Lindsay poem mixes line-lengths, too; so much so that it
ought to be termed *variable-podics*:

JOHN BROWN

    *(To be sung by a leader and chorus, the leader singing the body of
the poem, while the chorus interrupts with the question)*

I've been to Palestine.
    What did you see in Palestine?
I saw the ark of Noah—
It was made of pitch and pine.
I saw old Father Noah
Asleep beneath his vine.
I saw Shem, Ham and Japhet
Standing in a line.
I saw the tower of Babel
In the gorgeous sunrise shine—

By a weeping willow tree
Beside the Dead Sea.

I've been to Palestine.
    What did you see in Palestine?
I saw abominations
And Gadarene swine.
I saw the sinful Canaanites
Upon the shewbread dine,
And spoil the temple vessels
And drink the temple wine.
I saw Lot's wife, a pillar of salt
Standing in the brine—
By a weeping willow tree
Beside the Dead Sea.

I've been to Palestine.
    What did you see in Palestine?
Cedars on Mount Lebanon,
Gold in Ophir's mine,
And a wicked generation
Seeking for a sign,
And Baal's howling worshippers
Their god with leaves entwine.
And . . .
I saw the war-horse ramping
And shake his forelock fine—
By a weeping willow tree
Beside the Dead Sea.

I've been to Palestine.
    What did you see in Palestine?
Old John Brown.
Old John Brown.
I saw his gracious wife
Dressed in a homespun gown.
I saw his seven sons
Before his feet bow down.
And he marched with his seven sons,
His wagons and goods and guns,
To his campfire by the sea,
By the waves of Galilee.

I've been to Palestine.
    What did you see in Palestine?
I saw the harp and psalt'ry
Played for Old John Brown.
I heard the ram's horn blow,
Blow for Old John Brown.

I saw the Bulls of Bashan—
They cheered for Old John Brown.
I saw the big Behemoth—
He cheered for Old John Brown.
I saw the big Leviathan—
He cheered for Old John Brown.
I saw the Angel Gabriel
Great power to him assign.
I saw him fight the Canaanites
And set God's Israel free.
I saw him when the war was done
In his rustic chair recline—
By his campfire by the sea
By the waves of Galilee.

I've been to Palestine.
    What did you see in Palestine?
Old John Brown.
Old John Brown.
And there he sits
To judge the world.
His hunting-dogs
At his feet are curled.
His eyes half-closed,
But John Brown sees
The ends of the earth,
The Day of Doom.
And his shot-gun lies
Across his knees—
Old John Brown.
Old John Brown.

Vachel Lindsay

In analyzing a poem, *keep your mind open*. Simply look at the poem and describe what you see. Whatever you perceive in the way of an *organizing principle* is its *prosody*. That prosody may be unique, or it may be traditional, but every successful poem has its prosody. Every unsuccessful poem has a prosody too, but the poet's use of his material has failed.

Let's analyze W. B. Yeats' "Crazy Jane and the Bishop":

CRAZY JANE AND THE BISHOP

Bring me to the blasted oak
That I, midnight upon the stroke,
(*All find safety in the tomb.*)

May call down curses on his head
Because of my dear Jack that's dead.
Coxcomb was the least he said:
The solid man and the coxcomb.

Nor was he Bishop when his ban
Banished Jack the Journeyman,
(*All find safety in the tomb.*)
Nor so much as parish priest,
Yet he, an old book in his fist,
Cried that we lived like beast and beast:
The solid man and the coxcomb.

The Bishop has a skin, God knows,
Wrinkled like the foot of a goose,
(*All find safety in the tomb.*)
Nor can he hide in holy black
The heron's hunch upon his back,
But a birch-tree stood my Jack:
The solid man and the coxcomb.

Jack had my virginity,
And bids me to the oak, for he
(*All find safety in the tomb.*)
Wanders out into the night
And there is shelter under it,
But should that other come, I spit:
The solid man and the coxcomb.

W. B. YEATS

i.   The Typographical Level

Prosody. By simply looking at the poem, we can see that it is *stanzaic*, and all lines are relatively of the same length, so it is probably *metrical* as well (accentual, syllabic, or accentual-syllabic). Each stanza is of seven lines, so the poem is written in *septets*. Therefore, it is obviously a *verse mode* poem, rather than a *prose mode* poem.

ii.   The Sonic Level

Since we have already decided this is a verse mode poem, it is likely that the prosody will be based on the sonic level.

If we scan the first few lines, it becomes obvious that there is some kind of meter operating: there are four beats in each line except the 4th, which has five, and the 7th, which is either three-beat or four-beat, depending upon how we pronounce "coxcomb"—

cóxcómb or cóxcŏmb.

So the poem is *tetra*-something. Here is my scansion of the first stanza:

1. $//\smile\smile/\smile/$
2. $\smile//\smile\smile/\smile/$
3. $/\smile/\smile/\smile/$
4. $\smile/\cdot/\smile\cdot\smile/$
5. $\smile/\smile/\smile/\smile/$
6. $//\smile\smile/\smile/$
7. $\smile/\smile\cdot\smile\smile//$

We can see that iambs predominate, but the only thing that actually stays relatively standard is the beat. There are four beats to the line. Thus, this is basically an *accentual* poem, not an accentual-syllabic poem (the syllable count varies between seven and eight). In fact, it is *tetrapodic,* not dipodic; there is no regular caesura in the center of the line to divide each line into hemistichs. This means that the poem is built, like dipodics, on a prosody halfway between straight accentuals and accentual-syllabics. It is too regular to be the former, not regular enough to be the latter.

Sonic Devices. The poem is rhymed: *aabcccb*. It also uses two refrains, both rhyming *b*. To show that they are refrain rhymes, we will capitalize the rhyme, *B*; and, to tell the refrains apart, we will call the first refrain *B¹* and the second *B²*, so the poem really rhymes *aaB¹cccB²*. Except for the refrains, the rhymes change in each stanza. Therefore, the second stanza rhymes *ddB¹eeeB²*, and so forth.

Unlike dipodics, in this poem all rhymes are *masculine*. Most rhymes are true, but the refrains *consonate*—they are off-rhymes.

There is much alliteration: *b*'s in the 1st line, hard *c*'s in the 4th, *d*'s in the 5th; lots of assonance: long *i*'s in the 2nd line, short *o*'s in the 7th. There is head-cross-rhyming in lines 3 and 4: *All* and *call*.

Obviously, the poem is some kind of *lyric*.

iii. The Sensory Level

In the first stanza there is very little complication of imagery. The tropes are of the simplest kind, descriptions, mostly, e.g., *blasted oak*. In the rest of the poem there is simile, as in stanza two ("like beast and beast"), or four ("like the foot of a goose"). Now and then there is a metaphor, as in stanza three ("But a birch tree stood my Jack"). Basically, the poem depends on the sonic level.

iv.   The Ideational Level

A) What does the poem say? If we isolate the *theme,* it might be put thus: "I mourn my lover, Jack."

B) The schemas of the poem are quite simple. Basically, the poem operates by means of simple statements in sentences. Each stanza is end-stopped, so each is also a paragraph. There is *parenthesis;* i.e., the *B¹* refrain breaks up a sentence in each stanza. The *B²* refrain is climactic and in parallel with the statement of each stanza.

v.   The Fusion

   "Crazy Jane and the Bishop" is a tetrapodic lyric on the subject of love and its loss. It is a *madsong,* as is "Odds Bodkin's Springsong," which is written in the form called *madsong stanza.*

suggested writing assignment

   Write a dipodic poem of twenty lines, or two poems of ten lines each, one of which is dipodic, the other in some other podic prosody. Use rhyme and as much sound as will make for a good lyric. In a headnote (or headnotes) describe your prosody (or prosodies) and the sonic devices you are using.

15

POETIC VOICE

In every single one of the poems you have written so far, someone
has been speaking. Who? Have you, the poet, been speaking from your
own particular point-of-view? Does the word *I* appear in your poems?
Have you been speaking about yourself? If so, you have been using the
egopoetic point-of-view, as in this poem:

AN ORDINARY EVENING IN CLEVELAND

I

Just so it goes: the day, the night—
what have you. There is no one on TV;
        shadows in the tube, in the street.
In the telephone there are echoes and mumblings
        the buzz of hours falling thru wires.

And hollow socks stumbling across
the ceiling send plaster dust sifting down
        hourglass walls. Felix the cat has
been drawn on retinas with a pencil of light.
        I wait grey, small in my cranny,

        for the cardboard tiger on the
kitchen table to snap me, shredded, from
        the bowl.

209

II

Over the trestle go
the steel beetles grappled tooth-and-tail—over and
over and over there smokestacks

lung tall hawkers into the sky's
spittoon. The street has a black tongue: do you
hear him, Mistress Alley, wooing
you with stones? There are phantoms in that roof's trousers;
they kick the wind. The moon, on a

ladder, is directing traffic
now. You can hardly hear his whistle. The
oculist's jeep wears horn rim wind
shields the motor wears wires on its overhead valves—
grow weary, weary, sad siren,

you old whore. It's time to retire.

III

The wail of the child in the next room quails
like a silverfish caught in a
thread. It is quiet now. The child's sigh rises to
flap with a cormorant's grace through

the limbo of one lamp and a
slide-viewer in your fingers: I cannot
get thin enough for light to shine
my color in your eyes; there is no frame but this for
the gathering of the clan. Words

will stale the air. Come, gather up
our voices in the silent butler and
pour them into the ashcan of
love. Look, my nostrils are dual flues; my ears are
the city dump; my eyes are the

very soul of trash; my bitter
tongue tastes like gasoline in a ragged
alley.

IV

The child cries again. Sounds
rise by the riverflats like smoke or mist in time's
bayou. We are sewn within seines

of our own being, thrown into
menaces floating in shadows, taken
without volition like silver
fish in an undertow down the river, down time
and smog of evenings.

V

The child cries.

VI

Do you hear the voice made of wire?
Do you hear the child swallowed by carpets,
    the alley eating the city,
rustling newsprint in the street begging moonlight with
    a tin cup and a blindman's cane?

VII

The lamps are rheumy in these tar
avenues. Can you sense the droppings of
    flesh falling between walls falling,
the burrowings of nerves in a cupboard of cans?
    Can you hear the roar of the mouse?

VIII

There is nothing but the doorway
sighing; here there is nothing but the wind
    swinging on its hinges, a fly
dusty with silence and the house on its back buzzing
    with chimneys, walking on the sky

like a blind man eating fish in an empty room.

Or, have you been talking *about* someone or something else
primarily? Perhaps the word "I" appears, but it is of something external
you have been speaking, rather than internal as in egopoesy. Have you
been telling a story about someone else? Or have you been telling your
own story, but telling it objectively rather than subjectively, as in
egopoesy? Do the words "he" and "she" appear often? If so, you have
been using the narrative point-of-view, as the poet does in this poem:

RACEWAY

My raceway of sheets last night became
a cool trotter, unwinding with grace. Today,
    autumn peeps imponderably out of
        the soggy drought July had posted
        on the foothills. It is August

    here in Saratoga; the races
open tomorrow. Yesterday a filly
    worked out her own odds, snapping two of her
        ankles while we watched. She was done in
        by a green syringe. She lounged on

the turf, staring from one farthest eye,
both her forehooves angled like ballerina
   slippers. With her, summer has staggered: it,
      too, soon will drop and the jockey sun
         grow grey above the world's brown hide.

      when a thoroughbred loses its
      pins, there's no more running. Snort if you
   will, but reason, too, exhausts itself when
cause falters. Men have run down when barred from the
      race. Summer is a fragile courser

      here in the North; our racers are
   all imports from the southland. Summer
will not slow for falling leaves, nor haul our
sleighs: it will linger, pawing its reluctance
      to leave, but its strength is of only

      short will, meant for one swift effort.
   Watch the summer run its oval, it's
a winner now—nothing can stop it! The
stands urge their encouragement upon open
      air; shouts fall and rise like the fall wind

      that moves out of the foothills now, sure,
      pervasive, wild.
                  Blooded summer shies.

Or have you been speaking from the point-of-view of someone entirely
different from yourself? Have you imagined yourself into the personality
of another individual—have you adopted a poetic mask, a *persona,* as
Shakespeare did when he imagined himself as Hamlet, when he *became*
Hamlet—as the poet does in the following poem when he imagines
himself as a scarecrow *and* a pumpkin. If so, you have been using the
dramatic point-of-view:

SCARECROW

FOR 'DOLPH

We pumpkins worship you. We orange globes,
harrowed in youth, hollow in our old age,
aspire to your straw. In the darkness
of our swelling and decay, in our days
of rook pestilence and the owl's blight
which scampers among the vines we spin in
furrows and the furbelows of weed, we
do you homage. All honor, Scarecrow! You
there, sunstruck, eminent among us, rag

lord of moonlight, crucified among stars,
sighted as none of us may be. The world
in which we root unrolls unendingly
beneath your gaze, furlongs your province.
We pumpkins worship you, we orange globes.

I cannot see. Buttons for eyes, what would
I see? If I could hear, the crows' whispers
could tell me only of some simple fields,
potato-eyed and corn-eared, extending
to limits that would only barb my sleeve
and rend my cloth, if I could walk to them.
You worship me? a pole for a spine, a
timber for my extended bone, fingers
of hay stolen by wrens? I bleach and shake,
I shudder in the moon's dark. Pumpkins, crowd
of orange globes, I whistle in the wind.

Scarecrow, we too would whistle in the wind.

Essentially, the egopoetic point-of-view is single-angled. It is the
poet taking a stance at the center of his world and telling about it as he
sees it:

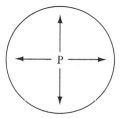

His method is autobiographical in nature and *exclusive* in effect. There
is but one angle of vision, and either the reader agrees with the poet
or he doesn't; those who do not agree are excluded from participation
in the subjective, ego-centered relation. The methods of egopoets are
usually those of rhetoric or *telling* rather than of persuasion or *showing*.
Much lyric poetry and most didactic poetry is written from the egopoetic
point-of-view.

The narrative point-of-view is *double-angled* at least, depending
on the number of characters whose story is being told in the poem.
The poet tells someone else's story, or perhaps his own story, but tells it
standing outside himself and taking an objective view of himself. But
even if it is someone else's story, *the poet is not excluded* from the story,
because we see the speaker (even if the speaker is "I," it is a narrative "I,"
not an egopoetic "I") reflected in the *way* he tells the story. The poet
may be telling it in an ironic way, or in a tragic way, or what-have-you.

The point is, we see both the world of the characters (or things) in the poem, and the world of the poet by *reflection*. We see them through the way he tells the story in a more-or-less objective, *inclusive* manner. The reader may *empathize* with one or more of the characters in the story or with the poet. The reader is not excluded, either way:

The dramatic point-of-view is similar, except that here the poet takes us *inside* another character's person, and both we and the poet *become* that person. Hence, we see the persona's world in the same way that we saw the poet's world from the egopoetic point-of-view. The main difference lies in the fact that we can still see the poet-speaker's point-of-view, by reflection, as in the narrative point of view *by the way in which the poet makes the persona speak*. The dramatic p.o.v. is most inclusive of the three. It is both objective and subjective, and the more personas the poet imagines in the poem, the more inclusive it is:

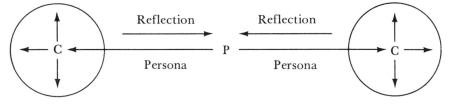

In fact, the dramatic p.o.v. is potentially universal in its effect. The poet may imagine a cosmos, including Paradise and the Inferno, as Dante did, or a whole society, as Chaucer did. This is impossible from the egopoetic p.o.v., and incomplete (because of its objective nature) from the narrative p.o.v.

Perhaps it would be better to say that the most universal of all points-of-view is a blending of all three. Both Chaucer and Dante blended narrative and dramatic points-of-view. In *The Canterbury Tales* Chaucer advanced his story line (or plot) narratively as the pilgrimage progressed, but he also had each of his characters tell a story, in the character's own persona, as they went along. In fact, both Dante and Chaucer included *themselves as characters* in their stories. Therefore, all three points-of-view are represented: egopoetic, narrative, and dramatic.

The final point to be made is this: a poem *always* has a speaker.

That speaker may be the poet telling his own story subjectively, or another person's story objectively (to a degree), or another person's story subjectively (by *becoming* that person); or the poet may choose to blend two or more poetic voices in one poem. The more points-of-view, the more inclusive the poem.

It is sometimes difficult to tell which p.o.v. the poet is using. It is relatively easy to tell the narrative p.o.v. if the poet uses the third-person "he" or "she" in his poem, or even the second-person "you." However, all three points-of-view can use the first-person "I": the egopoetic *I* ("I feel sad"), the narrative I ("I watched you feeling sad"), and the dramatic I ("I, Hamlet, feel sad"). In analyzing the poem, you will first have to judge whether the poet or someone else is speaking; and then, whether he is speaking about himself or somone else.

In essence, we see with various *I*'s.

For years it was thought that Emily Dickinson's poem "Dying" was written from the egopoetic point of view:

DYING

I heard a fly buzz when I died;
   The stillness round my form
Was like the stillness in the air
   Between the heaves of storm.

The eyes beside had wrung them dry,
   And breaths were gathering sure
For that last onset, when the king
   Be witnessed in his power.

I willed my keepsakes, signed away
   What portion of me I
Could make assignable,—and then
   There interposed a fly,

With blue, uncertain, stumbling buzz,
   Between the light and me;
And then the windows failed, and then
   I could not see to see.

EMILY DICKINSON

However, Hyatt H. Waggoner, in his book *American Poets from the Puritans to the Present** pointed out that Nathaniel Hawthorne was one of Dickinson's favorite authors, and that this poem is in fact written from the point-of-view of the *dramatic "I"*—the persona of the poem is Judge

* Boston. Houghton Mifflin, 1968.

Pyncheon in *The House of the Seven Gables,* at the moment of his death as he sat in front of a window.

Here, however, is a poem we can be nearly certain is written from the egopoetic point-of-view—the author of the poem usually writes from that point-of-view, and does it well, unlike so many who forget that confession is merely confession unless it is done artfully, at which point it becomes *art* rather than soap-opera:

FROM MY MOTHER'S MOTHER

I have you
In the fine red lines
Of your inner nostril
And your short sniff
When you answered father;

Then, at the brown upright piano,
On my right, at treble;
When I toss my head,
You say to stop
Showing off;

And last in your high bed;
You speak of a silk quilt
For my birthday;
I swing on the bedpost,
Almost kiss you.

My mother cried
When you left your wornout body.
I know what she meant,
But you didn't want it.
You are my mother's mother.

She never sniffs.
My daughter plays a white upright piano;
She sleeps in your bed
Under a nylon quilt.
My body is wearing out.

ALBERTA T. TURNER

Too many poets are victims of the *egopoetic fallacy*—the fallacious assumption that merely because something has happened to them, it will be of interest to others. The fact is, however, that readers are, for the most part, interested in *themselves.* The writer must consider:
1) how to interest the reader in what has happened to the writer;
2) how to hold the reader's interest once he has it; and 3) how to show

that what the writer is talking about is relevant *to* the reader as a human being, not merely as an individual.

One of the ways in which the best egopoets capture and hold the reader's attention is through lyricism. *Something* must carry the poem— something besides autobiography, that is. Unless, of course, one is either famous or infamous, in which case the reader may have some kind of interest in the writer aside from a literary interest, but this sort of interest is usually short-lived. This poem *sings* confession:

APRIL INVENTORY

The green catalpa tree has turned
All white; the cherry blooms once more.
In one whole year I haven't learned
A blessed thing they pay you for.
The blossoms snow down in my hair;
The trees and I will soon be bare.

The trees have more than I to spare.
The sleek, expensive girls I teach,
Younger and pinker every year,
Bloom gradually out of reach.
The pear tree lets its petals drop
Like dandruff on a tabletop.

The girls have grown so young by now
I have to nudge myself to stare.
This year they smile and mind me how
My teeth are falling with my hair.
In thirty years I may not get
Younger, shrewder, or out of debt.

The tenth time, just a year ago,
I made myself a little list
Of all the things I'd ought to know,
Then told my parents, analyst,
And everyone who's trusted me
I'd be substantial, presently.

I haven't read one book about
A book or memorized one plot.
Or found a mind I did not doubt.
I learned one date. And then forgot.
And one by one the solid scholars
Get the degrees, the jobs, the dollars.

And smile above their starchy collars.
I taught my classes Whitehead's notions;
One lovely girl, a song of Mahler's.

Lacking a source-book or promotions,
I showed one child the colors of
A luna moth and how to love.

I taught myself to name my name,
To bark back, loosen love and crying;
To ease my woman so she came,
To ease an old man who was dying.
I have not learned how often I
Can win, can love, but choose to die.

I have not learned there is a lie
Love shall be blonder, slimmer, younger;
That my equivocating eye
Loves only by my body's hunger;
That I have forces, true to feel,
Or that the lovely world is real.

While scholars speak authority
And wear their ulcers on their sleeves,
My eyes in spectacles shall see
These trees procure and spend their leaves.
There is a value underneath
The gold and silver in my teeth.

Though trees turn bare and girls turn wives,
We shall afford our costly seasons;
There is a gentleness survives
That will outspeak and has its reasons.
There is a loveliness exists,
Preserves us, not for specialists.

                                        W. D. Snodgrass

    Is this poem written from the egopoetic point-of-view, or is it written from the narrative p.o.v., or is it, perhaps, written in the dramatic voice?—

THE FOREST BEYOND THE GLASS

    Hundreds of yards of woodland
        smashed and torn.
  They had been a long while dying,
      these great beasts;
one, of a broken neck—the lucky
    one. Thirst took
the other: even on his side he'd dug
    a dozen

holes, deep as his hooves could delve,
    trying for
water. It had been one of those
    tremendous
agonies. There lie the two moose still,
    locked upon
love's combat, horns fused. All is as it was.
    The bulls are

    dead; so says the placard hung
    upon the
glass; thus they were found, silent in
    the forest.
The point and object of contention
    had long since
vanished when men happened upon these hulks
    steaming in

    a spring thaw. But it was not
    love that had
conquered; as usual, it was
    time. Engrossed
with death's petrified grove and with the
    heart's beasts calm
in the wildwood, we stand frozen by love's
    passing glance
reflected in the forest beyond the glass.

Whoever is the speaker, the author *lived* this poem, *at least in his imagination.* It is not possible for a writer to write out of anything *but* his experiences, whether he has actually lived them; or experienced them vicariously, through reading or viewing or some other way; or imagined the experience.

suggested writing assignment

A) Write a ten-line confessional poem. Simply write a "free verse" poem of some kind—don't even think about anything except what you want to say, letting the words fall as they will.

B) Rewrite your poem later on by casting it in the form of a sonic poem or an imagist poem. If you choose the former, write it in accentual-syllabics; if you choose the latter, write it in syllabics. Before you begin to write, however, *turn this page:*

"WINTER by Edmund C. Arlington

'Alone. Edge of the sea. I.
Listening. Watching. Waiting.
Gulls swoop, shriek. Waves tumble, crash.
Alone. Edge of the sea. I.'

Composed 9:35 A.M., December 4, 1971."

Henry Martin

16

major genres:
NARRATIVES

The four basic elements of narration are *character, plot, atmosphere,* and *theme*.

THEME is the thread of idea which underlies the story. All narrative elements support the theme, which is to be distinguished from *subject*. The subject of a narrative may be "love," but the theme is *always* expressible only in a complete sentence: "Love is hard to find."

CHARACTER has to do with the personal characteristics of the persons of the narrative. It is these personal characteristics which will determine the actions and reactions of the persons of a narrative in any given situation. The only person who is absolutely necessary is the *protagonist* (main character of the story). A narrative may also have a multiple protagonist (i.e., a group or village), though normally one person will represent such a composite protagonist.

A protagonist will have two qualities, basically: a *desire*—to *be,* to *have,* or to *do* something; and a dominant personality trait, such as courage, generosity, or fervor. His desire will aim him at an objective or *goal*.

The protagonist will be blocked in his desire to attain his goal by a logical *antagonist*. His antagonist may be another person who opposes him, a situation (being lost in a blizzard), a force (society), or himself, (an inner conflict). This opposition of protagonist and antagonist leads to conflict, which is essential to *the dramatic situation* (this is to be distinguished from the dramatic point-of-view).

PLOT concerns the story-line of actions and events that take place in the narrative, and the *resolution* of the conflict between protagonist and antagonist. Just as theme is the thread of thought that binds all elements of the narrative, plot may be defined as *the thread of actions and events* which carries the narrative and which serves to exemplify the theme.

ATMOSPHERE is the mood of the narrative, and mood is created by means of *setting* (locale and surroundings in which the narrative takes place), *attitude* (of the narrator and of the characters in the narrative), and *descriptions* (the sensory level).

Structure of the Narrative. Narratives may emphasize any one of the four basic elements. For instance, the author may choose to write a character sketch, a mood piece, a thematic narrative, or a complication story, and to subordinate other elements; or he may choose to write a narrative that emphasizes any combination of elements.

The author will choose to tell the story from a particular narrative *point-of-view*. In speaking of this subject, what we will be doing is breaking down *narrative voice* (covered earlier) into sub-categories:

i. ORIENTATION

A) In the *author-oriented* narrative point-of-view, it is the author who narrates the story.

B) In the *character-oriented* narrative point-of-view, it is a character (major or minor) in the story who narrates.

ii. PERSON

A) The story may be narrated in the *first person;* i.e., "I saw occurrences."

B) The story may be narrated in the *second person;* i.e., "You saw occurrences."

C. The story may be narrated in the *third person;* i.e., "He, she, it saw occurrences."

iii. ANGLE

A) In the *single-angle* only the actions of one character are followed; only what occurs in his presence is narrated.

B) In the *multiple-angle* (double, triple, etc.) what occurs in the presence of two or more characters is narrated.

C) In the *omnipresent-angle* the narrator has access to actions everywhere in the narrative.

iv. ACCESS

A) The narrator may have only *objective access* to occurrences; that is, he may narrate only actions seen externally.

B) Or the narrator may have *subjective access;* that is, he may be able to narrate not only external actions, but the thoughts and emotions of his characters as well.

As with all other elements, the narrator may choose to blend any combination of orientation, person, access, and angle. The OMNISCIENT POINT-OF-VIEW is a blending in which the author has chosen to blend *omnipresent angle* and *subjective access* to *all* characters. In other words, the author knows all about everything, internal and external, everywhere in his story, and narrates it thus.

The Complication Story. A *complication story* is one that emphasizes *plot.* A model complication story would be structured thus:

1) It will begin with *an inciting moment* or crucial point in the narrative, often *in medias res,* which means, literally, "in the middle of things," i.e., in the middle of the main action. Epics traditionally begin this way.

2) The *exposition,* which follows, gives necessary background information and provides partial answers to the questions *who?* or *what?, where?, when?,* and sometimes *why?*.

3) Following the exposition is the *body* of the narrative which is a series of *rising actions,* or increasingly stronger attempts on the part of the protagonist to achieve his goal. Each successive action culminates in a *crisis,* or critical moment, when protagonist and

antagonist are pitted against one another. In each attempt the protagonist either fails or only partially succeeds.

4) In time, the series of rising actions leads to a *climax,* or ultimate crisis when protagonist and antagonist are pitted against one another in a final effort. At this point the protagonist either overcomes his antagonist and achieves his desired goal, or he loses the conflict. The *black moment* is that point in the climax when things look darkest for the chances of the protagonist.

5) In the *denouement,* or winding down of the story, all actions are resolved, and the story is ended.

6) In the *conclusion,* the story is either *open* or *closed*; i.e., either all loose ends are tied up neatly in a closed package, or the story ends ambiguously—the actions may have been resolved, but not necessarily the attitudes of the narrator, the author, or the reader. Many modern narratives are open-ended; they are *inclusive.* Traditional narratives are often closed; they are *exclusive.*

Often a complication story will involve a subplot or secondary story-line that runs parallel to a main story-line—this is particularly true of longer narratives. The subplot, generally, involves secondary characters of the narrative, and the actions of these characters serve to *complicate* or impede the main action. Often the protagonist will have to deal with the subplot's impediments before he can go on to deal with the main conflict, hence the term *complication* for a narrative that emphasizes plot and action.

Here is a contemporary narrative poem, a ballad:

AN IMMIGRANT BALLAD

My father came from Sicily
  (O sing a roundelay with me)
With cheeses in his pockets and
A crust of black bread in his hand.
He jumped ashore without a coat,
  Without a friend or enemy,
Till Jesus nailed him by the throat.

My father came to Boston town
  (O tongue a catch and toss one down).
By day he plied a cobbler's awl,
By night he loitered on the mall.
He swigged his wine, he struck his note,
  He wound the town up good and brown,
Till Jesus caught him by the throat.

He'd heard of Hell, he knew of sin
  (O pluck that wicked mandolin),
But they were for the gentle folk,
The cattle broken to the yoke.
He didn't need a Cross to tote:
  His eyes were flame, his ears were tin,
Till Jesus nabbed him by the throat.

He met a Yankee girl one day
  (O cry a merry roundelay)
Who wouldn't do as she was bid,
But only what the good folk did.
She showed him how the church bells peal
  Upon the narrow straitaway,
And Jesus nipped him by the heel.

My father heard a sermon said
  (O bite the bottle till it's dead).
He quit his job and went to school
And memorized the Golden Rule.
He drained his crock and sold his keg,
  He swept the cobwebs from his head,
And Jesus hugged him by the leg.

The girl was pleased: she'd saved a soul
  (O light a stogie with a coal).
No longer need she be so wary:
Daddy went to seminary
To find how warm a Yankee grows
  When she achieves her fondest goal.
And Jesus bit him on the nose.

At last he had a frock to wear
  (O hum a hymn and lip a prayer).
He hoisted Bible, sailed to search
For sheep to shear and for a church.
He asked the girl to share his life,
  His choir-stall and shirt of hair,
For Jesus bid him take a wife.

My father holds a pulpit still
  (O I have had enough to swill).
His eye is tame, his hair is gray,
He can't recall a roundelay.
But he can preach, and he can quote
  A verse or scripture, as you will,
Since Jesus took him by the throat.

There are distinctions to be made between literary ballads, such
as "An Immigrant Ballad," and folk ballads, which were passed down
through oral traditions. First, literary ballads are usually written in
accentual-syllabics; oral ballads are often done in dipodics or some other
podic prosody. Second, The literary ballad's author is usually known,
whereas the folk-ballad's author is usually anonymous. Third, because
the literary ballad is still whole, it follows a more or less normal narrative
pattern. But as the folk-ballad was passed down from hand to hand, it
has usually become eroded, and only the high-points, or crises and
climaxes, remain. This phenomenon is called "leaping and lingering"—
the folk ballad leaps from high point to high point, and lingers on each
a while before it leaps again:

EDWARD, EDWARD

"Why dois your brand sae drap wi bluid,
                    Edward, Edward,
Why dois your brand sae drap wi bluid,
    And why sae sad gang yee O?"
"O I hae killed my hauke sae guid,
    And I had nae mair bot hee O."

"Your haukis bluid was nevir sae reid,
                    Edward, Edward,
Your haukis bluid was nevir sae reid,
    My deir son I tell thee O."
"O I hae killed my reid-roan steid,
                    Mither, mither,
O I hae killed my reid-roan steid,
    That erst was sae fair and frie O."

"Your steid was auld, and ye hae gat mair,
                    Edward, Edward,
Your steid was auld, and ye hae gat mair,
    Sum other dule ye drie O."
"O I hae killed my fadir deir,
                    Mither, mither,
O I hae killed my fadir deir,
    Alas, and wae is mee O!"

"And whatten penance wul ye drie, for that,
                    Edward, Edward?
And whatten penance will ye drie for that?
    My deir son, now tell me O."
"I'le set my feit in yonder boat,
                    Mither, mither,
I'le set my feit in yonder boat,
    And I'le fare ovir the sea O."

"And what wul ye doe wi your towirs and your ha,
        Edward, Edward?
And what wul ye doe wi your towirs and your ha,
  That were sae fair to see O?"
"I'le let thame stand tul they doun fa,
        Mither, mither,
I'le let thame stand tul they doun fa,
  For here nevir mair maun I bee O."

"And what wul ye leive to your bairns and your wife,
        Edward, Edward?
And what wul ye leive to your bairns and your wife,
  Whan ye gang ovir the sea O?"
"The warldis room, late them beg thrae life,
        Mither, mither,
The warldis room, late them beg thrae life,
  For thame nevir mair wul I see O."

"And what wul ye leive to your ain mither deir,
        Edward, Edward?
And what wul ye leive to your ain mither deir?
  My deir son, now tell me O."
"The curse of hell frae me sall ye beir,
        Mither, mither,
The curse of hell frae me sall ye beir,
  Sic counseils ye gave to me O."

ANONYMOUS

There are various traditional forms of narrative poems, aside from the common measure and ballad stanza forms. The *epic* is a long, heroic verse narrative; the *romance* is a long, lyric narrative; the *ballad* (which, though often written in specific stanza forms, really has no specific form) is a relatively short, lyric narrative; the *fabliau* is a short story in verse; the *lay* is a vignette in song form. An *epyllion* is a "little epic," originally composed in dactylic hexameter verse; the *beast epic* uses animals for its characters like the *fable*, which is a didactic allegory. The *chanson de geste* is a type of medieval French epic with marked lyric qualities. An *exemplum* is a brief verse narrative, anecdotal in nature, used to illustrate a particular didactic point.

    A number of French poem forms—such as the *ballade* family, including the *chant royal*, which is the longest of the forms (an example appears in the chapter on *didactics*)—have been used traditionally to tell stories. But, in fact, most poets make up their own forms, and stories have been told in every prosody.

SUNDAY MORNING

I

Complacencies of the peignoir, and late
Coffee and oranges in a sunny chair,
And the green freedom of a cockatoo
Upon a rug, mingle to dissipate
The holy hush of ancient sacrifice.
She dreams a little, and she feels the dark
Encroachment of that old catastrophe,
As a calm darkens among water-lights.
The pungent oranges and bright, green wings
Seem things in some procession of the dead,
Winding across wide water, without sound.
The day is like wide water, without sound,
Stilled for the passing of her dreaming feet
Over the seas, to silent Palestine,
Dominion of the blood and sepulcher.

II

She hears, upon that water without sound,
A voice that cries, "The tomb in Palestine
Is not the porch of spirits lingering;
It is the grave of Jesus, where he lay."
We live in an old chaos of the sun,
Or old dependency of day and night,
Or island solitude, unsponsored, free,
Of that wide water, inescapable.
Deer walk upon our mountains, and the quail
Whistle about us their spontaneous cries;
Sweet berries ripen in the wilderness;
And, in the isolation of the sky,
At evening, casual flocks of pigeons make
Ambiguous undulations as they sink,
Downward to darkness, on extended wings.

III

She says, "I am content when wakened birds,
Before they fly, test the reality
Of misty fields, by their sweet questionings;
But when the birds are gone, and their warm fields
Return no more, where, then, is paradise?"
There is not any haunt of prophecy,
Nor any old chimera of the grave,
Neither the golden underground, nor isle
Melodious, where spirits gat them home,
Nor visionary South, nor cloudy palm
Remote on heaven's hill, that has endured

As April's green endures; or will endure
Like her remembrance of awakened birds,
Or her desire for June and evening, tipped
By the consummation of the swallow's wings.

IV

She says, "But in contentment I still feel
The need of some imperishable bliss."
Death is the mother of beauty; hence from her,
Alone, shall come fulfilment to our dreams
And our desires. Although she strews the leaves
Of sure obliteration on our paths—
The path sick sorrow took, the many paths
Where triumph rang its brassy phrase, or love
Whispered a little out of tenderness—
She makes the willow shiver in the sun
For maidens who were wont to sit and gaze
Upon the grass, relinquished to their feet.
She causes boys to bring sweet-smelling pears
And plums in ponderous piles. The maidens taste
And stray impassioned in the littering leaves.

V

Supple and turbulent, a ring of men
Shall chant in orgy on a summer morn
Their boisterous devotion to the sun—
Not as a god, but as a god might be,
Naked among them, like a savage source.
Their chant shall be a chant of paradise,
Out of their blood, returning to the sky;
And in their chant shall enter, voice by voice,
The windy lake wherein their lord delights,
The trees, like seraphim, and echoing hills,
That choir among themselves long afterward.
They shall know well the heavenly fellowship
Of men that perish and of summer morn—
And whence they came and whither they shall go,
The dew upon their feet shall manifest.

WALLACE STEVENS

GOOSE

Trailing her father, bearing his hand axe,
    the girl thought she had never
   guessed what earthly majesty
      was before

then, as he strode unconcernedly
        holding a vicious gander
by the horny mitts and let
        the big wings

batter his knees. She was also surprised
        to feel a liberating
satisfaction in
        the coming bloodshed, and

that notwithstanding all the times she had
        been beleaguered and
had fled, today she did not fear
        the barnyard hubub.

Yet, as her father's clever stroke fell, as
        the pronged head skipped sideways
and the neck plumes stiffened with blood
        from the cleft,

she was angry; and, when the headless goose
        ran to the brook and was
carried off into the woods alive,
        she rejoiced,

and subsequently frequented those woods
        and avoided her father.
When the goose began to mend she
        brought him small

hominy, which was welcome though she had
        to press the kernels one
by one into the pink neck that
        throbbed into

her palm; when haemorrhage occurred she would
        not spare handkerchiefs,
and stanching the spot she felt a thrill
        of sympathy.

But for the most part there was steady progress,
        and growing vigor was
accompanied by restlessness,
        and one cool day

the blind thing was batted out of existence
        by a motorcycle.
She had no time for tears. She ran
        upstairs to miss

her father's barytone commiseration,
        then out onto the fields,

and, holding an old red pinwheel,
    ran ran ran ran.

Richard Emil Braun

This following poem is written in *Spenserian stanza*:

BLUEBEARD'S WIFE

Impatiently she tampered with the locks,
One by one she opened all the doors;
The music boxes and the cuckoo clocks
Stopped in alarm; dust settled on the floors
Like apprehensive footsteps. Then the stores
Of silence were exposed to her soft touch:
Mute diamonds and still exquisite orcs.
She had not thought the squalid world had such
Treasure to proffer, nor so easy, nor so much.

She did not listen to the hinges' groans,
Complaints in metal, warnings in the wood,
But room by room progressed from precious stones
To tears, and at each secret understood,
Exclaimed, amused, "How simple!" or "How good!"
As she took up some fragile, painted jar.
Throughout the palace doors and windows stood
Whether in dread or sympathy ajar
Upon a pale horizon seeming very far.

The open doors of summer afternoons,
The scented air that passes in and out
Ferrying insects, humming with the tunes
That nature sings unheard! She could not doubt
She was unseen, no one was about,
The servants all had gone—she wondered where:
The calm within was dead as that without,
And all about her breathed the stealthy air.
She knew she was alone, that no one else was there.

Now she attained the room of artifice.
Not a thing that grew there but was made:
Venetian glass that counterfeited ice
So close it seemed to melt, and green brocade,
The wind's most subtle movements in a glade.
Nothing was modern, everything was old,
And yet it was not true that they should fade
Though time and fashion dim the emerald.
Each was at once an image and a deathless mould.

Dazzled, she shut the door, but through the next
Saw greater good than any she had seen:
A window open on the sacred text
Of natural things, whose number had not been
Created or conceived, nor did they mean
Other than what they were, splendid and strange.
One leaf is like another, and between
Them all the worlds of difference range;
The world is not destroyed and does not cease to change.

The final door resisted all her strength,
No key would fit, the bars and bolts stuck fast.
But there she pried and worried, till at length
She opened it, knowing it was the last.
They hung on hooks, their finery surpassed
Each her predecessor's, in their lives
Less fortunate than she. There hung the past,
Putrid and crowned. And thinking, 'Love survives
The grave,' she stepped inside to join the other wives.

DARYL HINE

OU PHRONTIS

TO E. M. FORSTER

The bells assault the maiden air,
The coachman waits with a carriage and pair,
But the bridegroom says I won't be there,
    I don't care!

Three times three times the banns declare
That the boys may blush and the girls may glare,
But the bridegroom is occupied elsewhere,
    I don't care!

Lord, but the neighbours all will stare,
Their temperatures jump as high as a hare,
But the bridegroom says *I've paid my fare,*
    I don't care!

The bride she waits by the bed so bare,
Soft as a pillow is her hair,
But the bridegroom jigs with the leg of a chair,
    I don't care!

Say, but her father's a millionaire,
A girdle of gold all night will she wear,
You must your foolish ways forswear.
    I don't care!

Her mother will offer, if she dare,
A ring that is rich but not so rare
If you'll keep your friendship in repair.
    I don't care!

Her sisters will give you a plum and a pear
And a diamond saddle for your mare.
O bridegroom! For the night prepare!
    I don't care!

Her seven brothers all debonair
Will do your wishes and some to spare
If from your fancy you'll forbear.
    I don't care!

Say, but a maid you wouldn't scare
Now that you've got her in your snare?
And what about your son and heir?
    I don't care!

She'll leap she'll leap from the highest stair,
She'll drown herself in the river there,
With a silver knife her flesh she'll tear.
    I don't care!

Then another will lie in the silken lair
And cover with kisses her springing hair.
Another the bridal bed will share.
    I don't care!

I shall stand on my head on the table bare,
I shall kick my lily-white legs in the air,
I shall wash my hands of the whole affair,
    I don't care!

Note: The words *Ou Phrontis* were carved by T. E. Lawrence over the door of his cottage at Clouds Hill, Dorset. They come from the story in Herodotus, on which this poem is based.

                                          CHARLES CAUSLEY

The *character sketch* is in the tradition of narrative verse, too:

CLIFF KLINGENHAGEN

Cliff Klingenhagen had me in to dine
With him one day; and after soup and meat,
And all the other things there were to eat,
Cliff took two glasses and filled one with wine
And one with wormwood. Then, without a sign
For me to choose at all, he took the draught

Of bitterness himself, and lightly quaffed
It off, and said the other one was mine.

And when I asked him what the deuce he meant
By doing that, he only looked at me
And smiled, and said it was a way of his.
And though I know the fellow, I have spent
Long time a-wondering when I shall be
As happy as Cliff Klingenhagen is.

EDWIN ARLINGTON ROBINSON

YOU'RE THE ONE

where you been   i been
all over looking for you
been between countless legs
trying to find you
with a bump and a grind
hoping to find you with your elusive self
you was always one jump ahead
been partying steady
hoping to catch you
in a boogaloo
been going out of town too
they said you
liked traveling and seeing
new faces
even tried church one time
thinking perhaps
you was the religious kind
and might like to save me
from myself (it was a silly
desperate act) then finally i figured
a real black woman   a real black happening
was where you'd be
so i came
and at last   at last i found you
just when the crook in my arm
and the kiss in my mouth
was beginning to wear out
i found you
and as long as i've known you
i only wish to god you'd
stop shaking your head
and saying
you're not the one

MERVYN TAYLOR

suggested writing assignment

A) Write a narrative poem of from 16–20 lines in either accentual–syllabics or dipodics.

B) Write a character sketch of at least eight lines any way you want to.

17

major genres:
DRAMATICS

In Chap. 1 it was pointed out that the fictionist and the dramatist are both concerned with narrative, and that both use exactly the same elements of narrative: plot, theme, character, and atmosphere. It was also pointed out that the dramatist is usually limited to the language technique of dialogue, whereas the fictionist is not.

Neither is the dramatic poet, unless he writes plays specifically to be acted on the stage. The poet may choose to blend narrative and dramatic voices, as Frost does in "The Hill Wife":

THE HILL WIFE

　LONELINESS
　　Her Word

One ought not to have to care
　So much as you and I
Care when the birds come round the house
　To seem to say good-by;

Or care so much when they come back
　With whatever it is they sing;
The truth being we are as much
　Too glad for the one thing

As we are too sad for the other here—
   With birds that fill their breasts
But with each other and themselves
   And their built or driven nests.

HOUSE FEAR

Always—I tell you this they learned—
Always at night when they returned
To the lonely house from far away,
To lamps unlighted and fire gone gray,
They learned to rattle the lock and key
To give whatever might chance to be,
Warning and time to be off in flight:
And preferring the out- to the in-door night,
They learned to leave the house door wide
Until they had lit the lamp inside.

THE SMILE
Her Word

I didn't like the way he went away.
That smile! It never came of being gay.
Still he smiled—did you see him?—I was sure!
Perhaps because we gave him only bread
And the wretch knew from that that we were poor.
Perhaps because he let us give instead
Of seizing from us as he might have seized.
Perhaps he mocked at us for being wed,
Or being very young (and he was pleased
To have a vision of us old and dead).
I wonder how far down the road he's got.
He's watching from the woods as like as not.

THE OFT-REPEATED DREAM

She had no saying dark enough
   For the dark pine that kept
Forever trying the window-latch
   Of the room where they slept.

The tireless but ineffectual hands
   That with every futile pass
Made the great tree seem as a little bird
   Before the mystery of glass!

It never had been inside the room,
   And only one of the two
Was afraid in an oft-repeated dream
   Of what the tree might do.

THE IMPULSE

It was too lonely for her there,
    And too wild,
And since there were but two of them,
    And no child,

And work was little in the house,
    She was free,
And followed where he furrowed field,
    Or felled tree.

She rested on a log and tossed
    The fresh chips,
With a song only to herself
    On her lips.

And once she went to break a bough
    Of black alder.
She strayed so far she scarcely heard
    When he called her—

And didn't answer—didn't speak—
    Or return.
She stood, and then she ran and hid
    In the fern.

He never found her, though he looked
    Everywhere,
And he asked at her mother's house
    Was she there.

Sudden and swift and light as that
    The ties gave,
And he learned of finalities
    Besides the grave.

ROBERT FROST

But if the dramatic poet *does* choose to write for the stage rather than the page, he may choose among forms and traditions, if not among a large range of objective and subjective writing techniques.

There are several stage forms.

TRAGEDY is a form of verse drama in which a heroic protagonist struggles to avoid his inevitable defeat (fate). Its elements are the balance of pathos and terror as the hero courageously faces the human predicament; the paradox of nobility of character combined with human fallibility; theatrical narration by means of concrete, mimetic stage actions; masked or stylized characters who are representatives *not* of abstractions as such, but, first, of historical or mythological figures and,

second, of types of people; two choruses, usually representative
of Everyman, which comment on the action; and a set formal structure
consisting of speeches, odes, choral odes, and stylized stage actions of
various kinds. An example of a modern tragedy is T. S. Eliot's *Murder in
the Cathedral.*

COMEDY is tragedy burlesqued. The protagonist is a humorous,
not an empathetic, character, and the stages by which he progresses
toward his defeat or, possibly, his triumph, are humorous as well .

TRAGICOMEDY is a verse or a compound-mode drama. It
combines tragedy and comedy, usually in a plot-subplot relationship.
Good is rewarded and vice punished.

THE MASQUE is a relatively short verse or compound-mode drama
performed by masked figures. It includes songs speeches, dances, mimes,
and spectacle. It was a forerunner of opera. Current masques are largely
literary rather than dramatic. Cummings wrote masques, among them
one called "Santa Claus", and Frost wrote some as well.

THE MORALITY PLAY is a verse or compound-mode allegory in
the form of a play. It rehearses the pilgrimage of man's progress toward
death and his hope of salvation from sin through repentance and
submission to God's mercy. Other than the pilgrimage, the elements are:
the *psychomachia,* or strife of the Seven Deadly Sins aided by the Vices
with the Four Cardinal and Three Theological Virtues over possession
of Everyman's soul; and the *totentanz* or Dance of Death. Other
personified abstractions are Conscience, Conviction of Sin, and
Repentance.

The MYSTERY PLAY is based upon the Biblical story of Man's
Creation, Fall, and Redemption.

The MIRACLE PLAY is concerned with the life and martyrdom
of a Saint.

The PASSION PLAY deals with the events in the life of Christ
before the Resurrection—between the Last Supper and the Crucifixion.

The NŌ PLAY is a Japanese compound-mode drama, somewhat
similar to the masque and to tragedy. It is allusive and impressionistic.
It uses traditional subjects, masked figures, a chorus, mime, dance, music,
and choreographed movement. William Butler Yeats wrote plays that
were influenced by the nō.

Most poets today, however, write primarily for the page, and there
are three loose forms that often exist outside the drama proper:

A *dialogue* is a conversation among characters. In Housman's
"Terence, This Is Stupid Stuff," the only thing that shows this is
a dialogue is the stanza division. In the first stanza a drinking companion
asks the poet to stop fooling around with poetry and do something
useful—like getting drunk. The following stanzas is the poet speaking in

reply. Thematically, it is interesting to compare this poem with Robinson's "Cliff Klingenhagen" (p. 233).

"TERENCE, THIS IS STUPID STUFF"

"Terence, this is stupid stuff:
You eat your victuals fast enough;
There can't be much amiss, 'tis clear,
To see the rate you drink your beer.
But oh, good Lord, the verse you make,
It gives a chap the belly-ache.
'The cow, the old cow, she is dead;
It sleeps well, the hornéd head':
We poor lads, 'tis our turn now
To hear such tunes as killed the cow.
Pretty friendship 'tis to rhyme
Your friends to death before their time
'Moping melancholy mad':
Come, pipe a tune to dance to, lad."

Why, if 'tis dancing you would be,
There's brisker pipes than poetry.
Say, for what were hop-yards meant,
Or why was Burton built on Trent?
Oh many a peer of England brews
Livelier liquor than the Muse,
And malt does more than Milton can
To justify God's ways to man.
Ale, man, ale's the stuff to drink
For fellows whom it hurts to think:
Look into the pewter pot
To see the world as the world's not.
And faith, 'tis pleasant till 'tis past:
The mischief is that 'twill not last.
Oh I have been to Ludlow fair
And left my necktie God knows where,
And carried half-way home, or near,
Pints and quarts of Ludlow beer:
Then the world seemed none so bad,
And I myself a sterling lad;
And down in lovely muck I've lain,
Happy till I woke again.
Then I saw the morning sky:
Heigho, the tale was all a lie;
The world, it was the old world yet,
I was I, my things were wet,
And nothing now remained to do
But begin the game anew.

Therefore, since the world has still
Much good, but much less good than ill,
And while the sun and moon endure
Luck's a chance, but trouble's sure—
I'd face it as a wise man would,
And train for ill and not for good.
'Tis true, the stuff I bring for sale
Is not so brisk a brew as ale:
Out of a stem that scored the hand
I wrung it in a weary land.
But take it: if the smack is sour,
The better for the embittered hour;
It should do good to heart and head
When your soul is in my soul's stead;
And I will friend you, if I may,
In the dark and cloudy day.

There was a king reigned in the East:
There, when kings will sit to feast,
They get their fill before they think
With poisoned meat and poisoned drink.
He gathered all that springs to birth
From the many-venomed earth;
First a little, thence to more,
He sampled all her killing store;
And easy, smiling, seasoned sound,
Sate the king when healths went round.
They put arsenic in his meat
And stared aghast to watch him eat;
They poured strychnine in his cup
And shook to see him drink it up:
They shook, they stared as white's their shirt:
Them it was their poison hurt.
—I tell the tale that I heard told.
Mithridates, he died old.

A. E. HOUSMAN

My apologies to the shade of Mr. Housman for editing it—adding italics and so forth—to make it more obvious that this is a dialogue. Actually, this poem is more a *debat* than simply a dialogue—a verse argument, usually between two poets. In this case, Housman has taken both sides. A set Spanish form of the debat is the *pregunta,* in which one poet asks a question ("requesta") or series of questions, and another gives his reply ("respuesta") or series of replies.

Even more difficult to see is the dialogue in Henry Reed's "Naming of Parts." In all stanzas but the last one, two people are speaking. The recruit, who is thinking the poem, stands and listens to a noncom explaining the parts of the rifle. His mind then wanders off into the spring day. In the last stanza the statement is made by means of *dramatic irony* (through the revery of the recruit)—*war is madness*:

NAMING OF PARTS

Today we have naming of parts. Yesterday,
We had daily cleaning. And tomorrow morning,
We shall have what to do after firing. But today,
Today we have naming of parts. Japonica
Glistens like coral in all of the neighbouring gardens,
      And today we have naming of parts.

This is the lower sling swivel. And this
Is the upper sling swivel, whose use you will see of,
When you are given your slings. And this is the piling swivel,
Which in your case you have not got. The branches
Hold in the gardens, their silent, eloquent gestures,
      Which in our case we have not got.

This is the safety-catch, which is always released
With an easy flick of the thumb. And please do not let me
See anyone using his finger. You can do it quite easy
If you have any strength in your thumb. The blossoms
Are fragile and motionless, never letting anyone see
      Any of them using their finger.

And this you can see is the bolt. The purpose of this
Is to open the breech, as you see. We can slide it
Rapidly backwards and forwards: we call this
Easing the spring. And rapidly backwards and forwards
The early bees are assaulting and fumbling the flowers:
      They call it easing the Spring.

They call it easing the Spring: it is perfectly easy
If you have any strength in your thumb: like the bolt, ·
And the breech, and the cocking-piece, and the point of balance,
Which in our case we have not got; and the almond-blossom
Silent in all of the gardens and the bees going backwards and forwards,
      For to-day we have naming of parts.

Henry Reed

Reed never says it, he shows it. It is the essence of dramatic irony that the reader knows what the noncom does not, and the recruit may not know. The *reader knows more* about the situation in which the characters are placed than the characters do themselves.

Here is a poem in which silence is utilized as one of the characters in a drama:

POCOANGELINI 7

Pocoangelini. Sir. Your head. It is stuck into the sand.

Mr. Earth.

Pocoangelini. I'm not sure I understand. You hear me, don't you, even with both your earholes squat up against those furrows? I say, YOUR HEAD IS STUCK IN A BRAIN'S HARROWING. There's dirt up your nose, and ants are crawling about your neck. YOUR HEAD'S STUCK IN THE FILTHY SAND!

Mr. Earth.

Pocoangelini. The moon is out. It's playing with your spine. The shafts of starfire are sticking in your shoulderblades, making you appear to be a sort of celestial porcupine. What are you looking for? What color is the inside? Have you found whether stones push each other when they are together alone?

Mr. Earth.

Pocoangelini. Look, I'll scoop you out so we can talk like human beings. It's a cold night. Your thoughts must be chilly. This is no hour for such silver. I'll dig. Now pull, and tell me . . .

Mr. Earth.

Pocoangelini.   Oh.

from Pocoangelini: A Fantography

The second form is the *monologue,* a speech by one character with a listening audience assumed; the speaker addresses himself to his listener or listeners, who may be the reader or a silent character. In this poem by Browing, a corrupt Bishop of the Renaissance is addressing those who are gathered around his deathbed:

THE BISHOP ORDERS HIS TOMB
AT SAINT PRAXED'S CHURCH

Rome, 15—

Vanity, saith the preacher, vanity!
Draw round my bed: is Anselm keeping back?
Nephews—sons mine . . . ah God, I know not! Well—
She, men would have to be your mother once,
Old Gandolf envied me, so fair she was!
What's done is done, and she is dead beside,
Dead long ago, and I am Bishop since,
And as she died so must we die ourselves,
And thence ye may perceive the world's a dream.

Life, how and what is it? As here I lie
In this state-chamber, dying by degrees,
Hours and long hours in the dead night, I ask
"Do I live, am I dead?" Peace, peace seems all.
Saint Praxed's ever was the church for peace;
And so, about this tomb of mine. I fought
With tooth and nail to save my niche, ye know:
—Old Gandolf cozened me, despite my care;
Shrewd was that snatch from out the corner South
He graced his carrion with, God curse the same!
Yet still my niche is not so cramped but thence
One sees the pulpit o' the epistle-side
And somewhat of the choir, those silent seats,
And up into the aery dome where live
The angels, and a sunbeam's sure to lurk:
And I shall fill my slab of basalt there,
And 'neath my tabernacle take my rest,
With those nine columns round me, two and two,
The odd one at my feet where Anselm stands:
Peach-blossom marble all, the rare, the ripe
As fresh-poured red wine of a mighty pulse.
—Old Gandolf with his paltry onion-stone,
Put me where I may look at him! True peach,
Rosy and flawless: how I earned the prize!
Draw close: that conflagration of my church
—What then? So much was saved if aught were missed!
My sons, ye would not be my death? Go dig
The white-grape vineyard where the oil-press stood,
Drop water gently till the surface sink,
And if ye find . . . Ah God, I know not, I! . . .
Bedded in store of rotten fig-leaves soft,
And corded up in a tight olive-frail,
Some lump, ah God, of *lapis lazuli*,
Big as a Jew's head cut off at the nape,
Blue as a vein o'er the Madonna's breast . . .
Sons, all have I bequeathed you, villas, all,
That brave Frascati villa with its bath,
So, let the blue lump poise between my knees,
Like God the Father's globe on both his hands
Ye worship in the Jesu Church so gay,
For Gandolf shall not choose but see and burst!
Swift as a weaver's shuttle fleet our years:
Man goeth to the grave, and where is he?
Did I say basalt for my slab, sons? Black—
'T was ever antique-black I meant! How else
Shall ye contrast my frieze to come beneath?
The bas-relief in bronze ye promised me,

Those Pans and Nymphs ye wot of, and perchance
Some tripod, thyrsus, with a vase or so,
The Saviour at his sermon on the mount,
Saint Praxed in a glory, and one Pan
Ready to twitch the Nymph's last garment off,
And Moses with the tables . . . but I know
Ye mark me not! What do they whisper thee,
Child of my bowels, Anselm? Ah, ye hope
To revel down my villas while I gasp
Bricked o'er with beggar's mouldy travertine
Which Gandolf from his tomb-top chuckles at!
Nay, boys, ye love me—all of jasper, then!
'T is jasper ye stand pledged to, lest I grieve
My bath must needs be left behind, alas!
One block, pure green as a pistachio-nut,
There's plenty jasper somewhere in the world—
And have I not Saint Praxed's ear to pray
Horses for ye, and brown Greek manuscripts,
And mistresses with great smooth marbly limbs?
—That's if ye carve my epitaph aright,
Choice Latin, picked phrase, Tully's every word,
No gaudy ware like Gandolf's second line—
Tully, my masters? Ulpian serves his need!
And then how I shall lie through centuries,
And hear the blessed mutter of the mass,
And see God made and eaten all day long,
And feel the steady candle-flame, and taste
Good strong thick stupefying incense-smoke!
For as I lie here, hours of the dead night,
Dying in state and by such slow degrees,
I fold my arms as if they clasped a crook,
And stretch my feet forth straight as stone can point,
And let the bedclothes, for a mortcloth, drop
Into great laps and folds of sculptor's-work:
And as yon tapers dwindle, and strange thoughts
Grow, with a certain humming in my ears,
About the life before I lived this life,
And this life too, popes, cardinals and priests,
Saint Praxed at his sermon on the mount,
Your tall pale mother with her talking eyes,
And new-found agate urns as fresh as day,
And marble's language, Latin pure, discreet,
—Aha, ELUCESCEBAT quoth our friend?
No Tully, said I, Ulpian at the best!
Evil and brief hath been my pilgrimage.
All *lapis*, all, sons! Else I give the Pope
My villas! Will ye ever eat my heart?

Ever your eyes were as a lizard's quick,
They glitter like your mother's for my soul,
Or ye would heighten my impoverished frieze,
Piece out its starved design, and fill my vase
With grapes, and add a visor and a Term,
And to the tripod ye would tie a lynx
That in his struggle throws the thyrsus down,
To comfort me on my entablature
Whereon I am to lie till I must ask
"Do I live, am I dead?" There, leave me, there!
For ye have stabbed me with ingratitude
To death—ye wish it—God, ye wish it! Stone—
Gritstone, a-crumble! Clammy squares which sweat
As if the corpse they keep were oozing through—
And no more *lapis* to delight the world!
Well, go! I bless ye. Fewer tapers there,
But in a row: and, going, turn your backs
—Ay, like departing altar-ministrants,
And leave me in my church, the church for peace,
That I may watch at leisure if he leers—
Old Gandolf, at me, from his onion-stone,
As still he envied me, so fair she was!

ROBERT BROWNING

Here are two lovers' monologues, addressed to the loved-ones:

A VALEDICTION: FORBIDDING MOURNING

As virtuous men passe mildly away,
    And whisper to their soules, to goe,
Whilst some of their sad friends doe say,
    The breath goes now, and some say, no:

So let us melt, and make no noise,
    No teare-floods, nor sigh-tempests move,
T'were prophanation of our joyes
    To tell the layetie our love.

Moving of th'earth brings harmes and fears,
    Men reckon what it did and meant,
But trepidation of the spheares,
    Though greater farre, is innocent.

Dull sublunary lovers love
    (Whose soule is sense) cannot admit
Absence, because it doth remove
    Those things which elemented it.

But we by a love, so much refin'd,
　　That our selves know not what it is,
Inter-assured of the mind,
　　Care lesse, eyes, lips, and hands to misse.

Our two soules therefore, which are one,
　　Though I must goe, endure not yet
A breach, but an expansion,
　　Like gold to ayery thinnesse beate.

If they be two, they are two so
　　As stiffe twin compasses are two,
Thy soule the fixt foot, makes no show
　　To move, but doth, if th'other doe.

And though it in the center sit,
　　Yet when the other far doth rome,
It leanes, and hearkens after it,
　　And growes erect, as that comes home.

Such wilt thou be to mee, who must
　　Like th'other foot, obliquely runne;
Thy firmnes drawes my circle just,
　　And makes me end, where I begunne.

JOHN DONNE

A MALEDICTION, FORBIDDING MORNING

Because, my love,
There is no time but now to feel the Greek
Composure of your hips, or touch your sleek,
Harmonious thighs,
Because your eyes
Are purple shadows only while
Aphrodite's darkness keeps your smile
Dim and shy;
Therefore, I
Pursue your curving beauty—but my greed
Is greater than the night. *We need*
The curse of Eros on Apollo's steeds
And laws, my love.

Because, my dear,
There is no psalmist who can praise the night
As it deserves: not for the careless light
Of callous stars,
Not for the harsh
Moon, grim as an old Semitic coin,
But for the tangled darkness, where we join
Our souls

In passion, whole
As shadows; when our bodies clasp
And stagger sunrise with the grinding rasp
Of Joshua's mighty curse, *we will not grasp
At straws, my dear.*

Because, my love,
We lay up treasure solid as our lust
And permanent as darkness, trust
Desire
To fire
The forgeries of noon. When in the cold
Ash we run dark fingers through dark gold,
Waging our curse on dawn, *night will hold
No flaws, my love.*

PHILIP APPLEMAN

The third form, the *soliloquy,* is similar to the monologue, but the speaker is assumed to be alone, and his speech consists of his private thoughts put into words. Here is a series of soliloquies—they are necessarily soliloquies, since all speakers are members of a family, and all are dead:

GATHER THESE BONES

I. ONE SONG FOR OLD BONES

Father, come home.
The rat gnaws my bone.
  The mouse chews my hair.
Under my ear sleeps the flagstone;
  My eyes turn nowhere.

Father, it is a wide world.
The wind is cold.
  Cold is the mist of morningtime
When dawn is born to grow old—
  Cold as the turning tide.

Mother eases in the lizard's couch;
Sister hums in the oak crotch.
  Brother has sailed to murder time
With a cane handle; the head of a crutch.
  I stay behind.

My socket is sprung
Wide as the sea's life is long.
  White shall my bone dust be.
My jaw falls with song.
  The spider toils inside me.

II. SONATA FOR WIND AND WOOD

As my blood has run,
  So runs the wind
Under the moon,
  Over the limb.

In the branching of night
  Wind stills my breath.
In flues of recall grows lichen,
  And moss on the hearth.

An owl lives in my head,
  Shrews in the wood.
Hark! silent wings sense bread—
  Come, cowl and hood.

The world's yard lists
  Now windward, now lee.
Under my toenail twists
  The trysting tree.

As blood will run,
  Thus runs the wind
Under the moon,
  Over the limb.

III. THEME FOR A DUST DEVIL

My muscle is fertile, fair as the land;
  I do not lie fallow.
  My marrow is the tree's marrow.

My hair waxes green as the green leaf.
  Let no grief but air's grief slip
  Down the sky to whet my lip:

I want no pledge but the willow's oath.
  The dog digs in my mouth.
  When flocks forage further south,

Squirrels mistake my skull for a nut—
  I nod in assent,
  Grinning with the best intent.

Nor rave aloud, wife, for the wind will woo
  You in your bed with my voice.
  Listen, you will hear the noise

Of my lovemaking shaking the holly.
  Our cottage ticking was warm.
  Slow is the heat of the worm.

IV. PLAINCHANT AMONG
  THE MAIDENHAIR

There is no mercy here
  In the lizard's wood.
Children, beware.

The toad tunnels in my ear.
  Night has crept beneath my hood.
There is no mercy here

In this grove where
  Roots take my maidenhead.
Children, beware—

Dark is the maidenhair;
  Dark, the salamander's blood.
There is no mercy here:

The sycamores bear
  Old spores, new wood.
Children, beware

These precincts. Forswear
  My shallow bed.
There is no mercy here;
  Children, beware.

V. LIBRETTO IN WHITE

The urchin swims in my brow;
  As the moon drowns, it is stung.
I troll the snail's libretto
  With a slug for a tongue.
    The conch knows my song.

I wait in salt and coral.
  Searching for the worm's light,
Only the anemone's floral
  Ruin meets my starred sight
    In the tide's night.

I hear the sound of keels
  Scraping my sky.
About my heart, eels
  Breathe and swallow. The sigh
    Of the squid rakes my thigh.

This is no way
  For blood to come home.
Silt is my prey;
  My prayer is bone—
    My love, stone.

VI. EPITAPH IN A MINOR KEY
Willowillow,
Weep for me
  Buried neath
The blood root tree;

Socket clogged by
  Digging root;
  Nostril pierced
By
  Seedling shoot;

Rocks, miasmas
In my breast—
  Willowill
O
Guard my rest.

Here are some other dramatic poems:

OVERHEARD IN AN ASYLUM

And here we have another case
quite different from the last,
another case quite different—
Listen.

Baby, drink.
The war is over.
Mother's breasts
are round with milk.

Baby, rest.
The war is over.
Only pigs
slop over so.

Baby, sleep.
The war is over.
Daddy's come
with a German coin.

Baby, dream.
The war is over.
You'll be a soldier
too.

Yes, we gave her the doll—
Now there we have another case
quite different from—

ALFRED KREYMBORG

POEM TO WILLIAM, MY BROTHER

(b. 1945 d. 1948)

If will can move
A ghost, or love
Direct one, you
And I will kiss
One midnight. True
Though death be, I
Am truer: this
I swear in verse.
Since you first died,
Murdering me,
And slipped time's curse
For order's sake,
Confidently
Time's watched us seek,
And has done most,
Not meaning to,
For the aging ghost
That has sought you.

JAMES CRENNER

ENVOI

Go, little book. If anybody asks
Why I add poems to a time like this,
Tell how the comeliness I can't take in
Of ships and other figures of content
Compels me still until I give them names;
And how I give them names impatiently,
As who should pull up roses by the roots
That keep him turning on his empty bed,
The smell intolerable and thick with loss.

WILLIAM MEREDITH

GIVE BACK, GIVE BACK

If I married him for length,
none was so little so long.
How think to explain it?—
Words I have known are now his,
his weight rests under my pillow.
I have nothing for floating.

My children are of groceries,
and not of love. None
has fallen for years, none come crying,
as if the middle years were trying
to break me of my light warping.
I am not so lucky for looking.

On the white sheet of his will
my children inherited
the objects of original pleasure, his
for which I gave up pleasure,
for pleasure, in pleasure, to pleasure.
I am the lot of him, as is my wont.

Yet have wanted to wear the ring of him,
hear it and recreate it.
Into the night those marriages go
to which woman is bound to be used.
All over I hear the breathing pause
at the long entrance of the children.

MARVIN BELL

suggested writing assignment

Write a 24–30 line poem in syllabics—a dialogue, monologue, or
soliloquy.

18

major genres:
LYRICS

The third of the major genres (kinds) of poetry is *lyrics* or songs. But before we proceed to consider lyrics, and then go on to the minor genres, a point must be stressed: Many poems, just as they mix levels, likewise mix *genres*. For instance, shortly we will be considering the minor genre *occasionals*—poems written to celebrate a particular occurrence. Well, most occasionals are themselves lyrics. In fact, the two major forms of occasionals—odes and elegies—are lyric forms.

If we look back at the examples of poems given in the chapters on narratives and dramatics, it will occur to us that some of them might as easily have been called lyrics or something else, and some narratives might have appeared with our discussion of dramatics, et cetera.

The reason for analyzing the elements is *not* to pigeonhole each and every poem we read or write. Quite the contrary: It is to show *how elements blend,* to show how to use particular techniques *any way we want to use them,* to provide a *common vocabulary for discussion of poetry.* Nobody is trying to limit anyone. *The more one knows, the more he can do.* The boundaries of poetry are limitless, even in traditional forms and prosodies. We are limited only by our ignorance, by our inabilities, by the burdens of tradition—*not* by elements and techniques. Elements and techniques are what liberate us to become *makers, to* express what we need to express.

The three major genres of poetry, then, are: (1) *lyric poetry,*
(2) *narrative poetry,* and (3) *dramatic poetry.* These genres often, but
not always, correspond to the three poetic voices. For instance, lyric
poetry is often spoken from the egopoetic point-of-view; narrative poetry
from the narrative point-of view, and dramatic poetry from the dramatic
point-of-view. Even these—points-of-view—may be blended, as we have
seen in such poems as Robert Frost's "The Hill Wife." But if we need
to classify for purposes of discussion, what we need to decide is what
the poem is *mostly.*

Here is a college poem that is written in *short measure,* but it isn't
a ballad in particular. It is a song about death: *a dirge:*

TOTENTANZ

Lace the wind with rhythm,
   Heel and toe in time;
Tread a measure with the night,
   Heed the night's rhyme.

Hamlet on the parapet,
   Yorick in the ground;
Men are one, and one is man
   With the night's round.

Druids trod this measure once,
   Adam knew it well.
Shadow owns a harpsichord:
   Allemande, knell.

Brutus with his gory fist—
   Link hands, place your feet;
Judas swinging in the gale
   Keeps the slow beat.

Face your partner, courtesy;
   Time's fiddle arm soon flags.
Step aside, let others pace
   Ere the tune lags.

Fetter wind with rhythm,
   Heel and toe in time.
Tread a measure with the night.
Heed the night's rhyme.

And here is another:

A LYKE-WAKE DIRGE

This ae nighte, this ae nighte,
   —*Every nighte and alle,*

Fire and sleet and candle-lighte,
    And Christe receive thy saule.

When thou from hence away art past,
    —Every nighte and alle,
To Whinny-muir thou com'st at last,
    And Christe receive thy saule.

If ever thou gavest hosen and shoon,
    —Every nighte and alle,
Sit thee down and put them on,
    And Christe receive thy saule.

If hosen and shoon thou ne'er gav'st nane
    —Every nighte and alle,
The whinnes sall prick thee to the bare bane,
    And Christe receive thy saule.

From Brig o' Dread when thou may'st pass,
    —Every nighte and alle,
To Purgatory fire thou com'st at last;
    And Christe receive thy saule.

If ever thou gavest meat or drink,
    —Every nighte and alle,
The fire sall never make thee shrink;
    And Christe receive thy saule.

If meat or drink thou ne'er gav'st nane,
    —Every nighte and alle,
The fire will burn thee to the bare bane;
    And Christe receive thy saule.

This ae nighte, this ae nighte,
    —Every nighte and alle,
Fire and sleet and candle-lighte,
    And Christe receive thy saule.

                                            ANONYMOUS

On the other hand, here is a lyric written in syllabics:

MILLPOND

    This is the place where peace grows
like a green frond set among waters aerial
    with dragonflies. Where, at noon,
  the trees section the broad falling
leaf of light, and space color upon the millpond,
    yet do not move because motion
        might be lost upon silence.

This is the place where a stone,
given its occasional career, could disturb
     little with an arc and fall,
   for the pond would swallow all voice
and shrug circling ripples into its banks until
   moss had absorbed this small wet gift,
     showing a fancy darker.

This is the place where one may
abet his heart's romance, deceiving his eyes by
     unconsciously confusing
   slow change with no change. But even
here, dream makes way for declensions of wind and sun.
   The alders will grow, moss will dry.
   Wings will pulsate, then plummet.

This is the place where peace rests
like ferns beyond lilies. The trick is to wear it
     as a mantle, but to know
   cloaks for cloaks, shelters for shelters.
Beneath this revery of surfaces, fish wait
   for the dragonfly's mistake. The
     trick is to lose, but to own.

Besides the many lyric poem, stanza, and line forms* one may use, there are a number of loose forms that have been used by lyricists:

The AUBADE is a lovesong whose setting is dawn. Often each stanza ends with the word *dawn*. Here is an aubade written as a syllabic acrostic:

AUBADE TO SAY THE LEAST

*M*orning. A dull silver. The fields
*A*re an ore of straw. The
*R*ust of maples and oaks fires this
*G*old of August in our falling—
*A*nd the house is adrift,
*R*unning through the sluice of dream. Now,
*E*vening is over on its way
*T*oward windows like quicksilver.

ANACREONTICS praise wine, women, and song:

---

* See *The Book of Forms* by Lewis Turco, New York: E. P. Dutton, 1968 (paperback) for a complete listing of verse forms used in English.

OUT FOR A NIGHT

It was No, no, no, practicing at a chair,
And No at the wall, and one for the fireplace,
And down the stairs it was No over the railing,
And two for the dirt, and three Noes for the air,

And four in a row rapidly over the bar,
Becoming Maybe, Maybe, from spittoon to mirror,
It was shrugging cheeks on one face after another,
And Perhaps and So-So at both ends of a cigar,

Five, and it was Yes as a matter of fact
Who said it wasn't all the way down the bottle,
It was Hell Yes over and lightly underfoot,
And tongue like a welcome mat for the bartender,

And Yes in the teeth, Yes like a cracked whistle,
And one for you, and two for the rest of us,
Indeed, Indeed, the chair got up on the table,
And Yes got up on the chair and kissed the light

And the light burned, and Yes fell out of the chair,
And the chair slid off the table, and it was Maybe
All over the floor, tilted, it was squat,
And plunge to the rear, and smack lips like a baby,

It was five for the fingers Absolutely,
Four in the corners, it was three for the show,
And two descending eyebrows to make a ceiling,
And No to the knees and chin, and one Goodbye.

                                        DAVID WAGONER

The BALADA is a dance song with an insistent refrain. A CACCIA
or CATCH is a longer ROUNDELAY—any simple lyric that utilizes
a refrain. This one was written by a college student:

THE ISLE IS FULL OF NOISES

What if, tomorrow, after your coffee,
after your Wheaties, while you're buttoning your clothes—
a dove descends and inspects your chimney?
        (What if it doesn't?)
                Expect nothing.   Suppose.

What if, while putting your room in order,
after you've stashed every thing where it goes—
you see that your mirror's haloed in foxfire?
        (What if it isn't?)
                Expect nothing.   Suppose.

What if, during your smoke on the parkbench,
after your cogitations, before your doze—
who should kiss you but a leftover virgin?
    (What if she doesn't?)
        Expect nothing.   Suppose.

What if, suddenly, deep in a bookstore,
a ghost voice comes leap-frogging over the rows—
the voice says, "I love you." It's your father's.
    (What if it isn't?)
        Expect nothing.   Suppose.

What if, one evening, watering your bean patch,
kite-caught, you quicken: you know what God knows—
the salt of your tears withers the sproutlings—
    What if it doesn't?
        Suppose.   Suppose.   Suppose.

SAM HUDSON

    The CANSO, CANZO, or CANZONE is a song about beauty
and love:

THE PASSIONATE SHEPHERD TO HIS LOVE

Come live with me and be my Love,
And we will all the pleasures prove
That hills and valleys, dale and field,
And all the craggy mountains yield.

There will we sit upon the rocks
And see the shepherds feed their flocks
By shallow rivers, to whose falls
Melodious birds sing madrigals.

There will I make thee beds of roses
And a thousand fragrant posies,
A cap of flowers, and a kirtle
Embroider'd all with leaves of myrtle.

A gown made of the finest wool,
Which from our pretty lambs we pull,
Fair linéd slippers for the cold,
With buckles of the purest gold.

A belt of straw and ivy buds
With coral clasps and amber studs:
And if these pleasures may thee move,
Come live with me and be my Love.

Thy silver dishes for thy meat
As precious as the gods do eat,
Small on an ivory table be
Prepared each day for thee and me.

The shepherd swains shall dance and sing
For thy delight each May-morning:
If these delights thy mind may move,
Then live with me and be my Love.

CHRISTOPHER MARLOWE

A CANTICLE is a lyric rooted in liturgy:

A CANTICLE TO THE WATERBIRDS

Written for the Feast of Saint Francis of Asissi, 1950

Clack your beaks you cormorants and kittiwakes,
North on those rock-croppings finger-jutted into the rough Pacific surge;
You migratory terns and pipers who leave but the temporal clawtrack written
    on sandbars there of your presence;
Grebes and pelicans; you comber-picking scorers and you shorelong gulls;
All you keepers of the coastline north of here to the Mendocino beaches;
All you beyond upon the cliff-face thwarting the surf at Hecate Head;
Hovering the under-surge where the cold Columbia grapples at the bar;
North yet to the Sound, whose islands float like a sown flurry of chips
    upon the sea:
Break wide your harsh and salt-encrusted beaks unmade for song
And say a praise up to the Lord.

And you freshwater egrets east in the flooded marshlands skirting the sea-level
    rivers, white one-legged watchers of shallows;
Broad-headed kingfishers minnow-hunting from willow stems on meandering
    valley sloughs;
You too, you herons, blue and supple-throated, stately, taking the air majestical
    in the sunflooded San Joaquin,
Grading down on your belted wings from the upper lights of sunset,
Mating over the willow clumps or where the flatwater rice fields shimmer;
You killdeer, high night-criers, far in the moon-suffusion sky;
Bitterns, sand-waders, all shore-walkers, all roost-keepers,
Populates of the 'dobe cliffs of the Sacramento:
Open your water-dartling beaks,
And make a praise up to the Lord.

For you hold the heart of His mighty fastnesses,
And shape the life of His indeterminate realms.
You are everywhere on the lonesome shores of His wide creation.

You keep seclusion where no man may go, giving Him praise;
Nor may a woman come to lift like your cleaving flight her clear contralto song
To honor the spindrift gifts of His soft abundance.
You sanctify His hermitage rocks where no holy priest may kneel to adore,
    nor holy nun assist;
And where his true communion-keepers are not enabled to enter.

And well may you say His praises, birds, for your ways
Are verved with the secret skills of His inclinations,
And your habits plaited and rare with the subdued elaboration
    of his intricate craft;
Your days intent with the direct astuteness needful for His outworking,
And your nights alive with the dense repose of His infinite sleep.
You are His secretive charges and you serve His secretive ends,
In His clouded mist-conditioned stations, in His murk,
Obscure in your matted nestings, immured in His limitless ranges.
He makes you penetrate through dark interstitial joinings of His thicketed
    kingdoms,
And keep your concourse in the deeps of His shadowed world.

Your ways are wild but earnest, your manners grave,
Your customs carefully schooled to the note of His serious mien.
You hold the prime condition of His clean creating,
And the swift compliance with which you serve His minor means
Speaks of the constancy with which you hold Him.
For what is your high flight forever going home to your first beginnings,
But such a testament to your devotion?
You hold His outstretched world beneath your wings, and mount
    upon His storms,
And keep your sheer wind-lidded sight upon the vast perspectives
    of His mazy latitudes.

But mostly it is your way you bear existence wholly within the context
    of His utter will and are untroubled.
Day upon day you do not reckon, nor scrutinize tomorrow, nor multiply
    the nightfalls with a rash concern,
But rather assume each instant as warrant sufficient of His final seal.
Wholly in Providence you spring, and when you die you look on death
    in clarity unflinched,
Go down, a clutch of feather ragged upon the brush;
Or drop on water where you briefly lived, found food,
And now yourselves made food for His deep current-keeping fish,
    and then are gone:
Is left but the pinion-feather spinning a bit on the uproil
Where lately the dorsal cut clear air.

You leave a silence. And this for you suffices, who are not of the ceremonials
    of man,
And hence are not made sad to now forgo them.

Yours is of another order of being, and wholly it compels.
But may you, birds, utterly seized in God's supremacy,
Austerely living under his austere eye—
Yet may you teach a man a necessary thing to know,
Which has to do of the strict conformity that creaturehood entails,
And constitutes the prime commitment all things share.
For God has given you the imponderable grace to *be* His verification,
Outside the mulled incertitude of our forensic choices;
That you, our lessers in the rich hegemony of Being,
May serve as testament to what a creature is,
And what creation owes.

Curlews, stilts and scissortails, beachcomber gulls,
Wave-haunters, shore-keepers, rockhead-holders, all cape-top vigilantes,
Now give God praise.
Send up the strict articulation of your throats,
And say His name.

WILLIAM EVERSON

A CAROL originally was merely a joyous hymn, but it has come by tradition to apply specifically to hymns about the Nativity, whether joyous or not. Carols have a specific form, as illustrated in the following poem, but they need not be written in any set form:

THE SIGN

Once in the night there shone a Sign.
Now darkness lies upon Palestine.

My father spoke to me of birth
In his old age. He said, "Man's worth
Cannot be measured here on earth.
Once, in the night, there shone a Sign."

My mother never spoke of death
Except in periphrasis—breath
And murmur. We hung our wreath:
Now darkness lies upon Palestine.

I grew through Christmases and bells,
Through firs adorned, the sundry hells
And heavens where every child dwells.
Once, in the night, there shone a sign:

A star atop an evergreen,
A creche beneath. Let none demean
What was intended, what has not been,
Now darkness lies upon Palestine.

Now I inform my child, "This star
Foretold a birth. From afar
The wise men came. Though there is war,
Once in the night there shone a Sign. . . ,

"But it foretold a man's death, too.
I saw more clearly as I grew
Older; I saw, and so will you.
Now darkness lies upon Palestine."

And if these twins lie in the straw
Together, twined in fear and awe,
Then we must kneel before The Law—
Once, in the night. There shone a Sign;

Now, darkness lies upon Palestine.

A CHANT is a work song or religious recitiative that has a refrain;
a CHANTEY is a sailor's work song:

HAUL AWAY, JOE

Away, haul away, oh! haul away together,
Away, haul away, oh! haul away, Joe!

When I was a little lad, my mother told me
Away, haul away, oh! haul away together
That if I did not kiss the girls my lips would grow moldy
Away, haul away, oh! haul away, Joe!

Louie was the king of France, before the revolu-shi-ann
Away, haul away, oh! haul away together
But then he got his head cut off, it spoiled his consti-tu-shi-ann

Away, haul away, oh! haul away, Joe!
But now I've got an Irish girl, and she nearly drives me crazy—

Away, haul away, oh! haul away together
Away, haul away, oh! haul away, Joe!

                                                    ANONYMOUS

The DITHYRAMB is a wild song honoring revelry:

JOLLY RUTTERKIN

Rutterkin has come to town—
    Hey! jolly Rutter, hey!
Without a cloak nor coat nor gown,
But a good green hood upon his crown
    Like a hoyden rutter!

Rutterkin has no English—
   Hey! jolly Rutter, hey!
His tongue runs on like butterfish
Smeared with grease upon his dish
   Like a hoyden rutter!

Kiss Rutterkin and change your luck—
   Hey! jolly Rutter, hey!
He takes his ale down at a suck
Till he be wiser than a duck
   Like a hoyden rutter!

When Rutterkin gets up from board—
   Hey! jolly Rutter, hey!
He'll piss a gallon in a gourd,
Then take the lasses like a lord,
   Like a hoyden rutter!

ANONYMOUS

A DITTY is any simple lyric meant to be sung:

I CARE NOT FOR THESE LADIES

I care not for these Ladies,
That must be woode and praide,
Give me kind Amarillis
The wanton countrey maide;
Nature art disdaineth,
Her beautie is her owne;
   Her when we court and kisse,
   She cries, *Forsooth, let go.*
   But when we come where comfort is,
   She never will say no.

If I love Amarillis,
She gives me fruit and flowers,
But if we love these Ladies,
We must give golden showers,
Give them gold that sell love,
Give me the Nutbrowne lasse,
   Who when we court and kisse,
   She cries *Forsooth, let go.*
   But when we come where comfort is,
   She never will say no.

These Ladies must have pillowes,
And beds by strangers wrought,
Give me a Bower of willowes,
Of mosse and leaves unbought,

And fresh Amarillis,
With milk and honie fed,
　Who, when we court and kisse,
　She cries, *Forsooth, let go,*
　But when we come where comfort is,
　She never will say no.

THOMAS CAMPION

The ELEGY—one of the two major forms of *occasionals*—is
a serious lyric meditation, often on the subject of death:

FOR CLEMENT LONG, DEAD

lines written in the dark

Lord listen, or heaven is undone.
He will not spell your name or take your hand,
will hee-haw at the gate with a held breath,
will run away to the end where death is real.

Lord if you chase him like a wheatfield fire
till halelujahs and a choir of angels
sing him coming and the grand gates open,
still he will stand against your house
where no sin ever is and no flesh fails.

If even he has treasures, let the mouse
discover the grain, take the worm to the tree.
Give his potential pleasures to the poor.
Or watch him. And watch him well. And watching see
how he subverts the angels, whispering this:

ninety and nine returned and deserve attending;
surely the faithful one, the unoffending
son should have the calf; God, it's a small grace
to be a counter of coins in the first place.

MILLER WILLIAMS

Other, more intense lyrics of lamentation are the CORONACH, DIRGE
(see "Totentanz" and "A Lyke-Wake Dirge," above), MONODY and
THRENODY.

The EPITHALAMION or EPITHALAMIUM is a marital elegy or
wedding song. Originally, it was written in three movements or *strophes*:
The first part was to be sung at the chamber door of the bridegroom
and bride, and it was congratulatory in nature. It urged the newlyweds
to lusty combat, and was designed to muffle the sounds of that combat.
The second strophe was intended to refresh the combatants and urge

them to fresh efforts during the night. The third movement, sung in the morning, congratulated the couple on their performances, urged a truce until the next evening, and instructed them in their domestic and marital duties. A meditative lyric on the same subject is called a PROTHALAMION or PROTHALAMIUM:

WEDDING SONG

Orpheus calling. The grass parts, the seas
   lie down for Orpheus, the one
      calling, without harp or hymn,
         with his favored flesh, running
            white as a summer's day,

warmer than grass and stone
   where the sun lay.
      Everyone running, running before
         Orpheus, who loses again
         and again, himself, calling.

The grove beats with voices, sees
   a wedding walking, trees
      harping and crying, Eurydike
         runs in a white dress, her train
            catching the burrs and the leaves falling.

We, strangers on a bridge, look down.
   The moss-wedded water shows
      a wedding walking through water cress
         and wild flags, turning, flows
            into the muddy bed.

Procession in weedy dress
   spins us around too late. For us
      the air burns with their having
         been, like a swing rocking
            where the child has fled.

The serpent that gnaws
   at love lies sunning
      in the song. Orpheus calling.
         Through the woods they pass,
            hand in hand, running,

the Word calling, the grass
   parts and the sea lies down
      before the hymn, himself, before
         this man who loves, who was
            before sea, grass, and all falling.

                                        NANCY WILLARD

The LAY is a short narrative song—not to be confused with the French *lai,* which is a set form: This example of the lay is written in the form of an *English sonnet*:

THE HARLEM DANCER

Applauding youths laughed with young prostitutes
And watched her perfect, half-clothed body sway;
Her voice was like the sound of blended flutes
Blown by black players upon a picnic day.
She sang and danced on gracefully and calm,
The light gauze hanging loose about her form;
To me she seemed a proudly-swaying palm
Grown lovelier for passing through a storm.
Upon her swarthy neck black shiny curls
Luxuriant fell; and tossing coins in praise,
The wine-flushed, bold-eyed boys, and even the girls,
Devoured her shape with eager, passionate gaze;
But looking at her falsely-smiling face,
I knew her self was not in that strange place.

CLAUDE MCKAY

The MADRIGAL is a lyric concerning love, and is meant to be sung:

YOU KNOW MY HEART

You know my heart, my lady dear,
　That since the time I was your thrall
I have been yours both whole and clear,
　Though my reward has been but small:
　So am I yet, and more than all,
　　And you know well how I have served;
As if you prove it shall appear
　　How well, how long,
　　　How faithfully,
　　And suffered wrong
　　　How patiently!
　　Then, since that I have never swerved,
　　Let not my pains be undeserved.

You know also, though you say nay,
　That you alone are my desire;
And you alone it is that may
　Assuage my fervent, flaming fire;
　Succour me, then, I you require.

You know it were a just request,
Since you do cause my heat, I say,
    If that I burn,
        That you will warm,
    And not to turn
        All to my harm,
    Sending such flame from frozen breast
    Against all right for my unrest.

And I know well how frowardly
    You have mistaken my true intent,
And hitherto how wrongfully
    I have found cause for to repent:
But death shall ride me readily
    If your hard heart do not relent;
        And I know well all this you know,
            That I and mine,
                And all I have,
            You may assign
                To spill or save.
        Why are you then so cruel foe
        Unto your own that loves you so?

                            THOMAS WYATT

For examples of the MADSONG—a lyric sung by a madman or
a fool—see Yeats' "Crazy Jane and the Bishop" on p. 204, and "Odds
Bodkin's Springsong" on p. 201.

A NURSERY RHYME is a song for children:

BUGS

Big Bug, Little Bug,
Middle Bug, Beetle,
One named Tweedledum,
Another named Tweedle.
The third named Sam,
And he went for a ride
With a pretty little Ladybug
Sitting at his side.

The ODE is one of the two major form of *occasionals,* the elegy
being the other. It is a celebration of some event. (See the chapter on
Occasionals.)

The PAEAN is a song of praise to the gods; a PANEGYRIC or
ENCOMIUM praises men:

THE AFTERHOUR JOCKEYS

everytime after the next time
anybody gives us one a those
        "i gotcha" grabs

  we'll sky high in slippery ways
  leaving behind pairs of hands
  hurting from taking too much for granted

from then on out we'll be into
  an afterhour jockey stretch

    'round 'bout midnight
      thelonius monk gon turn up
      as one of our slanted priests
        teaching us how to be doubly exposed
        without coming out negative
  how to develop in dark rooms
  using the new braille charts
    how to play the crooked blues
    and if need be break the rules

All this info will spread itself
  so homefolks everywhere can get into
  a medley of sabbatical leaves

      we'll be untrackable
        bending census polls to question marks
        as seven dimensional sleepwalkers
          we'll crash the dreams of choreographers

we're about a knocktoed bowfooted slewlegged
pigeonkneed breed on an off minor orbit
      who every once and again
      unlax in an oldie but goodie shack
      to check out where our tracks have been

wherever we are is already a minute ago
  cause we're somewhere else
    and not there for too long

                              WESLEY BROWN

        The PASTORAL and similar forms are treated in the chapter on
bucolics.
        The REVEILLE is a waking song for morning—see "Awaken,
Bells Falling" p. 135.
        A RUNE is an incantation or magic charm, often in the form of
an *acrostic* or *anagram*—see "The Husband's Message" on p. 90, and
"A Talisman" on p. 114.

Coming full circle, the SERENADE is like the aubade, except that its setting is the evening:

SERENADE

Way, moon, sky Cub and Bear are low this summer.
The maples fatten, pigeons rounder grow.
A humid clover makes the rabbit heavy:
Bucks wait for does although they can't be slow.

My pretty, pretty girl, come out for rubbing.
Call love a feel. The weather's very near.
This warm air lolling in my hands is ready.
Leaf, bush, bough—O my pretty.   O my dear.

ROBERT HUFF

Actually, this poem is similar to a *horning,* a mock serenade sung to a bride.

suggested writing assignment

Write two lyrics, amounting to 24–28 lines altogether. Write one of them in accentuals or accentual-syllabics, the other in any way you wish.

19

minor genres:
DIDACTICS

Didactic poetry is *teaching* poetry. It is expository in nature, and it often winds up being more verse essay than poem because the writer is so intent upon *what* he is saying that he sometimes forgets *how* to say it well. Much contemporary protest poetry is didactic and propagandistic in nature. The eighteenth century was also particularly fond of didactic poetry.

Here is a didactic poem that was written in the University of Iowa's Writers' Workshop in response to a poem by someone who seemed to be defending the theory that poetry must be naked and free of any kind of form at all:

A COFFEE-HOUSE LECTURE

Come now, you who carry
  Your passions on your back,
Will insolence and envy
  Get you the skill you lack?
Scorning the lonely hours
  That other men have spent,
How can you hope to fathom
  What made them eloquent?

273

Blake tells you in his notebooks,
  If you could understand,
That Style and Execution
  Are Feeling's only friend,
That all Poetic Wisdom
  Begins in the minute,
And Vision sees most clearly
  While fingering a lute.

Robert Burns in Ayreshire
  With meter and with gauge
Studied the strict exactitudes
  That luminate his page,
Ignored the vulgar grandeur
  That you and yours revere,
And labored with his body
  And his perfected ear.

Paul Valery gripped a scalpel
  And sweated at his task,
Bent over bleeding Chaos
  In spotless gown and mask;
And in reluctant lectures
  Spoke of the cruel art
And cold precise transactions
  That warm the human heart.

How many that have toiled
  At the hard craft of verse
Had nothing more than music
  To fill their empty purse,
But found it was sufficient,
  In making out a will,
To pay for their mortality,
  And they are living still.

ROBERT MEZEY

A brief look at the elements of exposition may prove helpful at this point.

i. expository elements

The four basic elements of expository writing are the *subject* being examined, the *thesis* or statement of the point which the author is trying to prove, the *argument* or backing for the thesis which consists of data and facts to serve as proof for the thesis, and the *conclusion* or restatement of the proved thesis.

The CLASSICAL DISCOURSE is a model structure for expository writing.

ii. structure of the classical discourse

1) *Subject*

The subject of the discourse is given in the title.

2) *Thesis*

The *exordium* is the statement of the subject being examined and an introduction to the author's thesis. It differs from the subject in that it is a *complete statement*, usually given in one independent clause or sentence.

3) *Argument*

A. The *narratio* is the exposition of necessary background information concerning subject and thesis.

B. The *confirmatio* is the list of arguments, proofs, and facts backing the thesis. It is usually arranged in the order of weakest argument to strongest (climactic).

C. The *refutatio* is the rebuttal of all possible arguments to the contrary. It is usually arranged in the order of strongest argument to weakest (anticlimactic).

4) *Conclusion*

The *peroratio* is an appeal to emotion as well as to logic, the restatement of the proved thesis, and the conclusion of the discourse.

Some didactic techniques—commonly found in the classical discourse, and in other arguments, are these:

METASTASIS is the technique of flitting from one argument to another quickly, much as a boxer bobs and weaves so that his opponent can't get a good shot at him.

STASIS is the technique of dwelling at length upon one's strongest argument.

PARAGON is the argumentative technique of quickly summing up and rejecting all reasons for making a particular point, except the one reason which the arguer believes to be valid.

PARECNASIS is the technique of digression: leaving one's main argument for a time to talk of other things which, for the moment, may

not seem pertinent, but which in fact bolster the main point when one
returns to it.

APOPHASIS is the rhetorical technique of denying one's intention
to speak of a particular point, at the same time that one mentions it;
i.e., "I don't intend to mention the fact that Mr. Soandso was convicted
for larceny."

"The Old Professor" comes fairly close to following the form of the
classical discourse. It was written in college about a real person, and it
is cast in the form of a *chant royal*:

THE OLD PROFESSOR

Each day he drags his scholar's armament
   Along these limb-hung walks toward an old
Stone building, every ancient nerve intent
   Upon the threadbare lecture he has told
Since time was wound. His faculties impaled
By blunting years of teaching: cured and nailed
  To walls of hoarded knowledge none have seen
  Him lately scale, he trudges to the clean,
   Bland faces waiting in his daily void.
He owns but one idea that's pristine:
   At least the old professor is employed.

That hour has long grown moss when discontent
   Could nip his heels along the trails he's strolled
Spring, fall and winter. The ennoblement
   Of education was a manna sold
For fodder: feasts too rich had been curtailed
Because his fresh young banquets all had staled,
  Unsavored, on his desk. Now the routine
  Is constant, undisturbed. And the cuisine
   He offers is cold statement unalloyed
With sweetmeats that might activate the spleen.
   At least the old professor is employed.

A poverty of mind seemed evident
   Among his pupils: most were of a mold.
He'd searched in vain for signs of argument;
   He'd flattered, bantered, battered and cajoled
When moons were blue. But nothing had availed.
Those freshman bastions could not be assailed.
  His foes reclined behind his walls, serene.
  They would not rally arms to fog the scene
   With sorties into knowledge. Thus, devoid
Of wars, the warrior turned Nazarene—
   At least the old professor is employed.

Oh, he'd unburied some intelligent
   Young bodies then and now, but few were bold
Enough, and some were even reverent!
   The best of these had thumbed and pigeonholed
His words for hoary use. He had regaled
No one with tales of beauties lying veiled
   In halls of thought wherein a libertine
   Of wisdom might disport himself unseen
      And lip the cider Eve swore never cloyed.
   Though none had truly broached his bright demesne,
      At least the old professor is employed.

Then has his coin of manhood been misspent
   Because he's been unable to uphold
Antique ideals to any fond extent?
   And has the campus chapel belfry tolled
The streaming hordes of moments he's been gaoled
In mental pillories; been flayed and flailed
   By apathy? Have all his sometime keen
   Abilities been dulled, transformed to mean
      Synaptic grooves? Can he become annoyed
No longer? Is he just a figurine . . . ?
      At least the old professor is employed.

There rusts an ancient harvesting machine
Deprived of acreage that once was green,
   But withered now by hoarfrosts that destroyed
The twig that never nurtured nectarine.
   At least the old professor is employed.

However, many modern didactic poems do not argue, they harangue; they become RANTS or FLYTINGS. A rant is a bitter invective, such as Robinson Jeffers' "Shine, Perishing Republic." A flyting is a debate between poets which can become bitter—we have already spoken of the *debat* in the chapter on dramatics.

SHINE PERISHING REPUBLIC

While this America settles in the mould of its vulgarity, heavily thickening to empire,
And protest, only a bubble in the molten mass, pops and sighs out, and the mass hardens,

I sadly smiling remember that the flower fades to make fruit, the fruit rots to make earth.
Out of the mother; and through the spring exultances, ripeness and decadence; and home to the mother.

You make haste on decay: not blameworthy; life is good, be it stubbornly long
   or suddenly
A mortal splendor: meteors are not needed less than mountains: shine, perishing
   republic.

But for my children, I would have them keep their distance from the thickening
   center; corruption
Never has been compulsory, when the cities lie at the monster's feet there are
   left the mountains.

And boys, be in nothing so moderate as in love of man, a clever servant,
   insufferable master.
There is the trap that catches noblest spirits, that caught—they say—God,
   when he walked on earth.

                                                 ROBINSON JEFFERS

PREFACE TO A TWENTY VOLUME SUICIDE NOTE

Lately, I've become accustomed to the way
The ground opens up and envelops me
Each time I go out to walk the dog.
Or the broad edged silly music the wind
Makes when I run for a bus—

Things have come to that.

And now, each night I count the stars,
And each night I get the same number.
And when they will not come to be counted
I count the holes they leave.

Nobody sings anymore.

And then last night, I tiptoed up
To my daughter's room and heard her
Talking to someone, and when I opened
The door, there was no one there . . .
Only she on her knees,
Peeking into her own clasped hands.

                                                 LEROI JONES

AN OPEN LETTER TO LEROI JONES

"Nobody sings anymore."—from *Preface to a*
Twenty Volume Suicide Note by LeRoi Jones.

When we were younger, when words were the things we loved;
when men were men, evil and good;
when there was hope;
when you could speak to all, though few would listen;

when I could speak to you, though I did not know you;
when I did not know you were black, but only that your words were black on
    a white page;

when the page spoke and did not scream;
when there was a way for minds to touch across great distances;
when I read you and, perhaps, you read me in the magazines only the young
    and the hopeful read;
when time and life meant something more than now they mean;
when there was art;
when we meant to change the world with reason and love;
when there was infinite possibility, in art as in life—

then the world stayed the same, and we did not change it;
then we grew older, and now we are bitter;

now you speak bitterly, to bitter men, and the words are black in your mouth;
now bitter men hear, but do not listen;
now the words you say are the old words—we have lost our art;
now we say what has always been said,
now everyone understands—there is comfort in what we say;
now what we avoided when we were poets has come to pass:
now we are cliches, and our words mirror us;
now you are a black man and I am white—only the colors remain, the colors of
    our words and pages:
now we do not speak, we only harangue;
now we do not tell what could be, but only what is, what always has been;

we have lost ourselves in slogan;
we have lost our art in the web of words;
we are devoured by unreason, by the spider within;
we have forgone that which is human: mind, love, and art:

"Nobody sings anymore."

We are no longer poets.

   Notice that this kind of poem is egopoetic and *exclusive*. It is closed:
no other point of view is represented but the poet's. The classical
discourse is also a closed form, but it allows for opposing arguments.
Therefore, it is inclusive at least to some degree. Of course, in a whole
flyting, opposing arguments are represented.
   Generally, the better didactic poems are very compact, but this isn't
always true. An excellent example of serious contemporary *georgics* is
David Wagoner's "Staying Alive." GEORGICS are verse handbooks in
the arts or crafts. Wagoner's poem, on the literal level, tells how to stay
alive in the woods. But on the allegorical level it says a good deal more
than that:

STAYING ALIVE

Staying alive in the woods is a matter of calming down
At first and deciding whether to wait for rescue,
Trusting to others,
Or simply to start walking and walking in one direction
Till you come out—or something happens to stop you.
By far the safer choice
Is to settle down where you are, and try to make a living
Off the land, camping near water, away from shadows.
Eat no white berries;
Spit out all bitterness. Shooting at anything
Means hiking further and further every day
To hunt survivors;
It may be best to learn what you have to learn without a gun,
Not killing but watching birds and animals go
In and out of shelter
At will. Following their example, build for a whole season:
Facing across the wind in your lean-to,
You may feel wilder,
But nothing, not even you, will have to stay in hiding.
If you have no matches, a stick and a fire-bow
Will keep you warmer,
Or the crystal of your watch, filled with water, held up to the sun
Will do the same in time. In case of snow
Drifting toward winter,
Don't try to stay awake through the night, afraid of freezing—
The bottom of your mind knows all about zero;
It will turn you over
And shake you till you waken. If you have trouble sleeping
Even in the best of weather, jumping to follow
With eyes strained to their corners
The unidentifiable noises of the night and feeling
Bears and packs of wolves nuzzling your elbow,
Remember the trappers
Who treated them indifferently and were left alone.
If you hurt yourself, no one will comfort you
Or take your temperature,
So stumbling, wading, and climbing are as dangerous as flying.
But if you decide, at last, you must break through
In spite of all danger,
Think of yourself by time and not by distance. counting
Wherever you're going by how long it takes you;
No other measure
Will bring you safe to nightfall. Follow no streams: they run
Under the ground or fall into wilder country.

Remember the stars
And moss when your mind runs into circles. If it should rain
Or the fog should roll the horizon in around you,
Hold still for hours
Or days if you must, or weeks, for seeing is believing
In the wilderness. And if you find a pathway,
Wheel-rut, or fence-wire,
Retrace it left or right: someone knew where he was going
Once upon a time, and you can follow
Hopefully, somewhere,
Just in case. There may even come, on some uncanny evening,
A time when you're warm and dry, well fed, not thirsty,
Uninjured, without fear,
When nothing, either good or bad, is happening.
This is called staying alive. It's temporary.
What occurs after
Is doubtful. You must always be ready for something to come bursting
Through the far edge of a clearing, running toward you,
Grinning from ear to ear
And hoarse with welcome. Or something crossing and hovering
Overhead, as light as air, like a break in the sky,
Wondering what you are.
Here you are face to face with the problem of recognition.
Having no time to make smoke, too much to say.
You should have a mirror
With a tiny hole in the back for better aiming, for reflecting
Whatever disaster you can think of, to show
The way you suffer.
These body signals have universal meaning: If you are lying
Flat on your back with arms outstretched behind you,
You say you require
Emergency treatment; if you are standing erect and holding
Arms horizontal, you mean you are not ready;
If you hold them over
Your head, you want to be picked up. Three of anything
Is a sign of distress. Afterward, if you see
No ropes, no ladders,
No maps or messages falling, no searchlights or trails blazing,
Then, chances are, you should be prepared to burrow
Deep for a deep winter.

                                             DAVID WAGONER

Another form of didactics is the EPISTLE (or letter), used for giving
good (?) advice:

TO HELL WITH REVISING, I'M WRITING A NEW POEM

Anyway, it's two years since we ended
that summer as if to end all of them,
drunk at the writers' conference, swinging like
crazy, and that poet threw logs over our transom,

trying to get in and watch. You are still young
and lovely, but I have worked those poems so many
times, so many ways, that I've had to think
about you and all we said and strain it through

a hundred metaphors, a thousand iambic feet,
trying to patch it into order with my cat,
which has since died of distemper, and my wife,
whom I like more than I guessed, and of course my kids,

until I'd simply like to forget the metaphysics
and say that I'm going to get outdoors again
and pick some unpressed flowers. Listen,
why don't you go out and find someone you can trust?

RICHARD FROST

The RIDDLE is a lyric that asks a question, and provides hints to
the answer:

*ON THE P***E****S*

Because I am by nature blind,
I wisely choose to walk behind;
However, to avoid disgrace,
I let no creature see my face.
My words are few, but spoke with sense;
And yet my speaking gives offence:
Or, if to whisper I presume,
The company will fly the room.
By all the world I am opprest:
And my oppression gives them rest.
    Through me, though sore against my will,
Instructors every art instil.
By thousands I am sold and bought,
Who neither get nor lose a groat;
For none, alas! by me can gain,
But those who give me greatest pain.
Shall man presume to be my master,
Who's but my caterer and taster?
Yet, though I always have my will,
I'm but a mere depender still:

An humble hanger-on at best;
Of whom all people make a jest.
    In me detractors seek to find
Two vices of a different kind;
I'm too profuse, some censurers cry,
And all I get, I let it fly;
While others give me many a curse,
Because too close I hold my purse.
But this I know, in either case,
They dare not charge me to my face.
'Tis true, indeed, sometimes I save,
Sometimes run out of all I have;
But, when the year is at an end,
Computing what I get and spend,
My goings out, and comings in,
I cannot find I lose or win;
And therefore all that know me say,
I justly keep the middle way.
I'm always by my betters led;
I last get up, and first a-bed;
Though, if I rise before my time,
The learn'd in sciences sublime
Consult the stars, and thence foretell
Good luck to those with whom I dwell.

JONATHAN SWIFT

A set form for writing didactics is the *PRIMER COUPLET,* which
is merely a dipodic rhymed couplet used for versifying aphorisms:
"In Adam's fall / We sinned all," "A stitch in time / Saves nine," etc.
"The Lark" on p. 198 is essentially written in primer couplets, except
that the first line is repeated after two couplets in each stanza. Here are
some other didactic poems. Notice that lyricism is often used to "carry"
the message of the poem, and when lyricism isn't used, imagery is:

THE LIE

Go, soul, the body's guest,
    Upon a thankless arrant:
Fear not to touch the best;
    The truth shall be thy warrant.
        Go, since I needs must die,
        And give the world the lie.

Say to the court, it glows
    And shines like rotten wood;
Say to the church, it shows

What's good, and doth no good:
　　If church and court reply,
　　Then give them both the lie.

Tell potentates, they live
　Acting by others' action,
Not loved unless they give,
　Not strong but by a faction:
　　If potentates reply,
　　Give potentates the lie.

Tell men of high condition
　That manage the estate,
Their purpose is ambition,
　Their practice only hate:
　　And if they once reply,
　　Then give them all the lie.

Tell them that brave it most,
　They beg for more by spending,
Who, in their greatest cost,
　Seek nothing but commending:
　　And if they make reply,
　　Then give them all the lie.

Tell zeal it wants devotion;
　Tell love it is but lust;
Tell time it is but motion;
　Tell flesh it is but dust;
　　And wish them not reply,
　　For thou must give the lie.

Tell age it daily wasteth;
　Tell honour how it alters;
Tell beauty how she blasteth;
　Tell favour how it falters:
　　And as they shall reply,
　　Give every one the lie.

Tell wit how much it wrangles
　In tickle points of niceness;
Tell wisdom she entangles
　Herself in over-wiseness:
　　And when they do reply,
　　Straight give them both the lie.

Tell physic of her boldness;
　Tell skill it is prevention;
Tell charity of coldness;
　Tell law it is contention:

And as they do reply,
So give them still the lie.

Tell fortune of her blindness;
    Tell nature of decay;
Tell friendship of unkindness;
    Tell justice of delay:
        And if they will reply,
        Then give them all the lie.

Tell arts they have no soundness,
    But vary by esteeming;
Tell schools they want profoundness,
    And stand too much on seeming:
        If arts and schools reply,
        Give arts and schools the lie.

Tell faith it's fled the city;
    Tell how the country erreth;
Tell, manhood shakes off pity;
    Tell, virtue least preferreth:
        And if they do reply
        Spare not to give the lie.

So when thou hast, as I
    Commanded thee, done blabbing,
Although to give the lie
    Deserves no less than stabbing,
        Stab at thee he that will,
        No stab the soul can kill.

WALTER RALEIGH

THE BLIND MEN AND THE ELEPHANT

A HINDOO FABLE

It was six men of Indostan
    To learning much inclined,
Who went to see the Elephant
    (Though all of them were blind),
That each by observation
    Might satisfy his mind.

The *First* approached the Elephant,
    And happening to fall
Against his broad and sturdy side,
    At once began to bawl:
"God bless me! but the Elephant
    Is very like a wall!"

The *Second*, feeling of the tusk,
  Cried, "Ho! what have we here
So very round and smooth and sharp?
  To me 'tis mighty clear
This wonder of an Elephant
  Is very like a spear!"

The *Third* approached the animal,
  And happening to take
The squirming trunk within his hands,
  Thus boldly up and spake:
"I see," quoth he, "the Elephant
  Is very like a snake!"

The *Fourth* reached out an eager hand,
  And felt about the knee.
"What most this wondrous beast is like
  Is mighty plain," quoth he;
" 'Tis clear enough the Elephant
  Is very like a tree!"

The *Fifth* who chanced to touch the ear,
  Said: "E'en the blindest man
Can tell what this resembles most;
  Deny the fact who can,
This marvel of an Elephant
  Is very like a fan!"

The *Sixth* no sooner had begun
  About the beast to grope,
Than, seizing on the swinging tail
  That fell within his scope,
"I see," quoth he, "the Elephant
  Is very like a rope!"

And so these men of Indostan
  Disputed loud and long,
Each in his own opinion
  Exceeding stiff and strong,
Though each was partly in the right,
  And all were in the wrong!

  THE MORAL:
So oft in theologic wars,
  The disputants, I ween,
Rail on in utter ignorance
  Of what each other mean,
And prate about an Elephant
Not one of them has seen!

                    JOHN GODFREY SAXE

Saxe's poem is a FABLE: a small allegory—see the *fabliau* in the chapter on *narratives*.

A NEGRO SERMON—SIMON LEGREE

(To be read in your own variety of negro dialect)

Legree's big house was white and green.
His cotton-fields were the best to be seen.
He kept strong horses and fine swine.
He had cool jugs of cider and wine.
His garret was full of curious things:
Books of magic, bags of gold,
And rabbits' feet on long twine strings.
    But he went down to the Devil.

Legree he sported a brass buttoned coat,
A snake-skin necktie, a blood-red shirt.
Legree he had a beard like a goat,
And a thick hairy neck and eyes like dirt.
His puffed-out cheeks were fish-belly white,
He had great long teeth and an appetite.
He ate raw meat 'most every meal,
And rolled his eyes till the cat would squeal.
His fist was an enormous size
To mash poor niggers that told him lies:
He was surely a witch-man in disguise.
    But he went down to the Devil.

He wore hip boots and would wade all day
To capture his slaves who had fled away.
    But he went down to the Devil.

He beat kind Uncle Tom to death,
Who prayed for Legree with his parting breath.
Then Uncle Tom to Eva flew,
To the high sanctoriums bright and new;
And Simon Legree stared up beneath,
And cracked his heels, and ground his teeth:
    And went down to the Devil.

He crossed the yard in the storm and gloom;
He went into his grand front room.
He said, "I killed him, and I don't care."
He kicked a hound, he gave a swear;
He tightened his belt, he took a lamp,
Went down cellar to the webs and damp.
There in the middle of the mouldy floor
He heaved up a slab, he found a door—
    And went down to the Devil.

His lamp blew out, but his eyes burned bright.
Simon Legree stepped down all night—
Down, down to the devil.
Simon Legree be reached the place,
He saw one half of the human race;
He saw the Devil on a wide green throne,
Gnawing the meat from a big ham-bone,
And he said to Mister Devil:

"I see that you have much to eat—
A raw ham-bone is surely sweet.
I see that you have lion's feet;
I see your frame is fat and fine,
I see you drink your poison wine—
Blood and burning turpentine."

And the Devil said to Simon Legree:
"I like your style, so wicked and free.
Come sit and share my throne with me,
And let us bark and revel."
And there they sit and gnash their teeth,
And each one wears a hop-vine wreath.
They are matching pennies and shooting craps.
They are playing poker and taking naps.
And old Legree is fat and fine:
He eats the fire, he drinks the wine—
Blood and burning turpentine—
   Down, down with the Devil;
     Down, down with the Devil;
       Down, down with the Devil.

                       VACHEL LINDSAY

The speaker in Lindsay's dramatic poem, unlike the one in Saxe's, seems to become carried away with his own rhetoric and to forget the moral the reader is led to expect—Legree winds up having a fine time down with the devil instead of being damned forever. The same sort of thing happened in the first two books of John Milton's *Paradise Lost* —by far the most vivid of all the sections of the poem. The writer becomes so intrigued with his own character-of-imagination that he ends by admiring much more than damning.

Here are two more didactic poems by contemporary poets. Notice that statements are very important in these poems, but so is humor:

THE DIRTY FLOOR

The floor is dirty:
Not only the soot from the city air
But a surprising amount of hair litters the room.

It is hard to keep up with. Even before
The room is all swept up it is dirty again.

We are shedding more than we realize.
The amount of hair I've shed so far
Could make sixty of those great rugs
The Duke of China killed his weavers for,
And strangle half the sons of Islam.

Time doesn't stop even while I scrub the floor
Though it seems that the mind empties like a bathtub,
That all the minds of the world go down the drain
Into the sewer; but hair keeps falling
And not for a moment can the floor be totally clean.

What is left of us after years of shitting and shedding?
Are we whom our mothers bore or some stranger now
With the name of son, but nameless,
Continually relearning the same words
That mean, with each retelling, less.

He whom you knew is a trail of leavings round the world.
Renewal is a lie: Who I was has no more kisses.
Barbara's fierce eyes were long ago swept up from her floor.
A stranger goes by the name of Marianne; it is not she,
Nor for that matter was the Marianne I knew.

The floor having accumulated particles of myself
I call it dirty; dirty, the streets thick with the dead;
Dirty, the thick air I am used to breathing.
I am alive at least. Quick, who said that?
Give me the broom. The leftovers sweep the leavings away.

                                              EDWARD FIELD

SOME IMPORTANT ADVICE

There isn't any way to be perfectly safe.
Something terrible is possible
every time you touch the refrigerator
or flush the toilet. A long porcelain sliver
may ruin one kidney or destroy your liver
when you slide into the bathtub. If the pipes get crossed,
you can be scalded when you wash your face.
You can get knocked down, squashed, swallowed, or even lost.

You can be careful. When you sit anyplace,
watch for hidden scissors. Be wary
of poisonous banquets. If you cross the tracks,
keep your ankles far enough from the switch,
which will mangle you even if the train does miss.
Be normally alert. Watch out for pets.

If a cat's nail scratches, you know what the germs can bring.
Don't fondle dogs. And never kiss anything.

                                        RICHARD FROST

suggested writing assignment

Write a didactic poem of at least 30 lines. Use either lyricism or imagery to carry your message.

20

minor genres:

OCCASIONALS

We have already spoken of the ODE and the ELEGY—the two major forms of occasionals—in the chapter on lyrics. For an example of an elegy written in *elegiacs*, see "A Talisman" on p. 114. Here, following, is an elegy written in decasyllabics, followed by a PINDARIC ODE:

NOVEMBER 22, 1963

Weeping, I write this: You are dead. The dark
animal of the heart, the beast that bides
stilly in its web of flesh, has stolen
flight again out of the air. What is there
to say? That I wish we were gods? That the
mind of man were equal to his lusts? It
is not—not yet. You were a man, but more:
you were an idea dreamt in a sweet
hour while the spider slept. We make our
web: its habitant makes greatness of its
prey. We are ourselves victim and victor.
You were and are ourselves. In killing you
we murder an emblem of what we strive
to be: not men, but Man. In mourning you,
good Man, we grieve for what we are, not what

we may become.
     Sleep, my heart. We will try
once more. Sleep, sleep now. We will try again.

ODE ON ST. CECILIA'S DAY

NOVEMBER 22, 1964

I. OF THE PAST

Some music, then, for this day. Let it be
suitable to the mood of fallen snow,
the veil of a virgin saint. Quietly
let it come now, out of the silence; now
while the birds inexplicably forsake
the elm, the oak, the seed in the lilac. . . .
Instead, drumrolls muffled in an old year,
an echo of trumpets in the streets. Clear
but muted, there is a ragged tattoo
of hooves, image of a sable horse, wild-
eyed, resisting the rein, skittish among
the twin rows of witness citizens who,
their voices frozen, give up to the cold
air of the marble city an old song.

II. OF THE PRESENT

But it's another year, Cecilia's day
again, another part of the land. So,
let the phantoms of those cold days lie
under these new burdens of snow. Allow
that chorus of stricken men to dim like
shadows into blackening film, the dark
merging with the riderless horse. Feature
by feature, let the scene fade into near
distance, into perspective, then shadow.
This is music for St. Cecilia. Yield
to her the lyric due her. Let us sing
for her patronage: her martyrdom grew
out of a summer heart: she is our shield
against the winter. She is always young.

III. OF THE MOMENT

Here beyond the window the campus lies.
The students pass in mufflers and coats, eyes
almost hidden against the wind. The sound
of radio music settles around
the furniture, into the carpeting.
Choral voices: a requiem. Distant
and urgent, the November church bells ring.
Outdoors a dog rags something. An instant

pause in his play—he has caught a squirrel
which tosses and tosses in the grey air.
The mongrel, in the midst of his quarrel
with life, is assaulted by three girls. There,
at the base of a tree, the limp ruff falls
from insensate jaws, starts to inch up walls
of oak bark toward some invisible
sanctuary. The dog begins to howl.
The girls watch the squirrel into the limbs.
Cecilia's radio is shut of hymns.

A favorite occasion to be celebrated by the ode has been the day of St. Cecilia, patron saint of music.

The ode takes various forms. Wordsworth's ode on p. 107 an IRREGULAR ODE. Keats' "To Autumn" on p. 148 is an ENGLISH ODE or, rather, a variation on the form, which he invented. Milton's poem is a homostrophic ode; although it has two kinds of stanzas, the stanzas in each of the two strophes are alike:

ON THE MORNING OF CHRIST'S NATIVITY

1

This is the month, and this the happy morn,
Wherein the Son of Heaven's Eternal King,
Of wedded maid and virgin mother born,
Our great redemption from above did bring;
For so the holy sages once did sing,
    That he our deadly forfeit should release,
And with his Father work us a perpetual peace.

2

That glorious form, that light unsufferable,
And that far-beaming blaze of majesty,
Wherewith he wont at Heaven's high council-table
To sit the midst of Trinal Unity,
He laid aside, and, here with us to be,
    Forsook the courts of everlasting day,
And chose with us a darksome house of mortal clay.

3

Say, Heavenly Muse, shall not thy sacred vein
Afford a present to the Infant God?
Hast thou no verse, no hymn, or solemn strain,
To welcome him to this his new abode,
Now while the heaven, by the Sun's team untrod,
    Hath took no print of the approaching light,
And all the spangled host keep watch in squadrons
        bright?

4

See how from far upon the eastern road
The star-led wizards haste with odors sweet!
Oh run, prevent them with they humble ode,
And lay it lowly at his blessed feet;
Have thou the honor first thy Lord to greet,
   And join thy voice unto the angel choir
From out his secret altar touched with hallowed fire.

THE HYMN

1

   It was the winter wild,
   While the heaven-born child
All meanly wrapt in the rude manger lies;
   Nature, in awe to him,
   Had doffed her gaudy trim,
With her great Master so to sympathize:
It was no season then for her
To wanton with the Sun, her lusty paramour.

2

   Only with speeches fair
   She woos the gentle air
To hide her guilty front with innocent snow,
   And on her naked shame,
   Pollute with sinful blame,
The saintly veil of maiden white to throw;
Confounded, that her Maker's eyes
Should look so near upon her foul deformities.

3

   But he, her fears to cease,
   Sent down the meek-eyed Peace:
She, crowned with olive green, came softly sliding
   Down through the turning sphere,
   His ready harbinger,
With turtle wing the amorous clouds dividing;
And, waving wide her myrtle wand,
She strikes a universal peace through sea and land.

4

   No war, or battle's sound,
   Was heard the world around;
The idle spear and shield were high uphung;
   The hookéd chariot stood,
   Unstained with hostile blood;
The trumpet spake not to the arméd throng;
And kings sat still with awful eye,
As if they surely knew their sovran Lord was by.

5

But peaceful was the night
Wherein the Prince of Light
His reign of peace upon the earth began.
The winds, with wonder whist,
Smoothly the waters kissed,
Whispering new joys to the mild Ocean,
Who now hath quite forgot to rave,
While birds of calm sit brooding on the charmèd wave.

6

The stars, with deep amaze,
Stand fixed in steadfast gaze,
Bending one way their precious influence,
And will not take their flight,
For all the morning light,
Or Lucifer that often warned them thence,
But in their glimmering orbs did glow,
Until their Lord himself bespake, and bid them go.

7

And, though the shady gloom
Had given day her room,
The Sun himself withheld his wonted speed,
And hid his head for shame,
As his inferior flame
The new-enlightened world no more should need:
He saw a greater Sun appear
Than his bright throne or burning axletree could bear.

8

The shepherds on the lawn,
Or ere the point of dawn,
Sat simply chatting in a rustic row;
Full little thought they than
That the mighty Pan
Was kindly come to live with them below:
Perhaps their loves, or else their sheep,
Was all that did their silly thoughts so busy keep.

9

When such music sweet
Their hearts and ears did greet
As never was by mortal finger strook,
Divinely-warbled voice
Answering the stringèd noise,
As all their souls in blissful rapture took:
The air, such pleasure loth to lose,
With thousand echoes still prolongs each heavenly close.

10

Nature, that heard such sound
    Beneath the hollow round
Of Cynthia's seat the airy region thrilling,
    Now was almost won
    To think her part was done,
And that her reign had here its last fulfilling:
She knew such harmony alone
Could hold all Heaven and Earth in happier uniön.

11

At last surrounds their sight
    A globe of circular light,
That with long beams the shamefaced Night arrayed;
    The helméd cherubim
    And sworded seraphim
Are seen in glittering ranks with wings displayed,
Harping loud and solemn quire,
With unexpressive notes, to Heaven's new-born Heir.

12

Such music (as 'tis said)
    Before was never made,
But when of old the sons of morning sung,
    While the Creator great
    His constellations set,
And the well-balanced world on hinges hung,
And cast the dark foundations deep,
And bid the weltering waves their oozy channel keep.

13

Ring out, ye crystal spheres,
    Once bless our human ears,
If ye have power to touch our senses so;
    And let your silver chime
    Move in melodious time;
And let the bass of heaven's deep organ blow;
And with your ninefold harmony
Make up full consort to th' angelic symphony.

14

For, if such holy song
    Enwrap our fancy long,
Time will run back and fetch the age of gold;
    And speckled vanity
    Will sicken soon and die;
And leprous sin will melt from earthly mold;
And Hell itself will pass away,
And leave her dolorous mansions to the peering day.

15

Yea, Truth and Justice then
Will down return to men,
Orbed in a rainbow; and, like glories wearing,
   Mercy will sit between,
   Throned in celestial sheen,
With radiant feet the tissued clouds down steering;
And Heaven, as at some festival,
Will open wide the gates of her high palace-hall.

16

But wisest Fate says no,
This must not yet be so;
The Babe lies yet in smiling infancy
   That on the bitter cross
   Must redeem our loss,
So both himself and us to glorify:
Yet first, to those ychained in sleep,
The wakeful trump of doom must thunder through the deep,

17

With such a horrid clang
As on Mount Sinai rang,
While the red fire and smoldering clouds outbrake:
   The aged Earth, aghast,
   With terror of that blast,
Shall from the surface to the center shake,
When, at the world's last sessiön,
The dreadful Judge in middle air shall spread his throne.

18

And then at last our bliss
Full and perfect is,
But now begins; for from this happy day
   Th' old Dragon under ground,
   In straiter limits bound,
Not half so far casts his usurpéd sway,
And, wroth to see his kingdom fail,
Swinges the scaly horror of his folded tail.

19

The Oracles are dumb;
No voice or hideous hum
Runs through the archéd roof in words deceiving.
   Apollo from his shrine
   Can no more divine,
With hollow shriek the steep of Delphos leaving.
No nightly trance, or breathéd spell,
Inspires the pale-eyed priest from the prophetic cell.

20

The lonely mountains o'er,
And the resounding shore,
A voice of weeping heard and loud lament;
From haunted spring, and dale
Edged with poplar pale,
The parting genius is with sighing sent;
With flower-inwoven tresses torn
The Nymphs in twilight shade of tangled thickets mourn.

21

In consecrated earth,
And on the holy hearth,
The Lars and Lemures moan with midnight plaint;
In urns and altars round,
A drear and dying sound
Affrights the flamens at their service quaint;
And the chill marble seems to sweat,
While each peculiar power forgoes his wonted seat.

22

Peor and Baälim
Forsake their temples dim
With that twice-battered God of Palestine;
And moonéd Ashtaroth,
Heaven's queen and mother both,
Now sits not girt with tapers' holy shine:
The Libyc Hammon shrinks his horn;
In vain the Tyrian maids their wounded Thammuz mourn.

23

And sullen Moloch, fled,
Hath left in shadows dread
His burning idol all of blackest hue;
In vain with cymbals' ring
They call the grisly king,
In dismal dance about the furnace blue;
The brutish gods of Nile as fast,
Isis, and Orus, and the dog Anubis, haste.

24

Nor is Osiris seen
In Memphian grove or green,
Trampling the unshowered grass with lowings loud:
Nor can he be at rest
Within his sacred chest;
Nought but profoundest Hell can be his shroud;
In vain, with timbreled anthems dark,
The sable-stoléd sorcerers bear his worshiped ark.

25

He feels from Juda's land
    The dreaded Infant's hand;
  The rays of Bethlehem blind his dusky eyn;
    Nor all the gods beside
    Longer dare abide,
  Not Typhon huge ending in snaky twine:
Our Babe, to show his Godhead true,
Can in his swaddling bands control the damnéd crew.

26

So, when the sun in bed,
    Curtained with cloudy red,
  Pillows his chin upon an orient wave,
    The flocking shadows pale
    Troop to th' infernal jail;
  Each fettered ghost slips to his several grave,
And the yellow-skirted fays
Fly after the night-steeds, leaving their moon-loved maze.

27

But see! the Virgin blest
    Hath laid her Babe to rest.
  Time is our tedious song should here have ending:
    Heaven's youngest-teeméd star
    Hath fixed her polished car,
  Her sleeping Lord with handmaid lamp attending;
And all about the courtly stable
Bright-harnessed angels sit in order serviceable.

JOHN MILTON

LITTLE ELEGY

FOR A CHILD WHO SKIPPED ROPE

Here lies resting, out of breath,
Out of turns, Elizabeth
Whose quicksilver toes not quite
Cleared the whirring edge of night.

Earth whose circles round us skim
Till they catch the lightest limb,
Shelter now Elizabeth
And for her sake trip up Death.

X. J. KENNEDY

MINSTREL'S SONG

O! sing unto my roundelay;
  O! drop the briny tear with me;
Dance no more at holiday;
    Like a running river be.
      My love is dead,
      Gone to his death-bed
      All under the willow tree.

Black his hair as the winter night,
  White his skin as the summer snow,
Red his face as the morning light;
    Cold he lies in the grave below.
      My love is dead,
      Gone to his death-bed,
      All under the willow-tree.

Sweet his tongue as the throstle's note,
  Quick in dance as thought can be,
Deft his tabor, cudgel stout;
    O! he lies by the willow-tree.
      My love is dead,
      Gone to his death-bed,
      All under the willow-tree.

See! the white moon shines on high,
  Whiter is my true love's shroud,
Whiter than the morning sky,
    Whiter than the evening cloud.
      My love is dead,
      Gone to his death-bed,
      All under the willow-tree.

Come, with acorn-cup and thorn,
  Drain my own heart's blood away;
Life and all its good I scorn,
    Dance by night, or feast by day.
      My love is dead,
      Gone to his death-bed,
      All under the willow-tree.

THOMAS CHATTERTON

ELEGY JUST IN CASE

Here lie Ciardi's pearly bones
In their ripe organic mess.
Jungle blown, his chromosomes
Breed to a new address.

Was it bullets or a wind
Or a rip-cord fouled on Chance?
Artifacts the natives find
Decorate them when they dance.

Here lies the sgt.'s mortal wreck
Lily spiked and termite kissed,
Spiders pendant from his neck
And a beetle on his wrist.

Bring the tic and southern flies
Where the land crabs run unmourning
Through a night of jungle skies
To a climeless morning.

And bring the chalked eraser here
Fresh from rubbing out his name.
Burn the crew-board for a bier.
(Also Colonel what's-his-name.)

Let no dice be stored and still.
Let no poker deck be torn.
But pour the smuggled rye until
The barracks threshold is outworn.

File the papers, pack the clothes,
Send the coded word through air—
"We regret and no one knows
Where the sgt. goes from here."

"Missing as of inst. oblige,
Deepest sorrow and remain—"
Shall I grin at persiflage?
Could I have my skin again

Would I choose a business form
Stilted mute as a giraffe,
Or a pinstripe unicorn
On a cashier's epitaph?

Darling, darling, just in case
Rivets fail or engines burn,
I forget the time and place
But your flesh was sweet to learn.

In the grammar of not yet
Let me name one verb for chance,
Scholarly to one regret:
That I leave your mood and tense.

Swift and single as a shark
I have seen you churn my sleep;

Now if beetles hunt my dark
What will beetles find to keep?

Fractured neat and open bone—
Nothing single or surprised.
Fragments of a written stone,
Undeciphered but surmised.

JOHN CIARDI

FOR PHILIP STEPHEN ENGELS
   August 23–October 24, 1965

Swarming by your head
Red plastic butterflies
Danced patterns on their strings
Because that night you cried

And would not sleep; and I,
In my dark room, rejoiced
To know that bright beasts moved
Measured by your voice.

The sun came red as wings
To fix the swimming dust
In all our rooms; my son,
Your caught voice moves in us.

The house drowns in its lawns.
We watch the morning sun
Thrust deep into the sky
A honed and bloody tongue,

And in that roar of light
You sleep; above your head
The blazing wings grow dull
And larval on their threads.

You were no voice at best.
I measure what I tell:
The housed and swallowed bone
Grows hollow as a bell,

The breath swims in the throat,
The sun rings in the sky;
What color we remember
Burns inward from the eye.

JOHN ENGELS

THE PARDON

My dog lay dead five days without a grave
In the thick of summer, hid in a clump of pine
And a jungle of grass and honeysuckle-vine.
I who had loved him while he kept alive

Went only close enough to where he was
To sniff the heavy honeysuckle-smell
Twined with another odor heavier still
And hear the flies' intolerable buzz.

Well, I was ten and very much afraid.
In my kind world the dead were out of range
And I could not forgive the sad or strange
In beast or man. My father took the spade

And buried him. Last night I saw the grass
Slowly divide (it was the same scene
But now it glowed a fierce and mortal green)
And saw the dog emerging. I confess

I felt afraid again, but still he came
In the carnal sun, clothed in a hymn of flies,
And death was breeding in his lively eyes.
I started in to cry and call his name,

Asking forgiveness of his tongueless head.
. . . I dreamt the past was never past redeeming:
But whether this was false or honest dreaming
I beg death's pardon now. And mourn the dead.

RICHARD WILBUR

AN ATHLETE DYING OLD

*The Octogenarian, who had avoided doctors and
considered old age a bad habit, died today.*
Down at the Medical Center
    the nurses remember the day
when the sculptor who modeled in sinew
    left nothing but clay.

The intestine complained of the bile duct,
    the liver distended with rage,
as the boy who played tennis at eighty
    acted his age.

The bile was absorbed in the system
    till tissues were stained as with dye
from the laboring bowel to the languid
    and jaundiced eye.

Attendants walked softly in whispers
   putting the temperature down
and noting in keen expectation
    if his urine were brown.

Now he feels the support of subscribers
   applauding the pose from afar
as the thrust of the chin, well extended,
    is crossing the bar.

And he feels that the bowl of his belly
   spills into a liquid abyss.
The parachute jump in the Hudson
    was nothing to this.

They looked at, remarked, and admired
   the color of physical flaws,
relieved now to see the transgressor
    obeying the laws,

but nobody saw through the features
   into the yellowing sleep,
and nobody saw the last breath
    he tried to keep.

KNUTE SKINNER

DEAR JOHN, DEAR COLTRANE

    a love supreme, a love supreme
    a love supreme, a love supreme

Sex fingers toes
in the marketplace
near your father's church
in Hamlet, North Carolina—
witness to this love
in this calm fallow
of these minds,
there is no substitute for pain:
genitals gone or going,
seed burned out,
you tuck the roots in the earth,
turn back, and move
by river through the swamps,
singing: *a love supreme, a love supreme;*
what does it all mean?
Loss, so great each black
woman expects your failure
in mute change, the seed gone.

You plod up into the electric city—
your song now crystal and
the blues. You pick up the horn
with some will and blow
into the freezing night:
a love supreme, a love supreme—

Dawn comes and you cook
up the thick sin 'tween
impotence and death, fuel
the tenor sax cannibal
heart, genitals and sweat
that makes you clean—
a love supreme, a love supreme—
Why you so black?
cause I am
why you so funky?
cause I am
why you so black?
cause I am
why you so sweet?
cause I am
why you so black?
cause I am
a love supreme, a love supreme:

So sick
you couldn't play *Naima,*
so flat we ached
for song you'd concealed
with your own blood,
your diseased liver gave
out its purity,
the inflated heart
pumps out, the tenor kiss,
tenor love:
a love supreme, a love supreme—
a love supreme, a love supreme—

MICHAEL S. HARPER

THE ROOM

Through that window—all else being extinct
Except itself and me—I saw the struggle
Of darkness against darkness. Within the room
It turned and turned, dived downward. Then I saw
How order might— if chaos wished—become:

And saw the darkness crush upon itself,
Contracting powerfully; it was as if
It killed itself: slowly: and with much pain.
Pain. The scene was pain, and nothing but pain.
What else, when chaos draws all forces inward
To shape a single leaf? . . .
                              For the leaf came,
Alone and shining in the empty room;
After a while the twig shot downward from it;
And from the twig a bough; and then the trunk,
Massive and coarse; and last the one black root.
The black root cracked the walls. Boughs burst the window:
The great tree took possession.
                              Tree of trees!
Remember (when time comes) how chaos died
To shape the shining leaf. Then turn, have courage,
Wrap arms and roots together, be convulsed
With grief, and bring back chaos out of shape.
I will be watching then as I watch now.
I will praise darkness now, but then the leaf.

CONRAD AIKEN

suggested writing assignment

A) Write a syllabic elegy of about 15 lines.

B) Write an accentual-syllabic ode, preferably in one of the strict
forms, of between 15 and 24 lines.

21

minor genres:
BUCOLICS

The general form of *bucolics* is internal rather than external. That is, bucolics are intended to contrast simple modes with complex modes of life. Specifically, the subject matter of bucolics concerns the exaltation of the natural over the cultivated man, and of the country and rural life over the life of the town and city. Bucolics are essentially romantic in content and point-of-view. However, they have had a place in literature of the western world from classic times to the present.

Although there is no single set external form for the genre, several forms have been associated with it. A number of English-language bucolics have been written in *heroic sestet* ($a^5b^5a^5b^5c^5c^5$) and iambic tetrameter *sextillas* (*aabccb* or *ababcc*).

The PASTORAL or *idyl* is concerned, on its surface, with country ways, especially with the doings of shepherds or other rural people, but its allegorical level is concerned with more generally applicable topics. The ECLOGUE is a pastoral cast in the form of a dialogue or monologue spoken by country folk, and the PASTORAL ELEGY combines elegy and bucolics, as the name of the form would indicate:

THANATOPSIS

To him who in the love of Nature holds
Communion with her visible forms, she speaks

307

A various language; for his gayer hours
She has a voice of gladness, and a smile
And eloquence of beauty, and she glides
Into his darker musings, with a mild
And healing sympathy, that steals away
Their sharpness, ere he is aware. When thoughts
Of the last bitter hour come like a blight
Over thy spirit, and sad images
Of the stern agony, and shroud, and pall,
And breathless darkness, and the narrow house,
Make thee to shudder, and grow sick at heart;—
Go forth, under the open sky, and list
To Nature's teachings, while from all around—
Earth and her waters, and the depths of air—
Comes a still voice—Yet a few days, and thee
The all-beholding sun shall see no more
In all his course; nor yet in the cold ground,
Where thy pale form was laid, with many tears,
Nor in the embrace of ocean, shall exist
Thy image. Earth, that nourished thee, shall claim
Thy growth, to be resolved to earth again,
And, lost each human trace, surrendering up
Thine individual being, shalt thou go
To mix for ever with the elements,
To be a brother to the insensible rock
And to the sluggish clod, which the rude swain
Turns with his share, and treads upon. The oak
Shall send his roots abroad, and pierce thy mould.

   Yet not to thine eternal resting-place
Shalt thou retire alone, nor couldst thou wish
Couch more magnificent. Thou shalt lie down
With patriarchs of the infant world—with kings,
The powerful of the earth—the wise, the good,
Fair forms, and hoary seers of ages past,
All in one mighty sepulchre. The hills
Rock-ribbed and ancient as the sun—the vales
Stretching in pensive quietness between;
The venerable woods—rivers that move
In majesty, and the complaining brooks
That make the meadows green; and, poured round all,
Old Ocean's gray and melancholy waste,—
Are but the solemn decorations all
Of the great tomb of man. The golden sun,
The planets, all the infinite host of heaven,
Are shining on the sad abodes of death,
Through the still lapse of ages. All that tread
The globe are but a handful to the tribes

That slumber in its bosom.—Take the wings
Of morning, pierce the Barcan wilderness,
Or lose thyself in the continuous woods
Where rolls the Oregon, and hears no sound,
Save his own dashings—yet the dead are there:
And millions in those solitudes, since first
The flight of years began, have laid them down
In their last sleep—the dead reign there alone,
So shalt thou rest, and what if thou withdraw
In silence from the living, and no friend
Take note of thy departure? All that breathe
Will share thy destiny. The gay will laugh
When thou art gone, the solemn brood of care
Plod on, and each one as before will chase
His favorite phantom; yet all these shall leave
Their mirth and their employments, and shall come,
And make their bed with thee. As the long train
Of ages glide away, the sons of men,
The youth in life's green spring, and he who goes
In the full strength of years, matron and maid,
The speechless babe, and the gray-headed man—
Shall one by one be gathered to thy side,
By those, who in their turn shall follow them.

So live, that when thy summons comes to join
The innumerable caravan, which moves
To that mysterious realm, where each shall take
His chamber in the silent halls of death,
Thou go not, like the quarry-slave at night,
Scourged to his dungeon, but, sustained and soothed
By an unfaltering trust, approach thy grave,
Like one who wraps the drapery of his couch
About him, and lies down to pleasant dreams.

WILLIAM CULLEN BRYANT

There is great ambiguity between the moral, which appears as the last stanza of this poem, and the body of the poem. Such ambiguity seems to exist in much Victorian poetry.

Bryant's poem is written in blank verse; this following poem is written in decasyllabics. Compare the similarities and dissimilarities of the prosodies:

ANOTHER ONE

Softly, out of the old noon with its pumpkin sun still lifting the wraiths of the mist
from morning gulleys, the clear phoebe's call

assails the barn whose shingles, gray in all
lights, are nearer the heart of gray now in
the shadow of those deep eaves. Summer, like
a catchall huckster, winds over Blinn's hill,
having sold us a snippet of blue thread,
a needle, some ribbon—perhaps a pan
or two for Lori to bang on in time
to the oaten reed of phoebe's throat. The
falls still murmur out of the tannery's
sundered foundations, past the great mill stones
which lie beyond the new culvert crossing
under our road, and everything is the
same:
       The same poem issuing from my
pen, the same thread of ink stitching the same
flavors together—I sew fine taffy
samplers out of the sad hours of my
youth; the same summer stretching wistfully,
laconically, to that familiar
autumn perched like a chipmunk
atop the barrel by the chickencoop.

Melora and I feed the fighting song
sparrows with seeds the chipmunks steal: glutton
contends with glutton. The winter hovers
under the pelt or the plume, beneath these
lines, whether I will or no, whether I
fend off the incipient fall, forestall
the prime frost with my blunt point, or let fly
with silence.
       Or, if not the same, then at
least, I fear, similar. The fall comes, time
wanders. Melora, with her birds, waxes
fat and sleek, and for now I need not write
that lachrymose song I had in mind. Yet,
we reserve the right to return to that
old tune again one day, soon, when summer's
luster dims to the color of morning
mist—takes on the patina and hue of
pewter—and the dew is crystalline on
the vials of colored honeywater
hung on wires to catch the hummingbird.

The PASTORAL ODE, like the pastoral elegy, is a combination
of the two forms, except that the ode is more specifically commemorative
and may be set in one of the ode forms.
    Here is an eclogue written in the form of a *double sestina*:

SESTINA

STREPHON   KLAIUS

STREPHON

You Gote-heard Gods, that love the grassie mountaines,
You Nimphes that haunt the springs in pleasant vallies,
You Satyrs joyde with free and quiet forrests,
Vouchsafe your silent eares to playning musique,
Which to my woes gives still an early morning:
And drawes the dolor on till wery evening.

KLAIUS

O *Mercurie,* foregoer to the evening,
O heavenlie huntresse of the savage mountaines,
O lovelie starre, entitled of the morning,
Which that my voice doth fill these wofull vallies,
Vouchsafe your silent eares to plaining musique,
Which oft hath *Echo* tir'd in secrete forrests.

STREPHON

I that was once free-burgess of the forrests,
Where shade from Sunne, and sports I sought at evening,
I that was once esteem'd for pleasant musique,
Am banisht now among the monstrous mountaines
Of huge despaire, and foule afflictions vallies,
Am growne a shrich-owle to my selfe each morning.

KLAIUS

I that was once delighted every morning,
Hunting the wild inhabiters of forrests,
I that was once the musique of these vallies,
So darkened am, that all my day is evening,
Hart-broken so, that mole-hills seem high mountaines,
And fill the vales with cries in steed of musique.

STREPHON

Long since alas, my deadly Swannish musique
Hath made it selfe a crier of the morning,
And hath with wailing strength clim'd highest mountaines:
Long since my thoughts more desert be than forrests:
Long since I see my joyes come to their evening,
And state thrown downe to over-trodden vallies.

KLAIUS

Long since the happie dwellers of these vallies,
Have praide me leave my strange exclaiming musique,
Which troubles their dayes worke, and joyes of evening:
Long since I hate the night, more hate the morning:
Long since my thoughts chase me like beasts in forrests,
And make me wish myself layd under mountaines.

STREPHON

Me seemes I see the high and stately mountaines,
Transforme themselves to lowe dejected vallies:
Me seemes I heare in these ill-changed forrests,
The Nightingales doo learne of Owles their musique:
Me seemes I feele the comfort of the morning
Turnde to the mortall serene of an evening.

KLAIUS

Me seemes I see a filthie clowdie evening,
As soone as Sunne begins to clime the mountaines:
Me seemes I feele a noisome scent, the morning
When I doo smell the flowers of these vallies:
Me seemes I heare, when I doo heare sweete musique,
The dreadfull cries of murdred men in forrests.

STREPHON

I wish to fire the trees of all these forrests;
I give the Sunne a last farewell each evening;
I curse the fidling finders out of musique:
With envie I doo hate the loftie mountaines;
And with despite despise the humble vallies:
I doo detest night, evening, day, and morning.

KLAIUS

Curse to my selfe my prayer is, the morning:
My fire is more than can be made with forrests;
My state more base, than are the basest vallies;
I wish no evenings more to see, each evening;
Shamed I have my selfe in sight of mountaines,
And stoppe mine eares, lest I growe mad with Musicke.

STREPHON

For she, whose parts maintainde a perfect musique,
Whose beautie shin'de more than the blushing morning,
Who much did pass in state the stately mountaines,
In straightnes past the Cedars of the forrests,
Hath cast me wretch into eternall evening
By taking her two Sunnes from these darke vallies.

KLAIUS

For she, to whom compar'd, the Alpes are vallies,
She, whose least word brings from the spheares their musique,
At whose approach the Sunne rose in the evening,
Who, where she went, bare in her forehead morning,
Is gone, is gone from these our spoyled forrests,
Turning to desarts our best pastur'de mountaines.

STREPHON, KLAIUS

These mountaines witness shall, so shall these vallies,
These forrests eke, made wretched by our musique,
Our morning hymne is this, and song at evening.

PHILIP SIDNEY

THE FARMHOUSE

Our house is an old farmhouse, whose properties
The town has gradually purchased, leaving it
Only a city lot and a few trees
Of all that wood and busheldom and breeze
It once served. It is high and square,
And its lines, such as they are, have been muddled by several
Conflicting remodelers, whose care
In widening, lengthening, adding on, letting in air
Has left it with four kinds of windows, three porches
And a door that leads to a closet that is not there.

The city houses around us have borrowed from verse
And the Old Dominion; their cosmopolitan
Muddle is elegant next to ours.
We think of moving, and say we'll add no more dollars
To those already spent making a box
Of what was, is and will be, forever, a box,
When there's land, empty and unboxed, down a few blocks
Waiting.
We say this as we pull down, pull up, push out,
And generally persevere with our renovating—

That is, making new again—knowing
That houses like our house are not made new again
Any more than a man is. All that growing
Up and away from the land, that bowing
To impersonal social forces that transform
Wheatfields into rows of two-bedroom ramblers
Must be acknowledged; but the warm
Part of our country boy will not conform.
It remains, behind new windows, doors and porches,
Hugging its childhood, staying down on the farm.

REED WHITTEMORE

NEAR CARTER'S MILL

By walked-along water, the trees hang fire.
The roundhouse wind gives blood to my cheek.

In loved-down grass, by nesting air,
The hare lies gathered, tight and quick.
And near the shalebed, rundown stream,
The millwheel stands in the spraying flume.

From whistle-far town beyond the wheel
Where a Sunday sky, ringing with clouds,
Holds dusty horizons of October hills,
I fled this morning the well-drawn words
Of the preacher with his turning tongue
To the trembling wheel where racewaters lunge.

Under the quiet millstone reels
The browbeaten hill in an autumn rain,
The scored gulleys floundering downhill,
The bent-tined lightning, and the veins
Of thunder cracking the roiling ore.
The millstone trembles on the leafdrift floor.

When walked-alone water, by the falling trees,
Says, This is your book with a windy page,
Where the wet thumb counts and the wet eye grieves,
Then the deep heart thunders against the age.
By overboard water, I strike as stone.
I blow the grist and seize the grain.

O faraway town with your prince and poor,
I stand six miles up Lincoln Road
Where time held close, while the world went over
To the elbowing town where wheels go mad,
Where the factories spew by the granary,
With bread for you, but none for me.

                                                JOHN WOODS

SURVIVORS

1

Deserted by his flock, turned slightly yellow,
the sole survivor of some ancient ill,
the ivory shepherd boy catches my eye,
alone, unpacked, still resting near a window,
eyeing the crates stacked neatly near a wall
as if to pipe their final, soft goodbye.
Beyond him, past the glass, the lacy weave
of the huge elm tree forms its tracery
through which the white-slat houses of the block
appear like backgrounds to his steady gaze.
My stare goes out to some vague memory
strung like a wetwash in the inner eye

until a noise of traffic brings me back . . .
back to a morning I'd discovered him
while rummaging my grandmother's belongings,
and noticed in the eye two spotted tears
and on his back a ravaged, new-born lamb
and laid the tragedies to evil kings
who hired away an army of toy soldiers.
Now, years later, deserted by such realms,
I pack him out of habit when I leave
by choice or force one job for something better,
remapping what job-transferring assumes,
and having left all other boyhood games,
the armies having fallen to some grave,
marvel he still survives each hopeful future.

2

Only the last, quick, thorough scouring's left
before I load the crates into the car
and let go of the things we cannot take
for those to come like a considerate gift,
leaving the rooms we lived in all last year.
Looking about, I tackle this last work.
Strange, I had scoured them, too, when we arrived,
hoping by cleanser, ammonia, and soaps
to rid the former tenants from their walls.
Yet in the paint or a torn windowshade
they persisted, helping shape our hopes
which will assume their fulness someplace else.
I think of women, old friends once described,
who come to wash the dead with vinegar,
of the new tenants scrubbing us away,
and of the pictures hanging on our walls—
trees, people, landscapes, playful animals,
hearing in the small plaster holes we made
and where they used to hang, long hours of laughter,
hoping the sound survives their moving day.

3

So you can bid the animals goodbye,
we venture to the zoo to watch and sit
as we might do upon a sickroom visit
to someone close who is about to die.
But we're the ones who next week will be leaving.
The zebra with its thin stripes standing here,
after a spell indoors, will reappear
next year, never missing us or grieving.
So will the monkeys playing in their pen,
and the peacocks, those proud, deceptive things

who spread their god's-eyes to the sun mornings,
and, pacing the rocks, your favorite lion.
Propped on his bed, my father when he died
spoke of a magic voyage he would take
inside the cover of a Noah's Ark.
I remember this, standing at your side.
He showered me with all my favorite birds,
and made that going a processional
that transformed him into a special angel.
I missed and missed him deeply afterward.
It's we, the well, who always must be pampered.
And that you'll know this afternoon as happy
when these warm animals shrink to memory,
I offer cotton candy, popcorn, words.

4

Leaving this shady town for good,
car loaded down with moving crates,
I pass the willows and slow down,
my eyes still following the road
beyond a scattered file of graves,
and think of a bright afternoon
we picnicked in the willow groves.
Then you had asked, "What tree is that?"
"Willow," I said, and told a tale
of how the spirit of the tree
once changed into a shining girl,
married, and when the tree was cut,
at each ax blow showed agony.
A disbelief showed in your eye.

I told you, too, that Orpheus,
the greatest singer ever known,
when he went down to hell to bring
his love back carried such a bough,
and that some ancient shepherds sang
to flutes made out of willow trees.
An ivory shepherd, packed away,
reminds me of these days gone by—
uprootings, too, we've undergone,
and towns and friends we will incur,
as from one corner of my eye,
passing the county limits now,
I see a speed sign and glance down.
My speed's too slow. I press on faster.

Jerome Mazzaro

The French PASTOURELLE is a narrative poem, intended to be humorous, in which a knight (who narrates the story) takes advantage of a country wench, or in which the girl outwits him. This is a satiric form, a MOCK-PASTORAL:

A PASTORALE OF SORTS

When green buds burst and birds began
The summer's song, the cycle's plan;
   When grasses leapt for rain and sun,
   When snows had lost and warmth had won;
When cattle had been weaned from hay
And grazed again where rivers ran,
    I came to you, you came to me,
      Under the lemon tree.

No oranges for us, no pears,
No subtleties nor coy despairs.
   The yellow fruit, sweet to admire
   yet tart to taste, was our desire.
We'd wait together for the day
When ripeness took us unawares.
    I read to you, you read to me,
      Under the lemon tree.

We lingered there beneath those limbs;
We counted lambs and chanted hymns.
   Your pinafore soon came unstarched.
   Our mouths went dry, our throats grew parched;
My knickers turned from blue to grey.
The days were brights, the nights were dims.
    I tired of you, you tired of me,
      Under the lemon tree.

At last those golden fruits grew great
With pursing juices—bitter freight.
   We plucked our pleasure, slit the skins,
   And flavored nectar with our sins.
For several moments we were gay:
We puckered, giggled, sighed, and ate.
    I toasted you, you toasted me,
      Under the lemon tree.

When finally we looked around
The leaves were lying on the ground.
   The sun had gone, the frosts returned—
   We froze where lately we had burned.
The flocks had fled, bleated away.

Though we'd recall the joys we'd found,
I soured on you, you soured on me . . . ,
   Under the lemon tree.

suggested writing assignment

Write a pastoral poem of about thirty lines. Use either heroic sestets or sextillas (octosyllabic sestets rhyming *ababcc*).

22

minor genres:
CONFESSIONALS

Confessionals is *the* egopoetic genre. It is the poet speaking specifically about himself and his shortcomings, and it usually follows the *mea culpa motif*: "I am guilty."

Confessionals are strictly autobiographical in nature. Such poems are often popular for a while, especially if the poet who writes them captures the imagination of the public as a prominent figure. However, the poems often wear poorly after the poet fades from view. This usually means that the readers were more interested in sensationalism than in art, and the same was true of the poet.

Confessional poems can easily turn into overstatement, unless the poet remembers that the reader of literature, rather than simply the genre of autobiography, doesn't particularly *care* about the poet's personal problems. If the poet remembers that the *how* of what he is saying is at least as important as the *what,* he may capture the reader's interest through lyricism, as W. D. Snodgrass does in "April Inventory" on p. 217, or through imagery:

HOME THOUGHTS

Time buzzes in the ear. Somewhere
nearby, beyond my peripheral
vision, an insect throbs its heartsong

319

to the couch. A twilleter fuzzes
  against a burning lamp. Outdoors,

  a common goatsucker strings twelve
yellow streetlamps on its bill. Between
its hoarse shrieks, the town sky drops pieces
of clum among my snoring neighbors.
  If I close my eyes, a crack along

  the wall comes sliving my lids to
split the mind's dry sight. Look inward: a
plaster skull sifts dust down upon old
webs that hang, buzzing, as darkness moves
  ruthlessly to feast on something

small and hollow with blind, jewelled eyes.

Tact is important if the poet wishes to be heard by more than just
the vertical audience—those people, numbering in the millions, who
exist at any particular moment in time.

If the poet wishes to be read by the horizontal audience—those
people, numbering in the *hundreds* of millions, who will exist from the
moment the poem is written until people stop reading the poet's
language, or cease to exist as a race, the poet must use tact in order to
persuade those readers that what he is saying is important and
permanently relevant, not merely to himself but to others as well.

The poet cannot afford to close out the reader with exclusivity.
Unless the poet is writing primarily for an audience of one—himself;
or he is writing poetry as therapy, as several well-known contemporary
writers have done, he must find a way af getting and holding the
attention of the horizontal audience. If the poet considers his writing
to be a form of communication among human beings, he must give some
thought at some point to the question, "Whom am I trying to reach?"

Here are several poems, confessional in nature:

OF MY 33RD BIRTHDAY

Those that speak of the grey morning
Dream would say it's not the woman
Singing but the song wafted
Into the air like a thin slice
Of butter on the breakfast roll

Those that speak of waking dreamless
Hear the crow go back to sleep
And dream throwing a stone at the crow
Or dream ducks with silent squawks
Or thrushes with suspended whistles

The crow crows at the break of light
Who would say it has inclinations
Scares easily of squawking ducks
Head-on thrush collisions,
It's none of these but myself

Turning thirty-three on a grey morning

G. S. SHARAT CHANDRA

POPPIES IN OCTOBER

Even the sun-clouds this morning cannot manage such skirts.
Nor the woman in the ambulance
Whose red heart blooms through her coat so astoundingly—

A gift, a love gift
Utterly unasked for
By a sky

Palely and flamily
Igniting its carbon monoxides, by eyes
Dulled to a halt under bowlers.

O my God, what am I
That these late mouths should cry open
In a forest of frost, in a dawn of cornflowers.

SYLVIA PLATH

I GOT HARLEM

I got Harlem
And I got Harlem at the bottom of my shoes
I got that sweet, sweet soul,
That modern jazz
And I got that old time Harlem blues
I got young love deep in Harlem's heart
I wash my hands as tears fall from her eyes
While me and the wind
                    sit 'round the bend
Singin' jazzabies.

RONALD H. T. RHODES

ONE MORE PROSODY

The Dada poets invented a prosody based on the principle of randomness. They would take something they or someone else had written, and they would cut out each word separately. All the cut-out words were dropped into a bag, shaken up, and extracted one by one.

The words would be pasted on the page in random-length lines. The result was a Dada "poem." The method is similar to that of the contemporary composer John Cage who would set a tape recorder going, then drop a bag of marbles onto the exposed strings of a piano.

Even the Dada method is a prosody; its organizing principles are not absolutely random because you need certain things:

1) Words
2) A bag
3) Paper and paste
4) Someone to drop the words into the bag, shake it up, extract the words one by one, and arrange them in lines (a *maker*).

suggested writing assignment

Write a confessional poem any way you wish to write it, and as fast as possible. When you have finished it, cut out each word, and drop all the words into a paper bag; shake up the bag; take out the words one by one and arrange them in lines.

23

minor genres:
SATIRICS

Satire makes fun of things—it mocks them. All genres may be mocked—see the mock-pastoral "A Pastorale of Sorts" on p. 317. But satire can mock more than other genres; it can, in fact, mock anything, and several forms have been developed over the ages which are used almost exclusively for making fun.

The two major forms of satire are the EPIGRAM and the LITERARY EPITAPH. The epigram has been described as "terse verse with a cutting edge":

EVE'S DAUGHTER

Eve's daughter can entrance you with her eyes;
her hisses and her curves can mesmerize.
Good men, be wary of her. Shun the snake—
to do a Serpent in you need a Rake.

The pun, of course, is on the word *Rake,* and pun is often an element of satire.

The literary epitaph is similar, except that it is cast in the form of an inscription for a headstone; it has been described as "terse verse for the long gone":

AN EPITAPH ON SCHOLARS

Curse him who digs in yellow leaves
To scrape my twisted tongue
Of twisted songs that once I sang
Out of a twisted lung.

Rot take the worm that eats my dust.
May his bowels wither.
I shall see him eat my dust
When he grovels hither.

We have discussed *SKELTONICS* in the chapter on dipodics. *Odds Bodkin's Strange Thrusts and Ravels,* which closes this chapter, is written in Skeltonics. An opposite prosody is the *Nasher*—see the rhymed prose poem by Ogden Nash on p. 124. *Hudibrastics* are irregular tetrameter lines rhymed humorously in couplets. The *fabliau,* discussed earlier, is a satiric form, as is the *sirvente,* a lyric satire on religion or on public matters.

Rough meters such as Skeltonics and Hudibrastics are modes of *doggerel* verse. The term *doggerel* has often been used in a pejorative sense to mean verse written by someone with little skill, but doggerel can also be used deliberately for broad comic effect.

Here are some epigrams and epitaphs:

ON A WINDOW AT THE FOUR CROSSES IN THE WATLING-STREET ROAD, WARWICKSHIRE

Fool, to put up four crosses at your door,
Put up your wife, she's *crosser* than all four.

JONATHAN SWIFT

AT CHESTER

The church and clergy here, no doubt,
    Are very near akin;
Both weather-beaten are without,
    And empty both within.

JONATHAN SWIFT

EPIGRAM

You beat your pate, and fancy Wit will come:
Knock as you please, there's nobody at home.

ALEXANDER POPE

ANOTHER EPIGRAM ON SIR VOLUPTUOUS BEAST

Than his chaste wife though Beast now know no more,
He adulters still: his thoughts lie with a whore.

BEN JONSON

THE EXPLANATION

Charles, discoursing rather freely
  Of the unimportant part
Which (he said) our clever women
  Play in Science and in Art,
"Ah!—the sex you undervalue;"
  Cried his lovely cousin Jane.
"No indeed!" responded Charley,
  "Pray allow me to explain;
Such a paragon is woman,
  That, you see, it *must* be true
She is always vastly better
  Than the best that she can do!"

JOHN GODFREY SAXE

A DILEMMA

"Whenever I marry," says masculine Ann,
"I must really insist upon wedding a *man!*"
But what if the man (for men are but human)
Should be equally nice about wedding a *woman*?

JOHN GODFREY SAXE

ON A WOMAN WHO WAS SINGING BALLADS FOR MONEY TO "BURY" HER HUSBAND

For her Husband deceas'd, Sally chants the sweet lay,
  Why, faith, this is singular sorrow;
But (I doubt) since she sings for a dead man to-day,
  She'll cry for a live one to-morrow.

CHRISTOPHER SMART

THE BOSS

Skilled to pull wires, he baffles Nature's hope,
Who sure intended him to stretch a rope.

JAMES RUSSELL LOWELL

THE EPITAPH

Here, five feet deep, lies on his back
A cobbler, starmonger, and quack;
Who to the stars, in pure good will,
Does to his best look upward still.
Weep, all you customers that use
His pills, his almanacks, or shoes;
And you that did your fortunes seek,
Step to his grave but once a-week;
This earth, which bears his body's print,
You'll find has so much virtue in't,
That I durst pawn my ears, 'twill tell
Whate'er concerns you full as well,
In physic, stolen goods, or love,
As he himself could, when above.

JONATHAN SWIFT

EPITAPH ON THE DEATH OF DEMAR, THE USURER

Beneath this verdant hillock lies
Demar, the wealthy and the wise,
His heirs, that he might safely rest,
Have put his carcass in a chest;
The very chest in which, they say,
His other self, his money, lay.
And, if his heirs continue kind
To that dear self he left behind,
I dare believe, that four in five
Will think his better self alive.

JONATHAN SWIFT

EPITAPH ON FOP,

A dog belonging to Lady Throckmorton.

Though once a puppy, and though Fop by name,
Here moulders one whose bones some honour claim;
No sycophant, although of spaniel race,
And though no hound, a martyr to the chase.
Ye squirrels, rabbits, leverets, rejoice!
Your haunts no longer echo to his voice;
This record of his fate exulting view,
He died worn out with vain pursuit of you.
        "Yes"—the indignant shade of Fop replies—
"And worn with vain pursuit man also dies."

WILLIAM COWPER

NEAR WHITE

Ambiguous of race they stand,
  By one disowned, scorned of another,
Not knowing where to stretch a hand,
  And cry, "My sister" or "My brother."

Countee Cullen

A MEMORY OF MY FRIEND

A Jewish atheist stubborn as Freud
(the only Father he left undestroyed),
Who when you left his house at night would nod
And say, instead of "Good night," "Go with God."

Howard Nemerov

CREATION MYTH ON A MOEBIUS STRIP

This world's just mad enough to have been made
By the Being His beings into Being prayed.

Howard Nemerov

EPITAPH FOR A POSTAL CLERK

Here lies wrapped up tight in sod
Henry Harkins c/o God.
On the day of Resurrection
May be opened for inspection.

X. J. Kennedy

CONTEMPLATION

"I'm Mark's alone!" you swore. Given cause to doubt you,
I think less of you, dear. But more about you.

John Frederick Nims

LIFE

I met four guinea hens today,
Creaking like pulleys.

"A crrk," said one,
"a crrk," said two,
"a crrk," said three,
"a crrk," said four.

I agree with you cheerfully, ladies.

Alfred Kreymborg

RACE PREJUDICE

Little mouse:
Are you
some rat's little child?
I won't love you if you are.

ALFRED KREYMBORG

EPIGRAM 6 FROM *THE HELMSMAN*

Homer was poor. His scholars live at ease
Making as many Homers as you please,
And every Homer furnishes a book.
Though guests be parasitic on the cook
The moral is: *it is the guest who dines.*
I'll write a book to prove I wrote these lines.

J. V. CUNNINGHAM

EPIGRAM 3 FROM *DOCTOR DRINK*

Lip was a man who used his head.
He used it when he went to bed
With his friend's wife, and with his friend,
With either sex at either end.

J. V. CUNNINGHAM

There are longer forms of satire, as well; such as this, written by a college student for a creative writing class:

CARTOON SHOW

THE OLD SKIPPER

I announced every episode of
your lives,
knowing just what would happen;
that you would love, lust,
fight, go mad and a thousand other
meaningless passions.
And I sat on film with my fake beard
looking like Zeus and feeling like an
oldtimer in a Greek chorus.

BRUTUS

In my lumbering ox obscurity
I lusted over you, Olive Oyl.
With my thick lipped bearded mouth

I wanted your flesh, to take it by
force and never let it go.
I had not the strength of vegetables
nor white clothes and noble ideals,
only the desire of animals.
With the cunning of beasts
I tracked you until, each time,
that runt kicked me silly, and
running with my tail between my legs
my hatred filled the land like poison.
Why couldn't that bastard have left his
spinach at home just once?

POPEYE

I have tasted the spinach of victory,
transforming matter with my bare fists
turning bulls into packaged meat
and alligators into shoes and purses.
I have fought every creation of man and God
on every battleground from Alaska to Mars
to prove my love, Olive Oyl.
But still you questioned it,
flirting with that lummox
with the "nyah nyah" in your voice,
the challenge in your eyes.
And yes to protect your chastity
after you had aroused the animal,
I swallowed my spinach and became
your white knight again and again.
Each time hoping I would lose,
to escape your prison.
But when films flashed in my biceps
and tattoos danced across my chest;
I loved you more than the sea,
I loved you more than spinach.

OLIVE OYL

I am Helen of Troy.
I am Deirdre.
I am all the women men
have died for.
I am all the women men
have made fools of themselves
over.
But I asked to be no Goddess,
and I asked to be no object.
All I simply asked for was
a mayun.

SWEET PEA

My parentage was never explained.
Continually crawling in my
Doctor Dentons, a doubt.
A doubt that kept me young,
never dreaming of puberty or
responsibility, cut off from
the forbidden vegetable,
I wanted your breast, mother.
I wanted your piggyback, father.
So I continued to creep away
from those strange sailors and
their lady friend, looking for
answers in circuses and construction
yards, missing lions' jaws and
iron girders by inches. "Saved"
ad nauseam by the muttering bowlegged
warden with green teeth.

ALICE THE GOON

I have been fed on the dog-food of despair
and in my raging bitterness I saw your
foolishness, my lungs filling with hysterics,
my mouth rabid with foam.
And because you could not understand
my madness you thought yourselves sane
and ran from my outstretched arms,
trying to impress that wench Olive Oyl.
Because I am tired of screaming alone,
tired of crying in the hills,
I will ask you why?
Why, in a world of ugliness, was mine so
repulsive, my flesh so leprous?

WIMPY

I'm not bitter, nosireebob.
While you have talked of love and lust
I have devoured the hamburgers of fulfillment,
tasted the cheeseburgers of tranquility
and supped off the fat of the land.
You who laughed at Alice the Goon,
You who laughed at me, the roly-poly sponge,
I have watched your petty wars
waged for the smile of the ugliest
woman in the world.
I have watched you all chew your loco weeds.
And carrying my omniscience quite unobtrusively
I watched the cartoon roll by,

picking my teeth with celluloid
and farting noisily.

P. J. O'BRIEN

O'Brien's poem, it seems to me, does something remarkable: it satirizes *satire*—the Popeye cartoon show is already parody. And, in satirizing satire, he achieves a basic seriousness; he mythologizes the characters of the cartoon show, so that they no longer stand merely for parodies of humanity—they stand for humanity itself. They become symbols of being, and at the heart of the symbology is a paradox: Life is both comic and deeply serious. The poem, then, is inclusive, not exclusive. Both possibilities exist, and, in fact, *are*. So the poem does what life does: it holds both.

It also holds people, and O'Brien lets the people speak for themselves. In their voices we can hear each individual comic tragedy, and as a group, they represent this world: We can see *types* and *prototypes* in the characters. We can even see ourselves in them.

Here is a satire in the form of a dialogue. Or a monologue . . . or soliloquy. Or. . . .

SCRATCH

If I must stay where I am, My God,
How will I survive on this patch?
God said, Scratch

And if I'm so sick of this world
Its mere thought makes me retch?
God said, Scretch.

But what shall I do, my God,
To cure me of this Heavenly itch?
God said, Scritch

And if Your time be here, how will
I know, having lost my watch?
God said, Scrotch

And if the Messiah comes today,
How, my God, will I get in touch?
God said, Scrutch

But if I must go speak Your Word,
Where will I say it? to whom preach?
God said, Screetch

And though I sweat and struggle, what if
The Devil puts me in his pouch?
God said, Scrautch

But if he bears me off with him,
How will I find You, how approach?
God said, Scroatch

And if, my God, Your door be locked,
And I cannot cannot lift the latch?
God said, Scratch

O, where are You? Your voice like
A record worn, only one word I catch!
Scratch, God said, Scratch

IRVING FELDMAN

The last poem to be included here is a long satire on contemporary poetry and poets, including some of those whose work is presented in this text:

ODDS BODKIN'S STRANGE THRUSTS AND RAVELS
PROLOGUE

Sirs, my name is Odds,
of hods a worshiper, of clods
descended, an eater of pods—
my surname Bodkin,
of bad stock and odd kin
offsprung; can nod, can
grin, do odd jobs, japes,
queer faces, apes,
may jingle and rime
when the mood moves and the time
is promiscuous. Sirs, I'm
harmless, a happy man,
rimer, chimer—none sublimer
in my fashion, no climber
I, I suit my station, pan
my branch for glitter and,
sirs, though there be not much
gold forthcoming, such
is my lot—I am content,
I bend as I am bent.

But I have eyes, sirs, eyes
to see what shall pass, arise,
what grubs, grovels, flies,
becomes, is, shall be, dies—
I have a nose
for good verse, bad prose,
a breast that sighs,

fingers to scratch,
two ears that nigh match, a tongue
to tell and a good lung
with a loud breath
to back the telling. Death
shall still me, it may
be, but I shall stay
till I've said all I have to say,
and then it will not matter
how the sickle may tatter
my rags, rump, and marrow. Flatter
I shall lie, but not lie to flatter.

For I purpose to tell,
if it takes an ell
of foolscap, a fathomless well
of ink and one hell
of a heap of gall,
of my fellow rimers: all
their foibles and fables, small
honors and tall tales
told in school and out,
of the fleshless and the stout—
poor fish all: sucker, trout,
flounder, eel, grouper; bales
of pickled herring—of these
and many another: anchovies
in tins, oiled and boiled,
soiled, moiled, foiled, roiled,
salted and spoiled,
anemones, clams
served up in stuffings, chopped,
garnishing hams, Spams. . . . Stopped
by thy jaw, Odds!
Ye gods, how you do yaw! Cods
and codpieces! get on with it—
swallow or spit!

FIT THE FIRST
Of the Schoolmen first
let me speak. They thirst
after learning. Let them be curst,
and do their worst,
for they have no best,
only degrees—
Ph.D.'s,
scrolls, keys,
and they can sonnetize,

for they are wise,
wary in the ways
of the iambus. Lays
they make not, only lais
circum-scribed and -cized
their symbols compromised,
polished and pampered.

    Unhampered by lust, dampered
and damned, evenly,
objectively, correlatively,
with never a fallacy,
only a phallusy
stuck in cleverly
now here, now there,
now everywhere—
quickly they come and
slowly they go, hand
in hand with the Dean
of Women, never mean,
not clean but not obscene—
no, never, nothing do they sing
nor say, nor dare—publishing
not to be Red or read
but to Get Ahead—
they may get a head or twain,
but alas, they'll never get a brain
unless it be bottled.
Would they were throttled!
None know their names or
works. Call them professor,
each one and all—they'll answer,
smother you with mummy's
air, their vested tummies
rumbling with deep ponderings
like good Dutch gut. Wanderings,
maunderings, meanderings,
amongst the dikes, the little teas:
these you'll find, but no Odysseys.

    Sirs, the Schoolmen have Hollandaise
thrice each year. They amaze
the waiters and the caterers
as they polish off-rimes and *hors d'oeuvres*,
good burghers all, good Hollanders.*

* John Hollander

FIT THE SECOND
    Odds, in this, thy second
fit, let thy wreckings be unreckoned;
if they stick out their necks,
off with their nobs! Take next,
for thy next mistake
(for muckrake you must
once you've begun to raise dust,
for, to settle the air,
to everyone be fair
or unfair rather, without care,
that is, care less rather than more
how you effect your cure,
you must sprinkle dews
on the dust, not as you choose,
but as you list, though your shoes
get muddy, cruddy, fuddy-duddy
and folderol—muckrake,
for Christ's sake,
without excuse.
Odds, sprinkle abuse,
make the most use
of your spleen's bile,
gay all the while.
Though your flesh grow grey
your soul shall wax fey—
the one greyer and gayer,
t'other feyer and fair
till all shall come clean
and turn splendid your spleen). . . .

    As I started to say, next,
though they will be vexed,
let us take, lightly, my lords,
from the vine those bright gourds,
Winners of Awards,
bound in buckram and Ingram—
Merrily prized and surprised
to have done so well writing.
Who'd have thought that inditing
alone could have done it?

    No one. Each poet won It
by studying Under
and plotting like thunder
with him to win wonder,
fame, fashion, renown,

and a day on the town,
as soon as old Under should
sit on a jury. Good
gravy! *One* jury?
More likely, ten. Fury
hath never a peer
like Under making it appear
his protege's a steer
in a pen full of calves.

    He'll not go it by halves—
he's all riots and raves,
teeth, tonsils, and nails,
rails, wails. He assails
till he has won home
for his favorite's tome.
Then—smiles out of ferment
while the losers lament
and plot to snare the Lamont
or the Yale pot instead . . . ,
or the *whole* loaf of bread:
just think, if a pullet, sir,
should win the Pulitzer!
(Though there's little dough in it,
'tis glory to win it.)
Or: the National Book
with pictures in *Look*,
Life, *Time*, and Eternity.

    O! for plums in the furmety
ere incipient infirmity
defame and deflower us
in middle age's ominous,
omnivorous omnibus,
for ageing is Messy,*
or is it spelled Muzzy,
Mousey, Moose, Massy . . .
Merde, Odds. Give it over,
muckraker. Word-lover
was never *Lovemaker*
to phonemes in line,
but to grand sounds and rime.

FIT THE THIRD
    Hast ever heard,
sirs, of the word

---

* Robert Mezey

spelled S-*-*-T? Turd
is the comelier expression.
Poets there are
who use worse by far.
In this, our third lesson,
we shall speak of the bellows,
bleats, burdensome lines writ by fellows
whom often fame mellows,
who like not the world,
whose verse is all snarled and ragged,
whose lives are all jagged,
jazzy, jostling, jivey, junky, whirled
along on the rails
like a gangle of snails
living *Life* to the fullest
—If often its dullest—
who pull their heads in,
examine
their innards, grins
hidden in pot, in beards, busts,
crotches, crotchets—croquet mallets
swinging, they come off their pallets
(called "pads" by the swingers)
sweet singers of croaks, clingers
to clunkers, calliopes of weed, wingers
to Erewhon. Whenever you hear one,
good sirs, plug your eardrum
with a plug or a chaw
or you'll hear the raveners caw
long after they're done
dinning. One by one their ill-won
privy secrets are scrawled,
Zenned, men's-room-walled . . . ,
like, man, gadzooks! cool it,
like, don't be a square, dad, rule it
out, way out. daddyo,
or you'll be found on some patio
with a tubeless radio
playing some broken air,
a bearded, blue-jeaned
hoyden, uncleaned,
disclaimered, unclaimed,
uncombing your hair.

   Forswear, sirs, for swearing
in the name of world-caring
is but the id unbearing

its iddiness, giddiness,
ungodliness, gaudiness—
gad, sirs, good Odds
begs you beg off those broads
and their lousy beards,
if not merely to please
poor Bodkin, sirs, for fleas
or the social disease
you may carry home
and or whereas or else you roam
for, sir, on my life,
though *you* may not, *I* love your wife.
Sirs, be not so Coarse, oh!*
nor soak up White Horse so—
nay! do not soak Horse so!

FIT THE FOURTH

    Let us now sally forth,
not to the white North,
but to the South where all
winters merely fall
and the frigid call
of the mourning dove's cooing
goes sliding and slewing
down no skittish slalom
nor no falls where salmon
in icebreakup time, like finned Solomons,
go intuitively jumping
to their humping,
lumping and thumping
under maples pumping
sap into cauldrons,
but under the palms rather.

    Quickly, sirs, at once,
to list to old Father
Time conning Mother
Nature in words mysterious,
curious, delirious, somewhat deleterious,
it's true, to the meaning.
Let the reader go gleaning
as he can, as he may,
like the mouse frisky
in the woodlot. 'Tis risky,
mayhap, to hear the groans
of stones, or of bones,

* Gregory Corso

the moans of tones,
natural though they be
as the bumblebee
saying things deep as Hell
and falling, buzzing down, down in the well—
rumbling true things and fell,
frail things and immense,
dark, dim, grim, dense—
hence, Odds! Of whom speak you?

　　Sirs, may I bespeak you,
respectfully I greet you,
crave boons of you, entreat you
to listen full well
to the Druidical school.
Lest you appear a fool,
follow this rule,
though no two lines follow,
as: "The frog in the hollow.
Come, jasper and horned toad,
Diced blacksnake on the black road.
Oh, lowly is the roly-poly goad
Of Death, mahout.
Beward the twirly snout . . . ,"
be sure, sirs, you nod
your nose like a cod
aware of his liver. Odds
warns you, sirs, else you'll
be deemed but a damn fool
and they'll send you to school
to read weighty reviews
in *The Swanee Creek News.*
The high priest,* now ageing,
still goes a-raging
somewheres to the North,
but the sub-deacon
under Mason-Dixon
is fixing,
sirs, to overthrow
the old nasty dynasty. Now
hear his sad tunes. How
can you mistake them? Cow
bells, sirs? Oh, no,
they're nothing like. Moo
moo, sirs, say you?
Few would agree. See,

* Theodore Roethke

here comes the mummer
huckster now—now it is summer
and the lumber goes greening,
the dim bird goes preening,
somewhat overweening,
cocksure perhaps, pompous, fly-popper—
fop, maybe, but no flop. . . .

    Oh, sirs, do not try,
though you may be tempted,
to catch him. Unkempted,
unkept, and untameable,
he sings nigh Unnameable
and highly uninflammable tunes,
dark runes; chieftain of loons,
peacocks, sad ducks, geese—
sir! drop that salt shaker,
not even a Quaker
dare sprinkle the tail
of the Dickey bird,* lest he fail
and be roundly cursed,
should worst come to worsted,
and be reimbursed
with a feral hex. Shake not,
sirs, but nod, nod, nod, nod.

FIT THE FIFTH

    Who shall help me end my fifth?
Mnemosyne, goddess, boon me the gift
of second wind, a good draft
to take in one draught
as I drift helpless among
these lines, stung
in the lung, ding dong dung,
by an unworldly wordlessness.
Oh, what a mess
is this paper. I guess
poor Bod's hopeless. I am unlettered,
sirs, a man fettered
by ignorance. Ignore,
if you will, my bespattered
page, for I've been but smattered
with lore here and there.
Beware
the dull pen, sirs—it may tell lies
or, worse, my lords, truth,

* James Dickey

if you watch not your way. Odds, have ruth
if she will have ye. If not,
smooth over and go on. The pot
boils, the pudding thickens
though the plot sickens.
The dickens away with ye,
Odds, let's see
if you can tame,
if not your shame in rime,
at least your line.

Sirs, I propose to go
next where the writers go
to learn, in good faith, how to write just so,
nicely, precisely, concisely,
icily, neat verse feet,
contrite and sweet,
dulcet even; Stephen, Saint,
stoned for thy faith,
help me finish this fifth
an thou wouldst save your
poor Bodkin, Tartar
though I be, but willing martyr
to a Muse.
I shall do as the School uses,
the goodly School set in snow,
the Workshop windows all aglow.

Sirs, if you will, come now with me,
the Midwest weather handily
allowing it, to note the joys
of gentlewomen and genteel boys
penning scandal, lust, and vice
amid the grim midwinter ice,
cliquing and claquing and infighting
whilst they learn the art of writing;
manufacturing paper icicles
to print in the finest periodicals
which none shall open save each other
so all will know whom to name Brother
and who the enemy is this week,
who's Ascendant and whose lines creak.
Sirs, let us be off to learn the rule
which takes the measure of Writing School:

Take first the famous Angler,*
forever politic.

* Paul Engle

He wheedles shekels for his boys
who always do the trick;

then, the Lawyer of the Workshop†
enjoying a rhythmic game.
His first theme was nostalgia . . . ,
his last theme is the same.

     Here stands the Roman Statue—‡
his feet have been dyed blue
by the juices of The Vine.
His verses have dyed too.

     See modern Aristotle**
whose pentametric power,
now centered in this Middle West,
shall storm the Yvory tower;

and consider the Romantic*
who smokes a hellish pipe.
His verse has been called gutsy—
in fact, it's mostly tripe.

     Here's Homo Egoensis†
who pens immortal verse.
Though he dislikes the modern world,
he hates himself much worse;

and here is All America:‡
what's there to say of him?
He has a pretty wife.
He keeps his hair in trim.

     Take next, sirs, Akademos**
constructing solid rime.
His brow is smoothest marble;
on his foolscap there is lime.

     Note pretty Lydia Pinkham:††
her talent is immense.
A simple country girl at heart,
she straddles every . . . fence,
unlike the offbeat Dreamer*

† Donald Justice
‡ Peter Everwine
** Robert Mezey
* Lewis Turco (epigram written by Morton Marcus)
† Vern Rutsala
‡ James Crenner
** Edmund Skellings
†† Elaine Emmett
* Morton Marcus

whose beard surrounds his nose.
His rage, created by the world,
is vented on a rose.

And the Catholic Eclectic†
prays before he writes,
midst penitential candles,
according to his lights.

Look, here is the Reporter‡
printing up a book.
Though never his own chef,
he's everybody's cook.

Last, moral Boswell Boswell.**
The chair wherein he sat
still shows the true weight of
pontificating fat.

FIT THE SIXTH

Oh! it should not make you sick,
sirs—there's still sex,
tons of it. Hey?
The school's a madhouse? Nay,
a bedroom, maybe,
but Bedlam stands next door, grey,
agley, grand to see,
rampant with glib neuroses,
psychoses, diverse divor-ces and -cees.
Institutions breed
institutions, sirs, Please
take note: infections
spread, dejections come of rejections;
but once one succeeds, successions
of tyros will make inspections
of their schoolmate's confessions
and proceed to succeed
in the same bloody vein.
Rein in, sirs, contain
thine ardor—

I shall explain the order
before we inspect the boarders
of yonder mad manor in proper
manner:

† George Keithley
‡ Carl Kimber Merker
** Gerard Brissette

It seems
our real lives are dreams.
Reality is loneliness.
From this premise
proceeds the corollary that there is
no conviviality,
only cordiality extended
one's gizzard by one's id—
a sort of truce of flesh and spirit.
Meanwhile, the sad, clay-footed
superego yearns to sprout
wings and shout,
"Look out, immortality, here
I come!" But, she is dumb,
poor Psyche. She must come
at last to knuckle under
to the body's opposable thumb
which holds the only quill
she will ever know, and which may blunder
while scratching
on mortal parchment. No hatching
agony may be guaranteed
immortality thus. But greed
for life sows its seed,
so one writes verse which may
some day
be anthologized,
prized,
sized up for posterity.

Sirs, this is the case
with those in the madhouse
next door. The first inmate,*
great man, taught
at the school. The next† bought
the first's book, paid tuition, wrote
homelier poems on similar topics.
The third,* a girl, thought
all this was fine. Heliotropic,
she saw the light, entered the house
and, quiet as a rhinocermouse,
took up residence.
Now, sirs, advance

* Robert Lowell
† W. D. Snodgrass
* Anne Sexton

with me and we may enhance
our understanding. Slow, slow—
stand by the window
of the Confessional—Oh!
listen: Shhhh! Rejoice,
sirs, make no noise . . . ,
she speaks—her voice—

"Good gravy, all the nuts in here
are shell shucked. Zorba, grab my tongue;
put me to bed, lamb, up among
the bats that flap my inward fear
amongst the clappered shadow forms
where the young, afreud, hand down in swarms.

"Hang down in swarms, sir, I repeat.
Good gravy, all the nuts in here,
O Colonel Knight, are figments—mere
shades of fruits no girl may treat
unless, of course, she wants to leave,
the Muses granting her reprieve.

"I come to tell you my insides
are full of bladders filled with beer.
Good gravy, all the nuts in here
mistrust me. Here my psyche hides
amongst the glazing and the dough
that pads my cell. I loaf, I glow,

I bake! My inner fire looms near
the surface. Soon my blazing bowel
must flame forth! Search the High, the Low el—
good gravy! all the nuts in here
shall never find me, for I'll be
secreting myself well down inside me.

"Good Knight, your bells are of an odd brass.
You range my changes at strange hours
as May Day brazens out April showers.
I creep amongst the stems of Snide grass.
Good gravy, all the nuts in here,
and nearly all of them think me queer.

"Move over, citron. Can it, almond.
Give me room or give me ward.
I tug. Above, the belfry's chord
flounders in silence and is salmoned—
wrong meal. The mind's defloured: one tear:
good gravy! All the nuts in here!"

INTERLOGUE

    Much as doth the worm
at cocoon time,
we have come
to midterm,
sirs, at last. The germ
of endings freighted
with Bod's belated
farewells—said well, well stated—
may be anticipated.

    But ere we undertake
to take under this last quake
and quiver, ere we begin
to undo the thin
end-ravels of poesy in
our time, unbare
the remaining jinglers, jongleurs, spare
them nary an undy
to dress up in of a Sunday,
sirs, may I suggest,
since this is the Middle West
in Midwinter: too chill at best
for any kind of unbaring,
even polar, unless one is wearing
internal armor,
come, follow that farmer,
corncobbler, hograncher,
aprowl in this town
where cap and gown
are made of denim.
Fast, sirs, trail him—
he knows where to get warm
when he's not don on the farm.
Look, goodfellows, he's
entering Kenney's
where, for a few pennies
we may sip three-two
and pretend it's brew;
innocent celebration
from the heart of the Nation!
Catches, glees
out of the deepfreeze—
good nature up to our knees
all night (till midnight) long,
sweet voices, song!—

"Winters* be hanged from a cherry tree
—O niggle a roundelay, olé!—
and never more shall he Frost† the vine,
nor peck at the Muses' bill-bored sign.
He swings so limply: see him sway
from the limb of the blooming tree, I lay!

"Winters slumps from the cherry branch
—O haggle a cheery catch, olé!—
and Snow* is thick on his shoulderblade
as he metronomes in the frigid glade.
He has such a Cunning ham,† it may
not wither until the May,‡ I lay!

"The Coffin** shall Swallow†† the swallowtail's tune
—O fling a classical rune away!—
for the Ivorie fountain spurts no more;
its satyrs and nymphs, nipped by the hoar,
are piles of ruins in Sappho's Way—
kick over the habit, gents, olé!

"Strip Winters' chill rime from the trunk and bark
the lai of the lark so fey, olé!
with a frog in its throat and a wart on its beak,
before the tears of the Summers*** leak
to mourn the ices that cannot stay
when the sunlight lights on the dark, I lay!"

FIT THE SEVENTH
We have had our hoots
and hollers, sirs. On with our boots
to tiptoe ever so
lightly, so clever, so
piddling correct—were never so
proper spies, gentlemen,
as we shall be. Enter then,
Odds bids you, the center pen
perched like a setting hen
hatching (slightly sulphurous,

* Yvor Winters
† Robert Frost
* Wilbert Snow
† J. V. Cunningham
‡ James Boyer May
** Robert P. Tristram Coffin
†† Alan Swallow
*** Hollis Summers

haply—sniff! don't the smell lure us
whither, kill us or cure us,
we shall now wander?) good eggheads
of the Critical Crypt. Hogsheads
and bedbugs! What prickly hedgehogs
we shall encounter! Ah, what'll
we find Aristotle
has spawned? What the mottle
or pattern on thin skin
or shell? Shall we find a thin
cowbird within?
Or shall we find Plato
*in hoc reincarnato**
propped on a potato
nearsightedly watching
for signs of the hatching
whilst tatting and patching
a quiltwork of verses?

    Catcalls and curses!
Pay no attention
(or none fit to mention)
to the lackeys of detention
scholastic who'll try to
stop you, hop you, top you,
make you pay what they think is due
for the privilege of obtaining to
learning. Care not who reimburses
the registrars, the bursars,
P. R. men, the nurses,
coaches, lecturers,
custodians, dog-catchers, lechers—
what have you.

    Have at 'em
I say! and boldly,
not warmly, not coldly,
but straight out! Let's let 'em
know, though we're low stratum,
we're curious men.

    Broach the furious hen
ere we grow Elder!† Helter-skelter,
quipwit, crickcrank, shimmyshank, sir,
quick! to the lion's den,
catspaw and pawn!

* Hyatt H. Waggoner
† Elder Olson

Shall we shillyshally, shun
what we think must be done?

    In then! Put the question!—
A dillar a dollar
you Critical Scholar,*
and how do your verses grow?

    "I doggedly throttle
dog-eared Aristotle
until I am sure I know
just how art is built
out of mortar and gilt;
I polish my rimes just so.
I figure my plot out
with many a blotout
of words that are insincere,
then I chew on my pencil
and make out a stencil
and tug at my good tin ear.

    "Oh, is it mimetic,
somehow antithetic
to all that's didactic and dull?
If so, shall I portion
a social abortion
from various parts of my skull
and try out on paper
a gambit or caper
that shows up the state of my id?

    "Or should I lie fallow?
Ought I not to swallow
my feelings and hammer the lid
down on my libido?—
seek manna to feed O
the Classical Muses?

    "The problem confuses
me sometimes, I will admit.
But never you worry,
for I'm in no hurry!
I've plenty of knowledge and grit,
and one of these days
the sweetest of lais
shall issue from under my pen,
and all shall be smitten
by what I have written . . .

* Norman Friedman

"But I must get cracking again,
so if you'll excuse me,
my Muses abuse me,
accuse me of diligence lost.
It is very high time
I got back to my rime
which, you'll note, has been nipped by the Frost*

"My feminine ending
seems bent upon blending
with the tail of her masculine beau—
I quickly must stop it.
Back off there, you poppet!
Your id is beginning to show!"

A dillar, a dollar,
you Critical Scholar.
So that's how your verses grow!

FIT THE EIGHTH
Sirs,
I am one of your proslers,
no poet. In prose
anything goes.
Not so in pversetry,
or so they tell me
in the various schools.
I would beg to disagree,
if it were not that fools
such as yours truly
tend toward the unruly,
which is why there are rules.
A rose may be a rose may be a rose,
sirs, but rules are rules, and,
my lords, ain't they just grand?

And, gentlemen,
there's such a choice!
Nigh anyone who has a voice
has a set or two set out
at odd hours to flout,
foist, finger, or fumble.
Give any of them a tumble
and, quite humble,
close onto contrite,
they'll go slathering on all night.

*Robert Frost

Sirs, if you're prone to insomniac habits,
such folk are better than tablets.
I should recommend one, perhaps two—
no more. An overdose can kill you.

But to get back to poetry:
it's now called *snow-jobbery*.
That pundit most vociferous
in peddling what he's to offer us
at any given time
—in rime, on off-rime,
in language simple, sublime,
grimy or Limey, it makes
no great shakes
which, why, or whither—
is crowned King of White Weather
till shortly another
takes over—his brother,
most like! Everyone's snowing,
coming and going—
and disciples drift off,
to scathe and scoff
at what's no longer toff:
about to be had
by a newer fad.

But, sirs, I have been undressing
in public, digressing
from what is my true purpose.
One swig more from thermos,
jug, jubal, or flask,
sirs, for what I have to ask
of you now is a task
less taking even than this blizzard
chewing at my gizzard,
for that house shaped like a tome
topped by a most monstrous dome
is the Old Folks' Home
here on campus. We roam
circuitously here,
sirs, I most fearsomely fear.
Ere we come too near,
let us stop, take stock—hark!

Night falls; it grows dark,
but what chords, boys, do we hear
growing, slowing, winding, blowing
out of yon dorm?
What wails, flails,

sad quails, melancholic gales form
in the wind?

Well, it's warm
indoors at least. Blast
or no blast, chaps, hold fast
to our course till at last
we may ask what these alarums
may be, harum-scarums
and scritch-scratchings. Ah! here
comes someone wending near
now:

Hold, fellow!
What is this bellow
(neither pleasant nor mellow)
assailing ear and soul?
What goes on in that hole?
Tell us what you have seen,
said, or noticed therein—

"I just walked into the auditorium,
and there was Big Tom Eliot*
sawing away on a bass fiddle.
'Hi, Tom,' I said, 'how's it going?'
'Not badly,' he replied, 'I'm a little unstrung
by all this, though,
and my rosin's running out.'
'Anything I can do?' I asked,
checking Ezra† swiping
at his double mandolino.
'Hell,' Ez mouched over his big knuckles,
'quit that trilling, Crowe-baby,‡
that's baroque.'
'Anda-One, anda-Two,' Allen** huffed,
and he blew up *Dixie* on a sweet p'tater.
'No,' Tom said, 'there's nothing you can do;
we're almost through rehearsing,
so now comes the bomb.'
'Bomb?' I queried.
'Yeah,' Ez said, jabbing Allen in the chops
with the neck of his mandolino;
'the other boys never showed,
and we've gotta perform alone.'

* T. S. Eliot
† Ezra Pound
‡ John Crowe Ransom
** Allen Tate

'Like, who's missing?' I wondered
as I watched Conrad Weltschmerz, the janitor,
kicking butts under the curtain.
        'Three quarters of the double octet,'
Crowe-baby snorted, knocking spit
from his English kazoo.
        " 'Too bad,' I commiserated; 'you guys
been here long?'
        'Long and long,' Tom intoned, knocking some straw
out of his big fiddle.
'Okay,' Ez chewed, 'take it from Canto I.'
'Anda-Chop, anda-Chop,' Allen gritted,
wiping his brow with a big bandanna.
        'Bazoo, zoomeroo!' went the Crowe-baby's horn.
        'Come on, dammit! let's get with it!'
Erra yelled, his nails all tangled up
in his universal git box.
        'Not with a pow, either, but a tinkle,'
Big Tom added.
        "And old Conrad Weltschmerz*
swept the flat notes
under the curtain."

FIT THE NINTH

        Before they revamp us
completely, sirs, cramp us,
damp us, let us fast lamp us
the hell off of this campus,
or the smidgin of light left us
shall as well be bereft us
and we shall be staring, stark
out of the dark.
Off, sirs! Out of the park
they've made out of Eden.

        But we need not go speeding
off to Quito or Sweden
to regain our freedom.
Nay, we needn't fly,
dirt in our eye,
to Chile or Neruda
or the land of the Buddha
wrong, Wright,† blear, or Bly—‡
for what Swede or Quitan

* Conrad Aiken
† James Wright
‡ Robert Bly

can bleed Independence so well
when he has been bitten
by the Liberty Bell
weevil as he
who goes gnashing, gashing, crashing,
thrashing, and rehashing
the dicta of Whitman,*
Williams,† and Sandburg!‡ What man,
Sirs, I ask you, a white man,
Democrat to the bone,
head solid as stone,
stolid as Plymouth, can do more
to devastate yore
and traditional lore
than one who is common?

    Sirs, I beg you. Please come on,
nimmitypimmity, dressed up in dimity,
oh!—I beg your pardon,

                 I forgot
we're not (forgive me, there I go again. A lot of good it does me to
recall that we're not supposed to rime all the time) supposed to pay any
attention, at any time, to any of the requisites of versification, or prose
neither, I guess. We're supposed to take a vacation from elation and
speak flatly, conversationally, colloquially, not to say unemotionally
—get as close to good, substandard American diction as does poor fiction.
In fact, we're to write prose from here on in. It grows on one, don't it,
Jack? This here's real great stuff where what you do is pack all that
unslack claque flack away and write like I'm, minus rime—as I think I
mentioned before someplace—and that other stuff, such as rhythmical
lines and all that guff the eggheads do. Now this is how it oughta be—
this is really poetry, as I dig it. How democratic can you get?—everybody
can do it! Lordy, I like it. Strike it—strike that rime—oh, oh. I'm

slipping . . . quick grab me somebody! Grab my thumb,
my bum—damn! Strike me dumb,
oh! the undemocratic shame
of it, the lame-
brain unAmerican Grain,
sirs, of my inspiration. Pain,

* Walt Whitman
† William Carlos Williams
‡ Carl Sandburg

sorrow and stain
on the Bodkin escutcheon!

    I never had much on
the ball. Not at all,
but I did so hope
I'd be less of a trope dope,
drip, drab, flop,
birdbrain, bunnyhop . . .
Stop, foul fingers! Stop,
Odds, ye Gods!
Churl, knave!
This treason will pave
thy way to the grave
of the Unknown Poet.
Stow it, Odds, stow it,
quit, subversive! Strike it,
tear it, spare it not, mark it
out—it's no good for the market
(discount house, cut rate,
plateglass-walled, wide-aisled,
tiled: no mouse ever ate
off these shelves), the emporium
of euphonious euphorium,
Muzak-backgrounded, where dough
and neon signs galore glare *claro*
Stop! cheap bourgeois Nero,
Stop In And Shop, Hero!*

FIT THE TENTH

    Let us next take, sirs,
under our wing,
the Little Old Ladies,
for they love to sing.

    They like nothing better
than to shed a salt tear
for the soft, Godly sparrow
whom the buzzards do tear.
(Excuse me that rime, sirs,
I do greatly fear
it was slant rime, or slab rime,
or some suchlike beer.)

    The sweet little grannies
—God love 'em, God bless 'em—
if they were not Baptists

---

* Karl Shapiro

the priests could confess 'em,
and they'd not be driven
to meter such rhythms . . . ,
(I can't think of a rime,
so I'll have to use *spasms*,
although I don't like it—
it smacks some of Freud,
and Good Gracious! we know
that one must avoid
such deviate matter
lest aspersions be cast on
our cossets and corsets.
Has Victoria passed on
as yet, have you heard?
Oh! look at that bird.
I shall shortly have vapors,
he cuts such cute capers.)

    Bread, butter, and barristers,
gentlemen, good sirs—
dressed up in furs,
the good dames come
rumpletetumtum,
each flabby vacuum
smiling and waving
the latest engraving
of the vanity presses
under our noses;
all primps, squints, poses,
curtains for dresses
(or suits, sirs, I haste
to add, for these chaste,
matrons have not *all* been laid waste
by the feminine gender.)

    God save her, this tender,
offensive offender.
I would not offend her
for anything, comrades,
for each has strong lads
in mechanical institutes,
and, sirs, lick their hobheeled boots
one must, for the prizes,
foundations, societies,
are hers, bottom, top,
middle, fiddle, bowstring, prop
and living Foundation.
Besides that, the nation

would have your head on a platter
in merely a matter
of moments: she's a mother!
At least, sirs, a father.

   You ask me, why bother
to pelt her, to pother,
pimp, pander, pottle,
about an empty bottle?

   Ask me under fire,
under oath, Under mire—*
I would not answer. Please
check the anthologies
if, sirs, you would know
her kin, her kith
(the kiss of death). With
due respect, Pegasus' own Smith†
would not look a gift horse
in the rump, for of course
the gift horse is a trick—
Troy found it could kick.

FIT THE ELEVENTH
   Gentlemen, yours truly,
truly yours, sincerely and surely,
underweening and ungifted, surly
in some respects, certainly; unlettered
and oft bettered; nevertheless
I, Odds, I guess, by turns blest
and bloated, wish to request
that you give your best
(or next-to) to the rest
of this ramble, because, sirs,
having left the mothers
of verse
—having put to her what is hers—
we have but a short way to go
to the peace below:
we shall come to the root, know
how the juices flow
in the poetry plant. Odds
herewith hints strange sods
grow stranger pods,
are fed with weirder fodders

* Louis Untermeyer
† William Jay Smith

and folderol by odder gardeners
for still madder larders.

I speak, by devious routes,
of those hardy shoots—
perennials and annuals both: weeds,
most of them, scattering seeds
into wilding winds and dim fogs
to bloom in cotswolds, bogs,
on old logs—fungoid,
polyhedral, amoeboid,
amorphous, jellyish, rhomboid,
shapely or shapeless, devoid
of the ability to be destroyed
save by cataclysm.
Not even schism,
sirs, may break the prism
of regeneration caught in the kernel
of these sesquinfernal,
sempiternal, diurnal
(you name it) diarists
of both the higher mists
and the lower. Oh, why are wrists
so bloody to be cut? Wieners
and rutabagas! I speak of those preeners
in the arty eye, the Littlemagaziners.

Let us talk of the hothouses
themselves first, the outhouses
on the estate of journalistic
success. Mostly they are mystic
in that no one knows how they stick
to the scene. They're atavistic:
Sam Johnson, that ingroup outcast,
might've understood how they can last—
but he is dead; their age is past.
Nevertheless, they stick fast,
proliferate, grow vast
plantations. Everywhere they occur:
the largest is *The New Yorker.*
Great is its largess, grand forker-
over of loot to the cute, the chi-chi
and recherché. Aimed at the lurker
in salons and the tropic bar,
it is misnamed; *The Daily Nonworker*
would be more apropos.
For their kind of dough
call-girls and -boys come and go,

yet talking of Michael Angelo
whose last name, sirs, is Buonarotti:
he still hosts quite a languid party.

    Sirs, this is becoming epic.
Since I am tiring, growing sick
in soul and body, I need a trick
to spell me through this thick
core of choking smog that smothers
insight. (Hindsight
has long been darkened. Incite
to riot Odds must,
no matter who is fumed, fussed,
faddled, or fidgeted. Lust
is the lover's oil. Rust
clots the joints of art
in our age. The cart
must not go first, nor be upset by upstart,
tart, or elder statesman.
He who hates men
of small talent but great opinion,
if he has acumen,
would not do thus. Odds, sirs,
has no such blinkers
sewn to his ears.
Ass that he is, he is not bridled
by the new Niceguy Complex. Idled
he may be, sirs, by this, but unsaddled
he shall roam, or,
if need be, pasture.)

    Bod shall take a leaf from Homer
at this point. That tomer
made a catalogue of ships. My chronicles
shall consist of current periodicals
which the tide doth bear away
faster than plans can gang agley
ere they spring anew,
four for every two:
There's *Arbor* and *Bread, Anvil* and *Audit,*
Audience, Beàtitude, Bardic Echoes, Ambit;
Partisan, Experiment, sirs, and *Anarchy,*
Birth: BIM! Breakthru—ah! Liberté!
Flame! Inferno!—Icarus: Hearse;
Fat Abbot, Harlequin, Fellowship, Deuce;
Critical—Choice—Carp—Attack—Canon,
Hudson, december, Chicago, and *Kenyon;*
there's *ons* in and out: here comes *Carleton,*

Tricon, Nonplus, Yeah! (same as *Swing*),
Wormwood, rongWrong, Semina, Sharing . . . ,
I know it sounds absurd,
comrades, but pick a word,
any one: it will be the name
of one of these Inns of Fame.

It's too easy, sirs. I blush,
retch, thresh about, flush—
but, gentlemen, ere we crush
them to go gushing, ere my blushes
die, shall you ask who publishes
in these? Can *possibly*
so many poets not only
fill these pages, but *be*?
Who, sirs, you ask me,
can wear artistry
like a mask? Is no spirit free
simply to sing?
Need there be this much publishing?
Who told the wild Turk, "Hoe*
thy plot in the Abbey,† and lo!
thou shalt reap thy reward"? No
fame upon this Sward,‡ nay,
no *Trace* of the May**
shall sprout from Wit's†† grain
where there is Little‡‡ rain;
not even Mammon's
Evergreen shall grow good Almonds.***

FIT THE TWELFTH
       To a party now we go,
apartheid we shall go,
heigh! ho! sing derrydown!
where every swain
joins the daisy chain
to end our final fit.

       Come Pack††† the Hall‡‡‡ with song,
and sing the whole night long,

* Lewis Turco
† George Abbe
‡ Robert Sward
** James Boyer May
†† Harold Witt
‡‡ David Lyttle
*** A. R. Ammons
††† Robert Pack
‡‡‡ Donald Hall

heigh! ho! sing derrydown!
Stretch out your hand
to old England—
be sure the knuckles knit.

An orgy we shall have—
a gentle orgy have;
heigh! ho! sing derrydown!
for, sirs, today
is the First of May,
the Maypole stands erect,

and we twine it round
with ribands in a swound,
heigh! ho! sing derrydown!
because we come
in symposium
(so sweetly too) bedeckt

in lilies of the valley
found in some fragrant alley,
heigh! ho! sing derrydown!
to quite agree
*New Poets** are we
our verse belies our ages.

Oui, we are extra young,
young, young, young, young, young, young!
Heigh! ho! sing derrydown!
And we can write
all night, right, tight,
light rimes, or even heavy!

Look, gentlemen, behold!
Bedamned! Befogged! The bold
heigh! ho! sing derrydown!
latest immortals
have shut their portals!
Behold the beauteous bevy

through these convenient windows,
lined up in there in windrows,
heigh! ho! sing derrydown!
warming each other's noses,
all posies, squeaks, and poses,
making paper leis of reviews,

---

* *New Poets of England and America,* an anthology published in 1957 and edited by
  Donald Hall, Robert Pack, and Louis Simpson, New York: Meridian.

passing out, making passes,
tickling each other's fancies—
heigh! ho! sing derrydown!
Come, sirs, away.
Tis not *our* May.
Our welcome's worn out, our shoes

as well. It's time we left
the scene, slunk away bereft
of heigh, ho, sung derrydown.
We ought to break
into breakneck
Skeltonics just about now,

gentlemen, I know, but perhaps
we'll just let the meters break down
a tiny bit,
for, sirs, believe it
or not—Odds says take it or leave it
high, low, in the dairy down

there to be bottled,
curdled, or coddled,
or anything else—I vow
the milk of human kindness
flows in my veins, more or less
at last. It's the Second of May,
the night has passed away,
and I have passed most of my bile:
it has spilt from the vial
of Bodkin's vitriolic
soul. Sirs, it's the time,
perhaps, or a lack of rime—
or merely my birthday,
which it truly is. Sirs,
it could've been worse.
I might have had to pick
Christmas Eve to finish
this distillation of thinnish
varnish, or New Year's day!
My head thrums,
the tail comes
wagging behind the dog, flagging.

EPILOGUE
Odds Bodkin wishes you godspeed,
sirs. Go out and read

if you believe not
this rave and riot.
Pick up a book, buy it,
peruse it—then, once you have done,
use it as best it suits you.
                                                But none
shall finish this thing begun
when the first men sang the sun
into the night, spun
the lung's good breath
out in words to ward off Death
and the Devil. Nor can
man or men damage what began
as the sea's rhythm become blood.
Sparing the flood,
sirs, not even Bodkin
can end time—only God can,
and he's not a mind to. Jog
and jig, gentlemen! even the frog
must sing. Does the tail wag the dog?
I am undone.
                                    End here this Epilogue.

suggested writing assignment

Write a satire of at least epigram length on the subject of this
course. You've earned it. This, in outline, is what you have studied:

MODES OF WRITING

a) Prose   b) Verse

I.

II. PROSODIES

a) Accentuals
   1) Anglo-Saxon prosody
   2) Dipodics
   3) Sprung rhythm
   4) Variable Accentuals

b) Syllabics
   1) Normative syllabics
   2) Quantitative syllabics
   3) Variable syllabics

c) Accentual-syllabics
   1) Normative meters
   2) Quantitative meters
   3) Variable accentual-syllabics

d) Grammatics
   1) Parallelism
   2) Perfect parallelism
   3) Parenthetics

e) Word-count prosody

f) Spatials
   1) Calligrammes
   2) Concrete verse

g) To infinity: Invented Prosodies
   1) Moraics
   2) Dada prosody, etc.

III.

POETIC VOICES

a) Egopoetic: 1st person, single-angle.

b) Narrative: 1st, 2nd, or 3rd person, double-angle.

c) Dramatic: 1st person, multiple-angle.

IV.

GENRES

1) Lyrics; 2) Narratives; 3) Dramatics; 4) Didactics; 5) Bucolics; 6) Occasionals; 7) Confessionals; 8) Satirics.

select bibliography of recommended corollary texts

†Gross, Harvey, SOUND AND FORM IN MODERN POETRY, Ann Arbor: University of Michigan Press—Ann Arbor Paperback, 1968.

†Puttenham, George, THE ARTE OF ENGLISH POESIE, Kent: Kent State University Press, 1970.

*Turco, Lewis, THE BOOK OF FORMS: A HANDBOOK OF POETICS, New York: E. P. Dutton—Dutton Paperback, 1968.

* Recommended for all courses.
† Recommended for advanced courses.

INDEX

ABBE, George, 360.
abstraction—see *personification, trope*; also, 239.
acatalexis—see *counterpoint*.
accent, 24, 30, 100 *ff.*;
   see also *accent grave, accent ague, stress, stressed syllable, accentuals, accentual-syllabics*.
accent aigu, 24
accented syllable—see *stressed syllable*.
accent grave, 24
accentuals, 20 *ff.*, 24, 31-32, 45, 87 *ff.*, 99, 161 *ff.*, 195 *ff.*, 205-206 (analysis); see also *Anglo-Saxon Prosody, podics, sprung rhythm*.
accentual-syllabics, *Intro.*, 25 *ff.*, 39, 45, 92, 99 *ff.*, 195, 205-206 (analysis) 226; see also *counterpoint*.
access—see *narration*.
ACCONCI, Vito Hannibal, "Re," *Intro.*
acephalexis—see *counterpoint*.
acrostic, 90, 258, 270.
action, 14, 41, 43, 144, 153,

(action continued)
   224 (rising action), 239 *ff.* (stage action); see also *plot*.
acyron: Use of words inappropriate to the thing being described; *mixed metaphor*.
adjective, 115, 143.
adonic, 29.
adverb, 143.
afflatus—see *divine afflatus, inspiration*.
agreement—see *convention*.
AIKEN, Conrad, "The Room," 305; also 353.
alba—see *aubade*.
alcaics, 118.
Alexandrian: Pertaining to Hellenist writers of c. 330-30 B.C.
Alexandrine—see *line*.
Alexandrine couplet—see *couplet*.
ALIGHIERI, Dante, 214:
allegory—see *trope*; see also *Intro, similetic construction*, and pp. 227, 240, 279, 307 *ff.*
alliteration—see *parimion*,

tail-glide—see *elision.*
talent: Ability and aptitude.
talisman—see *rune.*
tanka, 166 *ff.*
taper—see *spatials,* Chap. 5.
taper reversed—see *spatials,* Chap. 5.
tapinosis—see *rhetorical trope.*
tasis—see *grace.*
TATE, Allen, 352.
tautologia: Overuse of sonic devices,
    such as alliteration, as in a line
    of verse containing nothing but
    alliterated words.
TAYLOR, Edward,
    "Acrostic Love Poem to
    "Elizabeth Fitch," 44.
TAYLOR, Mervyn,
    "You're the One," 239.
TBOF: The Book of Forms—see
    the Select Bibliography, p. 365.
teacher, *Intro.*
technique, *Intro.,* 15-16, 17-20,
    126.
telescoped metaphor—see *conceit.*
telestich: An acrostic made of final
    letters rather than initial letters—
    see *acrostic.*
tenor, 112 (tone), 145, 147-148;
    see also *metaphoric construction.*
tense, 183-184.
tension: The balance created
    between opposing principles,
    situations, or techniques. See
    balance, grace, proportion.
tercet, 167; also *triplet.*
terminal alliteration, 88.
terminal punctuation, 79.
tetrameter, 102, 324.
tetrapodics—see *podics.*
tetrastich—see *quatrain.*
text, 90.
texture, 106; see also *exargasia,
    verbal texture.*
theatrical narration—see *narration.*
theatrical techniques, 15.
theme, 14-15, 41, 43, 51, 82, 167,
    207 (analysis), 221 *ff.,* 237;

(theme continued)
    see also *ideational level.*
thesis, 15, 275; see also *argument,
    didactics.*
third distance—see *envelope stanza,
    quatrain, proportion.*
third-person—see *person.*
THOMAS, Dylan, *Intro.,* 24, 57,
    63-64, 65, 82-84, 106;
    "Fern Hill," 83;
    "Of Any Flower," 82;
    "Triolet," *Intro.*
    "Vision and Prayer," 58.
thought, 51; see also *ideational level.*
threnody, 266.
TICHBORNE, Chidiock, 179;
    "Elegy. On the Evening of
    His Execution," 179.
timbre—see *tone.*
tmesis—see *schemas.*
TOLKIEN, J. R. R., 197.
tone, *Intro.,* 106; see also *tenor.*
topographia—see *trope.*
topographical verse: Retrospective,
    meditative verse written on
    the subject of a particular
    locale. See *topographia.*
tornada—see *envoi.*
total alliteration, 88.
totentanz, 240, 256.
touchstone: A line or passage
    or whole work used as a
    criterion of excellence.
tradition, *Intro.* burden of tradition),
    20, 39, 84, 226-227 (oral tradition),
    227 *ff.* (narrative tradition), 239 *ff.*
    (dramatic tradition), 258 *ff.*
    (lyric tradition), 263.
traductio—see *antanaclasis.*
tragedy, tragic, 213, 239-240
    (definition), 331.
tragic flaw—see *hamartia.*
tragicomedy, 240.
Transcendentalism, *Intro.* see also
    Platonic poetry.
translation, 26-27, 90-92, 169.
transposition, 174.

Robert Frost, "The Hill Wife," reprinted from THE POETRY OF ROBERT FROST, edited by Edward Connery Lathem (copyright 1916 and 1969 by Holt, Rinehart and Winston, Inc.) by permission of Holt, Rinehart and Winston, Inc.

A.E. Housman, "Terence, This Is Stupid Stuff," reprinted from THE COLLECTED POEMS OF A.E. HOUSMAN (copyright 1939, 1940, and 1959 by Holt, Rinehart and Winston, Inc. and 1967, 1968 by Robert E. Symons) by permission of Holt, Rinehart and Winston, Inc.

Henry Reed, "Naming of Parts," reprinted with permission of Jonathan Cape Ltd., London.

Philip Appleman, "A Malediction: Forbidding Morning," reprinted from SUMMER LOVE AND SURF (Copyright 1968) by Vanderbilt University Press. By permission of the author.

Lewis Turco, "Gather These Bones," (Copyright 1961, 1972 by Lewis Turco), reprinted with permission of the author.

Alfred Kreymborg, "Life," and "Overheard in an Asylum," reprinted from THE SELECTED POEMS OF ALFRED KREYMBORG (1912-1944), copyright 1945 by Alfred Kreymborg, by permission of E.P. Dutton & Co., Inc.

Marvin Bell, "Give Back, Give Back," (Copyright 1969 by Marvin Bell) reprinted from A PROBABLE VOLUME OF DREAMS, by permission of Atheneum Publishers. Originally appeared in POETRY magazine.

David Wagoner, "Ou For A Night" and "Staying Alive" reprinted from THE NESTING GROUND (Copyright 1963) and STAYING ALIVE (Copyright 1966) with permission of Indiana University Press, Bloomington, Ind.

Brother Antoninus, "A Canticle to the Waterbirds," (Copyright 1959 by University of Detroit Press), reprinted from THE CROOKED LINES OF GOD by Brother Antoninus (William Everson), reprinted with permission of the author.

Lewis Turco, "The Sign," (Copyright 1971 DE KALB LITERARY ARTS JOURNAL). published in the DE KALB LITERARY ARTS JOURNAL, reprinted with permission by the DE KALB LITERARY ARTS JOURNAL, De Kalb College, Clarkston, Georgia.

Miller Williams, "For Clement Long, Dead," reprinted from SO LONG AT THE FAIR, (Copyright 1968 by Miller Williams), E.P. Dutton, with permission of the author.

Nancy Willard, "Wedding Song," reprinted from IN HIS COUNTRY by Nancy Willard. Generation. Copyright 1966 by Nancy Willard. By permission of the author.

James Crenner, "Poem to William, My Brother," reprinted from THE AGING GHOST (Copyright 1964 by Golden Quill Press), reprinted with permission of the author.

William Meredith, "Envoi," (copyright 1948 by William Meredith) reprinted from EARTH WALK: NEW AND SELECTED by William Meredith, by permission of Alfred A. Knopf, Inc.

Claude McKay, "The Harlem Dancer," reprinted from SELECTED POEMS OF CLAUDE McKAY (Copyright 1953) with permission of Bookman Associates, New York, N.Y.

Robert Mezey, "A Coffee House Lecture," reprinted from THE LOVEMAKER (Copyright 1961 by Robert Mezey), published by Cummington Press, with permission of the author.

Robinson Jeffers, "Shine, Perishing Republic," (copyright 1925 and renewed 1953 by Robinson Jeffers) reprinted from SELECTED POEMS OF ROBINSON JEFFERS by permission of Random House, Inc.

LeRoi Jones, "Preface to a Twenty Volume Suicide Note," reprinted by permission. Copyright 1961 by LeRoi JOnes and published by Crinth Books.

Lewis Turco, "An Open Letter to LeRoi Jones," (Copyright 1969), reprinted by permission of The New York Times Company.

John Frederick Nims, "Contemplation," (Copyright 1967 by Rutgers University Press), reprinted from OF FLESH AND BONE with permission of Rutgers Univ. Press, New Brunswick, New Jersey.

Robert Huff, "Serenade". . ., reprinted from COLONEL JOHNSON'S RIDE (Copyright 1959), Wayne State University Press, by permission of the author.

Richard Frost, "To Hell with Revising, I'm Writing a New Poem," and "Some Important Advice," published in THE CIRCUS VILLAINS (Copyright 1965 by Richard Frost) reprinted with permission of the author.

Edward Field, "The Dirty Floor," reprinted from STAND UP, FRIEND, WITH ME. (copyright 1963) published by Grove Press, Inc. by permission of the publisher.

Lewis Turco, "November 22, 1963," (Copyright 1965, 1968 by Lewis Turco) reprinted from AWAKEN, BELLS FALLING: POEMS 1959-1967 with permission of THE MISSOURI PRESS.

Lewis Turco, "The Auction" and "Ode on St. Cecilia's Day, 1964," reprinted with permission of the IOWA ALUMNI REVIEW, vol. 18, No. 2, Feb., 1965.

X.J. Kennedy, "Epitaph for a Postal Clerk," (copyright 1956 by X.J. Kennedy) and "Little Elegy," (copyright 1960 by X.J. Kennedy) both originally appeared in *The New Yorker* magazine, reprinted by permission of Doubleday & Company, Inc.

John Ciardi, "Elegy Just in Case," (Copyright 1955 by Rutgers University Press), reprinted from AS IF by permission of Rutgers University Press, New Brunswick, New Jersey.

John Engels, "For Philip Stephen Engels," reprinted from THE HOMER MITCHELL PLACE (copyright 1968 by the University of Pittsburgh Press, by permission of the author.

Richard Wilbur, "The Pardon," reprinted from CEREMONY AND OTHER POEMS (copyright 1948, 1949, 1950 by Richard Wilbur) by permission of Harcourt Brace Jovanovich, Inc.

Knute Skinner, "An Athlete Dying Old," (Copyright 1965 by Knute Skinner), published in the STRANGER WITH A WATCH, reprinted with permission of the author.

Michael Harper, "Dear John, Dear Coltrane," reprinted from DEAR JOHN, DEAR COLTRANE (copyright 1970), University of Pittsburgh Press, by permission of the author.

Conrad Aiken, "The Room," reprinted from COLLECTED POEMS (Copyright 1953 by Conrad Aiken.) by permission of Oxford University Press, Inc.

Lewis Turco, "Another One," (Copyright 1966 by SOUTHERN REVIEW), reprinted with permission of SOUTHERN REVIEW, University Station, Baton Rouge, LA.

Reed Whittemore, "The Farmhouse," reprinted from POEMS: NEW AND SELECTED by Reed Whittemore, copyright 1967, by permission of University of Minnesota Press, Minneapolis, Minn.

John Woods, "Near Carter's Mill," reprinted from ON THE MORNING OF COLOR by permission of Indiana University Press, Bloomington, Ind.

Jerome Mazzaro, "Survivors," reprinted from CHANGING THE WINDOWS, Ohio University Press. Copyright 1966 by Jerome Mazzaro. By permission of both author and publisher.

Lewis Turco, "Home Thoughts," reprinted from POETRY (January 1969) by permission of the Editor of POETRY.

G.S. Sharat Chandra, "Of My 33rd Birthday," reprinted from POETRY, xcix:2, Nov. 1971 (copyright 1971 by POETRY) by permission of the Editor of POETRY.

Lewis Turco, "Eve's Daughter" and "Odds Bodkin's Springsong" (copyright 1966), reprinted with permission of the RED CLAY READER. By permission of the author.

Sylvia Plath, "Poppies in October," reprinted from ARIEL by Sylvia Plath (copyright 1963 by Ted Hughes) by permission of Harper & Row, Publishers, Inc.

Countee Cullen, "Near White," reprinted from COLOR by Countee Cullen (copyright 1925 by Harper and Brothers and renewed 1953 by Ida M. Cullen) by permission of Harper & Row, Publishers, Inc.

Howard Nemerov, "A Memory of My Friend," reprinted from POETRY, cxix: 1, Oct. 1971, (copyright 1971 by POETRY), by permission.

P.J. O'Brien, "Cartoon Show," reprinted by permission of the author, Copyright 1972 by P.J. O'Brien.